Culture and Conflict in

While the scholarly study of culture as a politically contested sphere in Palestine/Israel has become an established field over the past two decades, this volume highlights some particular understudied aspects of it: the relations between Arab identity, Mizrahi identity, and Israeli nationalism; the nightclub scene as a field of encounter, appropriation, and exclusion; an analysis of the institutional and political conditions of Palestinian cinema; the implications of the intersectional relationship between gender, ethnicity, and national identity in the field of popular culture, and the concrete relations between particular aesthetic forms and symbolic power.

The authors come from diverse disciplines, including anthropology, architecture, ethnomusicology, history, sociology, and political science.

The chapters in this book were originally published as a special issue of *Ethnic and Racial Studies*.

Tamir Sorek is Liberal Arts Professor of Middle East History at Pennsylvania State University. He studies culture as field of conflict and resistance, particularly in the context of Palestine/Israel. His research has highlighted the political role of sports, poetry, and collective memory.

Ethnic and Racial Studies

Series editor: **John Solomos**, *University of Warwick, UK*

The journal *Ethnic and Racial Studies* was founded in 1978 by John Stone to provide an international forum for high quality research on race, ethnicity, nationalism and ethnic conflict. At the time the study of race and ethnicity was still a relatively marginal sub-field of sociology, anthropology and political science. In the intervening period the journal has provided a space for the discussion of core theoretical issues, key developments and trends, and for the dissemination of the latest empirical research.

It is now the leading journal in its field and has helped to shape the development of scholarly research agendas. *Ethnic and Racial Studies* attracts submissions from scholars in a diverse range of countries and fields of scholarship, and crosses disciplinary boundaries. It is now available in both printed and electronic form. Since 2015 it has published 15 issues per year, three of which are dedicated to *Ethnic and Racial Studies Review* offering expert guidance to the latest research through the publication of book reviews, symposia and discussion pieces, including reviews of work in languages other than English.

The *Ethnic and Racial Studies* book series contains a wide range of the journal's special issues. These special issues are an important contribution to the work of the journal, where leading social science academics bring together articles on specific themes and issues that are linked to the broad intellectual concerns of *Ethnic and Racial Studies*. The series editors work closely with the guest editors of the special issues to ensure that they meet the highest quality standards possible. Through publishing these special issues as a series of books, we hope to allow a wider audience of both scholars and students from across the social science disciplines to engage with the work of *Ethnic and Racial Studies*.

Race and Ethnicity in Pandemic Times
Edited by John Solomos

Culture and Conflict in Palestine/Israel
Edited by Tamir Sorek

For more information about this series, please visit:
www.routledge.com/Ethnic-and-Racial-Studies/book-series/ERS

Culture and Conflict in Palestine/Israel

Edited by
Tamir Sorek

Routledge
Taylor & Francis Group

LONDON AND NEW YORK

ETHNIC
◄ AND ►
RACIAL
STUDIES

First published 2022
by Routledge
2 Park Square, Milton Park, Abingdon, Oxon OX14 4RN

and by Routledge
605 Third Avenue, New York, NY 10158

Routledge is an imprint of the Taylor & Francis Group, an informa business

© 2022 Taylor & Francis

British Library Cataloguing in Publication Data
A catalogue record for this book is available from the British Library

ISBN: 978-1-032-14637-9 (hbk)
ISBN: 978-1-032-14638-6 (pbk)
ISBN: 978-1-003-24030-3 (ebk)

DOI: 10.4324/9781003240303

Typeset in Myriad Pro
by Newgen Publishing UK

Publisher's Note
The publisher accepts responsibility for any inconsistencies that may have arisen during the conversion of this book from journal articles to book chapters, namely the inclusion of journal terminology.

Disclaimer
Every effort has been made to contact copyright holders for their permission to reprint material in this book. The publishers would be grateful to hear from any copyright holder who is not here acknowledged and will undertake to rectify any errors or omissions in future editions of this book.

Contents

Citation Information

The following chapters were originally published in *Ethnic and Racial Studies*, volume 44, issue 6 (2021). When citing this material, please use the original page numbering for each article, as follows:

Chapter 2
Dancing with tears in our eyes: political hipsters, alternative culture and binational urbanism in Israel/Palestine
Merav Kaddar and Daniel Monterescu
Ethnic and Racial Studies, volume 44, issue 6 (2021), pp. 925–945

Chapter 3
Face control: everynight selection and "the other"
Yotam Hotam and Avihu Shoshana
Ethnic and Racial Studies, volume 44, issue 6 (2021), pp. 946–965

Chapter 4
The impossible quest of Nasreen Qadri to claim colonial privilege in Israel
Nadeem Karkabi
Ethnic and Racial Studies, volume 44, issue 6 (2021), pp. 966–986

Chapter 5
Mediterraneanism in conflict: development and settlement of Palestinian refugees and Jewish immigrants in Gaza and Yamit
Fatina Abreek-Zubiedat and Alona Nitzan-Shiftan
Ethnic and Racial Studies, volume 44, issue 6 (2021), pp. 987–1007

Chapter 6
Songs of subordinate integration: music education and the Palestinian Arab citizens of Israel during the Mapai era
Oded Erez and Arnon Yehuda Degani
Ethnic and Racial Studies, volume 44, issue 6 (2021), pp. 1008–1029

For any permission-related enquiries please visit:
www.tandfonline.com/page/help/permissions

Notes on Contributors

Fatina Abreek-Zubiedat, The Faculty of Architecture and Town Planning, Technion – IIT, Haifa, Israel.

Samira Alayan, Sociology of Education, Hebrew University of Jerusalem, Jerusalem, Israel.

Arnon Yehuda Degani, Avraham Harman Research Institute of Contemporary Jewry, Hebrew University of Jerusalem, Jerusalem, Israel.

Oded Erez, Department of Music, Bar-Ilan University, Ramat Gan, Israel.

Liora R. Halperin, Department of History, Jackson School of International Studies, University of Washington, Seattle, USA.

Yotam Hotam, Faculty of Education, University of Haifa, Haifa, Israel.

Amal Jamal, School of Political Science, Government and International Affairs – Tel Aviv University, Tel Aviv, Israel.

Merav Kaddar, Department of Political Science, The Hebrew University of Jerusalem, Jerusalem, Israel.

Nadeem Karkabi, Department of Anthropology, University of Haifa, Haifa, Israel.

Noa Lavie, Academic College of Tel Aviv – Yafo, Tel-Aviv, Israel.

Daniel Monterescu, Department of Sociology and Social Anthropology, Central European University, Wien, Austria.

Alona Nitzan-Shiftan, The Faculty of Architecture and Town Planning, Technion – IIT, Haifa, Israel.

Lana Shehadeh, Political and International Relations, Florida International University, Miami, USA.

Avihu Shoshana, Faculty of Education, University of Haifa, Haifa, Israel.

Tamir Sorek, Department of History, Pennsylvania State University, USA.

Introduction: Culture and politics in Palestine/Israel

Tamir Sorek

For many years, the study of power struggles in Palestine/Israel tended to iden-tify "power" with the state, military, and the economy (Stein and Swedenburg 2005). The "cultural turn" in the social sciences and the humanities since the 1970s was slow to gain ground in the Palestinian–Israeli context. For example, a Google Scholar search of materials that include the words "military" and "Palestine" in their title reveals that 54 per cent of these materials were published after 2000. However, the share of materials published after 2000 among items that include the words "Palestine" and "music" in their title is 70 per cent, of "Palestine" and "cinema"/"movies"/"films" is 73 per cent, while for "Palestine" and "sport(s)" or "theater" the share of the past two decades is 100 per cent. While the semiotic study of culture, especially in poetry and litera-ture, is an established academic field, it has been only in the last two decades when scholars begun to analyse the ways material processes and forces shape and being shaped by cultural representations and aesthetics (Stein and Swedenburg 2005).

Scholars have become more interested in the political implications of cul-tural consumption, in the ways cultural products are interpreted and, in their potential to shape consciousness and political mobilization. This process has been fuelled by the emergence of new modes of representation and com-munication, as well as by the rise of new discourses of rights and rootedness. Therefore, these studies have paid growing attention to the political processes that shape the culture industry, such as institutional censorship or the politics of funding. Furthermore, there has been an extension of the scholarly interest from "high culture" such as literature to the spheres of popular culture, such as popular music, sports, and cuisine. These studies have been inspired by the global spread of cultural studies, and have used various conflictual analytical lenses, including post-colonialism, feminism, and critical sociology of culture. They examined cultural spheres as contested terrains shaped by politics and illustrated how actions and discourses in these spheres promote various pol-itical goals, such as maintaining hegemony, political oppression, protest, or resistance.

The chapters in this book are part of these emerging trends. The authors come from diverse disciplines, including anthropology, architecture, ethnomusicology, history, sociology, and political science. They share, however, the understanding of culture as a dynamic sphere with political relevance, where new fields, configurations, and constellations are constantly emerging and other are fading away. They all respond to the political and theoretical developments that has taken place during the past decade, or take a fresh look at older history, informed by these recent developments. While the scholarly study of culture as a political sphere in Palestine/Israel is not rare anymore, the chapters in this book highlight some particular understudied aspects of it: the relations between Arab identity, Mizrahi identity, and Israeli nationalism; the nightclub scene as a field of encounter, appropriation, and exclusion; an analysis of the institutional and political conditions of Palestinian cinema; the implications of the intersectional relationship between gender, ethnicity, and national identity in the field of popular culture, and the concrete relations between particular aesthetic forms and symbolic power.

Antonio Gramsci believed in the power of intellectuals to disseminate ideas and shape political consciousness. He commented, though, that non-intellectuals do not exist. While everyone has the potential to disseminate ideas, some individuals have the social position and resources that enable them to function as intellectuals (Gramsci 1971, 9). These remarks lead us to examine who could function as an intellectual. Scholars agree that in the Palestinian context, poets have historically played a major role as public intellectuals who shaped anti-colonial consciousness (Ghanem 2009; Furani 2012; Nassar 2017). With the diversification of artistic media, artists from other fields took upon themselves a similar role. Amal Jamal and Noa Lavie studied the dilemmas of a particular group of artists – Palestinian women filmmakers in Israel. Unlike poetry, cinema is an expensive art and for filmmakers to function as intellectuals, they need access to resources, a necessity that confronts them with constant dilemmas. Palestinian independent resources are scarce, Israeli public funding is growingly conditioned on monitoring the film's content, and obtaining Western funding depends on adaptation to a Western gaze. Therefore, the way towards becoming functioning intellectuals already shapes the content of the cultural product.

The constraints and cross-pressures in this sphere are further complicated by the gender dimension. As long as debates about gender role and patriarchy are part of an internal Arab debate in the press or other Arabic public spheres, the moral and social fields shape most of the controversy. Once it is embodied in the form of cinematic production, it is potentially viewed by Jewish-Israelis and then the political field and the national conflict gain dominance. The existential anxiety and the reality of constant dispossession and marginalization experienced by Palestinians in Israel propelled the political dynamics to the front row and erodes the autonomy of the cultural field.

Samira Alayan and Lana Shehada's chapter about donning the Hijab in East Jerusalem and the rest of the West Bank illustrates Gramsci's assertion that everyone is an intellectual (even though Gramsci originally wrote "every man"), because the justifications these women give to donning the hijab are frequently political, which means that they embed this practice in the context of a struggle over consciousness. Like the study of Palestinian filmmakers, this chapter engages with the intersection of anti-colonial struggle, gender, and cultural choices as political acts. Relying on in-depth interviews, the authors compare the justifications women give for wearing the hijab under two different types of political subjugation. They found that Palestinian Muslim women in the West Bank, where interactions with the occupier are limited to tense encounters with soldiers, use the hijab as a defiant symbol against the Israeli occupation. In East Jerusalem, Palestinian women use the hijab as a visible representation of their identity and resilience, but at the same time, they are more cautious and consider the way the hijab might be viewed by Jewish-Israeli civilians, whom they encounter daily.

Two chapters in the book are based on ethnographies in nightclubs. They map the extreme potentials of nightclubs as a political space, and especially the complicated relations between Arab and Mizrahi identities, as well as Israeli and Palestinian nationalisms. Merav Kaddar and Daniel Monterescu studied a nightclub in Jaffa as a stage for the contours of an emerging new social type – the political hipster. This type, like the scene within it is acting, proposes a particular blend of centre and periphery. It offers the wild nightlife of the centre, complemented by the rugged authenticity of the binational periphery, on the seam line between "Palestinian" Jaffa and "Jewish" Tel Aviv. Anna Loulou, the bar under discussion, is a carnivalistic scene, which allows a non-binding integration of nationalism, identity politics(Palestinian and Mizrahi), postnational utopia, cosmopolitism, and artivism.

This fluidity stands in a sharp contrast to the narrative provided by Yotam Hotam and Avihu Shoshana in their chapter about a Jewish night club in Tel Aviv, where Arabness is excluded by Jewish gatekeepers, whose own Arabness would have prevented them from crossing the entrance of the club as guests. In this case, Mizrahi Jews are assigned with the role of identifying Arabness, represented by the stereotypical image of the *ars* (a pejorative term for a stereotypical Mizrahi men), and separating them from Ashkenazi guests and Mizrahi guests who abandoned enough signifiers of Arab identity. This is a symbolic dissection of Arab and Jewish identity, and since the dividing line between these identities exists within individuals rather than between them, the separation requires particular forms of symbolic violence. Hotam and Shoshana focus on the experience of the Mizrahi doormen, who report that customers' faces make it difficult for them to do their jobs and force them to engage in evading faces and suspending ethical judgments. Together the two chapters about nightclubs present the two extreme potentials of this contested nocturnal space.

Nadeem Karkabi, in his chapter about the attempt of a female pop-singer of an Arab-Palestinian origin to claim Jewish Mizrahi identity, portrays another type of relationship between Arab and Mizrahi identities. The singer Nasreen Qadri challenges Ashkenazi definition of Jews and Arabs as antagonistic ethnonational binaries but she falls short to cross into religious-national privilege in Israel/Palestine. Her failure to overcome colonial segregation is a testimony to the racialized politics of conversion in Israel. While Mizrahi Jews' entrance to the nightclub in Tel Aviv is conditioned on their will and ability to shed signs of Arabness (and especially Arab masculinity), Qadri's Arab identity is understood in racial terms, which makes her claim to be Jewish almost impossible. Her status as a pop icon amplifies her personal experience and provides exceptional echo to a widespread racializing practice.

Qadri's attempt to enter the gate of Israeliness has been done through transforming herself into a Jewish-Zionist Mizrahi popular singer. Mizrahi music as a genre emerged in Israel as a style that both retains the connection of Mizrahi Jews with the cultural origin of their families, while at the same time distances itself from Arabness, leaning towards "Mediterranianism", a label which is more socially acceptable under Zionist hegemony. The path chosen by Qadri, therefore, is not coincidental – it is based on the *raison d'être* of Mizrahi music and the longing for Mediteraniansim in Israeli public culture. In their chapter, Fatina Abreek-Zubiedat and Alona Nitzan-Shiftan point to a similar phenomenon in the fields of architecture and urban planning. Focusing on the Israeli development plan in the Gaza Strip and Northern Sinai from 1972 to 1982, they show how Mediterranean architecture embodied long-percolating Zionist ideals of belonging to a de-Arabized Middle East. Mediterranean architecture was posited by Israeli architects and engineers in Gaza as a way to transform the conditions of refugees and make them ordinary urban citizens. At the same time, in Yamit, the short-lived city Israel built in Northern Sinai, the use of Mediterraneanism intended to instil a sense of community and safety to a Jewish settler population in recently occupied territory surrounded by Arab neighbours.

In their chapter about Music Education and the Palestinian Arab Citizens of Israel, Oded Erez and Arnon Degani describe a similar attempt to use particular aesthetic to maintain power. Here the authorities did not attempt to de-Arabize music, but to de-nationalize Arab music. Music played a nationalist role in Palestine during British Mandate period (McDonald 2013), and during the Military Rule period (1948–1966). Palestinians who recently became Israeli citizens were exposed, through the radio, to Arab national songs, including specific references to the Palestinian Nakba and calls to liberate Palestine

(Massad 2003). Israeli education authorities used music to confront these trends and disseminate a cultural identification with a general "Arabness", deprived of explicit nationalist content. While Palestinian music educators after the Nakba attempted to navigate their way under these restrictive conditions and use their own voice, the way Arab music was used in the curriculum of Arab schools meant that Palestinians were integrated only as a group-apart, relating to the authority of the state using a separate musical idiom.

The Arab musical education in Israel, argue the authors, is an expression of what they call "subordinate integration" of Palestinians into the Israeli polity. The subordinate integration has taken place because of Israel's character as a settler–colonial project which, unlike most other settler–colonial polities, still consider the indigenous population as a threat. Therefore, the state was very careful with the integration it offers, simultaneously encouraging "a-political" cultural expressions while limiting independent political power.

Emphasizing Zionism's settler–colonial character is also the analytical prism Liora Halperin is taking in her chapter about the commemoration of early Zionist settlements in Palestine. Halperin's organizes her discussion around the term "firsting" which she borrowed from Jean M. O'Brien (2010), and was originally developed to explain settler–colonial discourse and practice in the United States. Firsting consists of repeated and exhaustive litanies of "first" people and things, identifying instances of land settlement as moments of historical rupture. The chapter is looking at the firsting process in commemorative sites including medals, military parades, local commemorations, and protocols of commemorative sessions in the Knesset, where Jewish settlements established in the 1880s are constituted as signifying a rupture with the past and a new beginning.

Together these studies illustrate various dimensions of culture as power and as a field of productive contention, at a time when the struggle for justice, freedom, and peace in Palestine/Israel seems to reach an impasse. With the demise of the two-state solution and no realistic paths for implementing alternative forms of de-colonization, the future of Palestinians and Israelis depends on the ability of creative forces to imagine new paths and mobilize support for their ideas. The cultural sphere is where this imagination could happen, and cultural producers have the potential to serve as intellectuals disseminating new ideas and building innovative forms of consciousness. The chapters in this book provide some potential leads to the ways it could happen, as well as indicate to the obstacles, limitations, and challenges we could face as we expect a political change to emerge from the cultural arena.

Acknowledgements

This book is based on papers presented on the conference "Culture and Conflict in Palestine/Israel" that took place on 1–3 February 2020 at the

University of Florida, funded by the Alexander Grass Chair in Jewish Studies at the University of Florida, the University of Florida Office of Research, and the Center for Global Islamic Studies at the University of Florida.

Funding

This work was funded by the Alexander Grass Chair in Jewish Studies at the University of Florida, the University of Florida Office of Research, and the Center for Global Islamic Studies at the University of Florida.

References

Furani, Khaled. 2012. *Silencing the Sea: Secular Rhythms in Palestinian Poetry*. Stanford, CA: Stanford University Press.

Ghanem, Honaida. 2009. *Reinventing the Nation: Palestinians Intellectuals in Israel* (in Hebrew). Jerusalem: Magnes Press.

Gramsci, Antonio. 1971. *Selections from the Prison Notebooks of Antonio Gramsci*. London: Lawrence & Wishar.

Massad, Joseph. 2003. "Liberating Songs: Palestine Put to Music." *Journal of Palestine Studies* 32 (3): 21–38.

McDonald, David A. 2013. *My Voice is My Weapon*. Durham, NC: Duke University Press.

Nassar, Maha. 2017. *Brothers Apart: Palestinian Citizens of Israel and the Arab World*. Stanford, CA: Stanford University Press.

O'Brien, Jean M. 2010. *Firsting and Lasting: Writing Indians out of Existence in New England*. Minneapolis: University of Minnesota Press.

Stein, Rebecca L., and Ted Swedenburg. 2005. *Palestine, Israel, and the Politics of Popular Culture*. Durham, NC: Duke University Press.

Dancing with tears in our eyes: political hipsters, alternative culture and binational urbanism in Israel/Palestine

Merav Kaddar ⓘ and Daniel Monterescu ⓘ

ABSTRACT

Excessive redevelopment and gentrification in Jaffa produced liminal extra-territories which serve as fertile grounds for the emergence of unruly urban agencies. Drawing on seven years of ethnographic observations, interviews, and social media analysis of Anna Loulou bar, we outline the contours of a new social type – the political hipster. Unlike the archetypical hipster that could flourish in any urban setting, this specific agent is the product of the particular blend of centre and periphery, characteristic of Jaffa and the Anna Loulou bar in particular. On the seam line between "Palestinian" Jaffa and "Jewish" Tel Aviv, Anna Loulou offers the wild nightlife of the centre, complemented by the rugged authenticity of the binational periphery. The bar serves as a unique intersection between two opposing fields – the cultural and the political. This allows the political hipster to juggle between the fields – commodifying identity and erotizing politics: dancing with tears in her eyes.

Dancing in the binational space

July 30th 2015 was a special day at the Anna Loulou Bar: it was the first time Tamer Nafar, the leader of DAM – "the first Palestinian rapper and godfather of Palestinian hip-hop" played a DJ set. He preferred addressing the binational crowd in Hebrew since most of the Jews do not speak Arabic, and presented an eclectic playlist that followed no specific genre, let alone challenging the sophisticated crowd who was looking for a "Palestinian" performance. From early nineties American hip-hop, through French rap, pop classics, Arabic hits, and up to the Israeli Balkan Beat Box, the captive audience danced to Nafar's unusual set. The crowd was cheerful and forgiving, but the Palestinian barman mumbled: "this music is rubbish". An hour later, Nafar played music which was alien to the space but struck a familiar chord. The smoky dancing floor froze as everybody realized it was the Israeli national anthem, "Hatikva" [the Hope]. The crowd was immediately split between Palestinian clubbers and Jewish dancers. The former reacted in restrained fury. The latter suddenly stood erect as they were taught in formal ceremonies in school. The awkwardness became tangible as the crowd exchanged confused looks: how should one react? Can one dance to the anthem? Is it a comic relief or a fierce act of protest? Soon enough the awkward silence turned into a burst of laughter and collective catharsis. The bar's owners, Niv Gal and Ilana Bronstein, seemed amused, and the mixed crowd watched Nafar as he moved to the rhythm of the Israeli anthem. The party continued and was lauded as a great success. During the interview, Gal would describe it as a "performance of organized rage".

Located in a hidden alley in Old Jaffa, the Anna Loulou bar was a local and global icon (Sagui Bezawe 2016). It was also the only place in Israel which allowed this kind of playful inversion. The bar defined a new alternative urban subculture (Hebdige 1979), and enabled a binational contact zone of radical political subversion packaged as a Dionysian party for Jews and Palestinians. Anna Loulou's success story began in late 2010, due to the growing interest in Arab and oriental culture, and reached its peak during the "Arab spring". The owners, a Jewish couple, were sensitive to the political implications of opening a bar in Jaffa in the midst of a contested and intensely gentrified area. Consequently, they promoted an alternative cultural agenda that reached out to a hip Palestinian crowd, as well as Mizrahi Jews[1] and other cultural and gender minorities. The reflexive use of orientalist imagery in the bar's design and publicity created a mimicking and self-mocking pastiche of the common Israeli vision of Jaffa as an exotic and conservative place (Monterescu 2015).

While Tel Aviv's nightlife scene is usually depicted as a hipster bubble, the Anna Loulou case allows us to conceptualize a social type which thrives in the binational space. We identify this type as the political hipster, who is dialectically both a product of the Loulou space and an urban agent that defines it. Political hipsterism expresses a new micro-identity in Tel Aviv-Jaffa's social life. We perceive political hipsters as an urban tribe (Maffesoli 1995) which establishes a distinct subculture by adopting unique behavioural practices, aesthetic style and anti-bourgeois ideology. The paper elaborates on how the political hipster ethically and ideologically differentiates herself from the "typical" hipster, by adding a political layer to consumerist sensibilities. We start by theoretically positioning the bar in the discourse on mixed cities and in the sociological debate on the "hipster paradox".

Jaffa's alternative scene: creative marginality on the periphery of the centre

Ethnically mixed towns, such as Jaffa, represent the dialectic between intimacy and violence which is characteristic of binational urbanism in Israel/Palestine. This "contrived coexistence" renders visible the copresence of the political Other who cannot be wished away from everyday life in the city (Monterescu 2015). Challenging both the Zionist and Palestinian national imaginations, "these cities bring to the fore the paradox of Palestinian citizens in a fundamentally Jewish state, while simultaneously suggesting, by the very spatial and social realization of 'mixed-ness,' the potential imaginary of its solution" (Monterescu 2009, 647).

Binational spaces have been mostly conceptualized in terms of what can be called the "marginality paradigm". While this approach rightly stresses the political economy of uneven development (Wacquant 2008), it also fails to acknowledge these places as lifeworlds on their own terms. Instead, these spaces are reduced to unidimensional territories of passive victimhood and nebulous resistance or conversely to ghettos of delinquent violence. Recognizing the critical power of such theories of exclusion (Yiftachel and Yacobi 2003), we warn against essentializing these spaces and offer a relational theory of urban difference. Against the nationalist and colonial logic of purification, we argue, there emerges an unruly display of creative marginality which energizes Otherness and turns dispossession into a lively and rugged countercultural backstage. From a postcolonial perspective, the Jewish-Arab "contact zone" (Pratt 2017) becomes thus a site of decolonializing rupture, subversive action and alternative urban identities. The binational city instantiates thus not a zero-sum game but a relational configuration of "hybrid urbanism" (Alsayyad 2001). In the process, cultural initiatives and rebel institutions imagine what Aharon-Gutman and Ram (2017) termed, following Max Weber, an urban "objective possibility".

The recent history of gentrification plays a major role in setting the scene to the alternative subculture we analyse. More than seventy years after the Palestinian Nakba, the Jaffa Arabs helplessly watch as their city turn into a bourgeois space of Jewish consumption. Three decades of intensive urban redevelopment and neoliberal planning, favoring wealthy Jews, have exacerbated social inequalities but also brought new publics and resources to the city (Monterescu 2015). The influx of Jewish gentrifiers changed the delicate balance between the diverse local communities, Palestinian and Jewish alike. While these processes are sometimes perceived by Palestinians as a Jewish colonial invasion, or an orchestrated economic transfer, they also produce new scopes of agency for the creative classes and social activists (Kaddar 2020). Consequently, social groups that relocated to Jaffa – from liberal to radical gentrifiers, whether Jewish or Palestinian – use the city as a creative platform for advancing new cultural and political agendas.

At the periphery of the centre, Jaffa encapsulates the aura of a rugged inner city, while benefiting from the cultural and economic resources hedonistic Tel Aviv has to offer. In the late 1980s, Smith (1987) identified the "rent gap" between entrepreneurs' investments and potential return which boosted urban redevelopment processes. Similarly, we claim that a parallel "culture gap" enables a unique alternative subcultural scene. As real estate prices continue to soar, the complete commodification of space could be suspended by creative outbursts that aim to resist these processes. Paradoxically, these initiatives are simultaneously active participants and victims of gentrification. While some of these initiatives would soon be coopted by the neoliberal city (Hubbard 2016), others, like the Anna Loulou, represent a fragile urban temporality – liminal and transitory.

The Loulou heterogenous crowd is comprised of (self-perceived) "radical" political activists, queers, tourists and urban artists consuming symbolic capital and adding a hip subversive dimension to the place. All of whom outline the contours of the political hipster: feeding off the tension involved with the night-time encounter with "otherness", while consuming the aesthetics that urban life enables. The bar is defined from within through the "political hipster" who cherishes the place as "a safe space for national and gender conflicts" in the words on one regular client, and from without through audiences which avoid it: the Tel Aviv bourgeoisie, low socio-economic Jaffan Jews, and some Jaffa Arab women who fear for their reputation and would rather have what one interviewee called "mainstream Palestinian cultural institutions".

At the Loulou, the binational encounter between excluded identities creates what we identify as "political Eros" – a collective effervescence caused by the mere contact with the political "Other". This encounter is charged with anxious excitement, simultaneous attraction and distance, and a sense of thrilling uncertainty which is part of the creeping gentrification of the city. By offering a binational space of pleasure and engagement, Anna Loulou is positioned at the forefront of the anti-gentrification struggle, while taking part in the very process it opposes.

The hipster paradox

Perceived as "the stormtroopers of gentrification" (Cowen 2006, 22), hipsters are largely identified with urban culture and ironic attitudes. In popular culture, the hipster is often ridiculed and labelled as "an urban harlequin", "a student of cool" and a "walking citation" (Wampole 2012). Greif (2010, 12) defines the hipster as a "rebel consumer", relentlessly developing and consuming styles in order to differentiate herself from the mainstream.

Others emphasize the aesthetic and consumerist preferences hipsters share: vintage fashion (Maly and Piia 2016); urban lifestyle (Cowen 2006); ideological cosmopolitanism; kitsch and irony (Moss, Wildfeuer, and McIntosh 2019); and a constant search for authenticity and individuality (Michael 2015). Although hipsters are perceived as essentially a-political, their cultural and aesthetic preferences protest against the middle-class ethos by distancing themselves from conversative tradition while valorizing thrift store chic (Moss, Wildfeuer, and McIntosh 2019).

The hipster operates dialectically by combining global and local trends and by weaving authenticity and imitation in his persona. The *hipster paradox* (Schiermer 2013) situates the hipster between the mainstream and the margins of society. Although the hipster militates against mainstream culture, s/he eventually finds her/himself an integral part of it. The hipster praxis oscillates between sophisticated nostalgia (vintage) and an intense search for authenticity. S/he is standing out by fitting in, and puts major efforts in cultivating symbolic capital which celebrates distinction and creative freedom.

While most of the sociological scholarship emphasizes the global facets of hipsters (Michael 2015; Maly and Piia 2016), in this paper, we focus on hipsters' local determinants, which are unique to Jaffa and the Israeli-Palestinian space. Though cosmopolitanism and global tastes are important elements of the hipster's image, local practices, like social and political engagement in a specific community, are also part of hipster culture and modus operandi (Moss, Wildfeuer, and McIntosh 2019).

How should one describe the social agent populating and feeding off the binational consumerist space? Bourdieu's field theory indicates reciprocal relations between and within the political, cultural and consumerist fields, and conceptualizes the activation of taste not only as cultural consumerism, but as a comprehensive and sophisticated practice (Bourdieu 1984). We emphasize the dynamic overlap between these fields. The exchange between politics, culture and consumption is embodied through social agents we define by the hybrid term "political hipster". This agent is not reducible to taste, class or ethnicity and allows a non-binding integration of nationalism, identity politics (Palestinian and Mizrahi), postnational utopia, cosmopolitism and artivism. The political hipster can thus enjoy a political graffito of a Palestinian terrorist/freedom fighter Leila Khaled, while discussing Arab-Jewish partnership and dancing to Palestinian Dabke (a traditional Arab dance) and Israeli hits. The alleged contradiction in terms reveals the tension facing the bar's clientele – their wish to transcend national definitions, while being constrained by their national identities. Hipsterism, as an ironic self-negating disposition was made clear to us when Bronstein's, the owner, described herself and the place as "hipsters against hipsters".

We analytically discern between the two social types: while the political and the standard hipster share the same cultural and aesthetic codes, they differ in three key elements. Firstly, the political hipster replaces the ironic attitude with a confrontational engagement. The typical hipster protests mass consumerism by changing his/her consumerist preferences, while the political hipster actively struggles against injustice and strives to change political and social power structures. Secondly, the political hipster regards him/herself as a political activist. Her/his activism oscillates between active participation in distinct political spheres such as demonstrations and rallies, to suggestively viewing a dance party as a subversive political event. Thirdly, by replacing liberal cosmopolitanism with trans-localism, namely the "simultaneous situatedness across different locales" (Brickell and Datta 2011, 4), the political hipster reacts to concurrent events in her/his immediate surroundings (Oakes and Schein 2006, 20). We claim that the political layer functions as a local solution to the "hipster paradox", trapped between mimicry and authenticity. Rather than standing out exclusively through consumerist and aesthetic preferences, the political hipster distinguishes her/himself through radical ideology and subversive political lifestyle.[2]

Methodology

This article follows the rise and fall of the Anna Loulou bar, a cultural institution that was active during 2010–2019. The paper's core draws on in-depth interviews conducted in Hebrew and Arabic in 2014–2015 with key players we define following Handelman (1991, 205–206) as "symbolic types". These actors personify a "perfect praxis" by possessing the power to create an authentic reality for other participants.[3]

Anna Loulou's founders, Niv Gal and Ilana Bronstein were interviewed three times during the research. Three "in-house" DJs, Muhammad Jabali, Eyal Sagui Bizawe and Ophir Toubul, who performed in consecutive periods at the Loulou, were interviewed once and approached for clarifications when needed. Each interview lasted between 90 minutes to 180 minutes.

Ethnographic fieldwork supplemented the recorded statements, and focussed on the bar's peak during 2013–2016, including weekly visits, followed by monthly visits until the bar closed down. Fieldwork was complemented by additional in-depth interviews (five in total) and 30 informal conversations with the bar's clientele and other Jaffa Palestinian and Jewish residents. Finally, the observations and interviews were complemented by print and social-media review in order to ground our findings in concurrent events and understand the public discourse on the bar specifically, and on Jaffa generally.

The authors are longtime Jewish residents of the city and well-grounded in its cultural and activist field. Daniel was born in Jaffa and spent three decades in the city. He is an anthropologist specializing in binational urbanism in Israel/Palestine. Merav is a political theorist and urban scholar, who spent five years in Jaffa documenting the city's creeping gentrification, in research and in activism. She was a frequent visitor and intimately familiar with the inner circle of Anna Loulou' customers.

"Looking for alterity in the night": the owners as marginality entrepreneurs

Perceiving the bar as a cultural and political vocation, the owners – a Jewish Ashkenazi couple – mobilized their cultural capital to keep the place alive and relevant. Gal holds a graduate degree in anthropology, and Bronstein is a former fashion designer. They wished to create an "alternative" cultural establishment even before they settled on a bar. Gal described the bar's history as "growth through play" which created a "self-aware oriental place". Self-Orientalism, defined in postcolonial scholarship as the abuse and reappropriation of western stereotypes (Kobayashi, Jackson, and Sam 2019, 161) endowed the place with multiple signs which positioned it as a radical cultural institution (see Figure 1). Bronstein added:

> Early on we understood that we were positioned in Jaffa, and when it comes to the Tel Aviv nightlife, which is pretty leftist, Arab music and culture are an asset. We felt it would be intuitively and organically interesting for the Tel Avivian crowd. People look for the margins, for alterity in the night … it's an asset – a cultural and economic capital. Otherness is avant-garde and sexy.

Their vision of opening a bar which "responds to its urban environment" blended naturally with the Mizrahi and Arab music trend in the city. Throughout the interview, they juggled between two presentations of self – radical political agents and cultural consumption entrepreneurs. Explanations followed by disclaimers, pride entailed by self-justification. Five years after opening the bar, they openly described their savvy use of Jaffa's environment – the "sex appeal of the margins" and the use of "Arab and Mizrahi music" – as part of the place's success.

Feeding off the volatile fusion of social and cultural extremes, the establishment's uniqueness was honed by what Gal termed an "orientalist fantasy". The owners' sensitivity to urban processes in Jaffa translated to the Loulou's hedonistic and consumerist space, in a way which set it apart from other places in Jaffa that were opened roughly in the same time (e.g. Shafa bar). While other places, they suggested, "copy-pasted" trends in order to attract the Tel Aviv crowds, Bronstein emphasized they chose to highlight "something that organically grows in Jaffa and is essentially

Figure 1. Self-Orientalism: the bar's interior design is playful and reflective. Photo credit: the authors.

good". As an urban institution Anna Loulou was soon to become the informal home for an alternative subculture: hip and political, local and progressive, authentic and cool. In the process, the owners became ever more careful about the power of institutions to "establish hegemony over those they dominated" (DiMaggio 1982, 48).

Gal and Bronstein perceived Arab music and culture in Jaffa as the basis of a shared experience: "in that context, due to circumstances beyond us, it became a much broader fantasy". Through Arab music the bar became a familiar and welcoming space for Palestinians, but also a magnet for left-leaning activists, up-to-date hipsters, tourists and other visitors. The owners described the typical client as a hipster with unique features, which we define as the "political hipster". Aesthetically sensitive, anti-conspicuous-consumption, politically aware, and activism savvy, the political hipster dances in the Loulou in a self-aware performance, as Gal described it:

> He is someone who is very aware that every move he makes in public space is a performance … Everything might be used as a prop – the beard, the narrative, history. Everything is part of his storytelling, and the hipster's story is a sensitive one. He is a consumerist but his consumer choices are political – he goes green, he boycotts. He's a person who sees through different worlds and combines them into something new.

As part of the performative counter-culture the place represents, the owners embody the "hipster paradox". "Yes – I'm a hipster," Gal said, "I've made up my mind. It's a term that grew on me". "I guess we are kind of a role-model for this thing" Bronstein added, "We are hipsters against hipsters.[4] The term was forced on us. So instead of resisting it we accept parts of it. Being mainstream means being apathetic to your surroundings". Though hipsters were not the only customers, the owners emphasized the "regulars" – political activists who wished to temper the depressing political stalemate with liberating Eros: "This group of leftie gentrifiers come with self-aware orientalism … They show up in order to protest … They are activists and they act as such everywhere. Even when they dance it's a political statement".

The Loulou's repertoire did not commit to one form of "authenticity". The cultural programme included almost every genre Israeli society regards as "authentic", from high to low culture, through fringe theatre, Mizrahi music and up to alternative Arab music. Party lines such as "Arabs do it better", "Queer here" and "Yemenites have fun" suggested a broad cultural variety which attracted different audiences. Fridays were Arab party nights – the bar's crown jewel. "This is the entry ticket to the Loulou", the owners attested, "if you handle this you can try more avant-garde nights".

While the audience was politically aware and active, the evening's political tone and the kind of protest it engenders were set by the DJ – the evening's "leader" as Bronstein put it: "The DJ here is more significant than in other places … usually DJ's are about music, not about persona. But here it's about their charisma, their political biography and their ideology. It is much more than perfect musical transitions". At the same time, music is strategically employed by the DJs as a tool for marking identities and conveying political messages (McDonald 2013). Subsequently, the following describes three symbolic types which offer three interpretations to the hipster dilemma: urban Palestinian, Mediterranean Levantine, and Middle Eastern Oriental (Mizrahiyut).

"The return to the Palestinian city": Muhammad Jabali's translocalism

Muhammad Jabali, to whom the owners refer to as their third founding partner, is a nomadic intellectual and cultural entrepreneur from the Palestinian city of Taybe. "I worked in all mixed cities in Israel excluding Acre ... As soon as I'll tick that box I'll be out of here", he smiled, exposing his ambivalence which oscillates between indigenousness and cosmopolitanism. His interest in urbanism and art led him to Jaffa where he taught Arabic and was involved in political activism. There he also encountered the difficulties preventing the city from living up to its potential.

His role in the Loulou corresponds with his ambitious project of reimagining the Palestinian city beyond the marginality paradigm as part of a translocal vision of restauring lost connectivity to the region. In the Loulou he found what he was missing in other places – full control over content and an audience open for experimentation:

> Jaffa is lacking in Palestinian projects and strategic approach. There are a lot of projects but no synergy. The main project is surviving the Zionist regime. My task is to reclaim the city, turning it into a Palestinian urban space rather than a poor ghetto. The Loulou provides nightlife which is crucial for real urbanism. This was my project for three years and it was one of the most challenging ones. Suicidal in some ways. But frankly if we had the same success rates in other cultural initiatives I was involved in – we would have a [Palestinian] city by now.

Akin to other agents involved, Jabali highlighted the Loulou's subversive dimension, in face of the Israeli hegemony on the one hand, and Arab conservatism on the other. The difficulty lay not only in establishing a radical space that brings Arabs and Jews together, but also in creating one that is "self-reflective" and leverages urban alienation. The Loulou, accordingly, was not a Palestinian "ghetto project", nor was it a mainstream Tel Aviv project or an Arab social club:

> The idea is subversive because it creates a Palestinian shared space, allowing for political Palestinian content – and this is not obvious. Jaffa's location establishes an open space for strangers – rather than an educational safe-haven – thus having a life of its own. But that's also what makes it so exhausting. These are not people carefully chosen. This is an open space. A culture the community creates and enforces ... Shared spaces are present everywhere. A falafel stand is a shared space, but not necessarily self-reflective one. The Loulou is a space that voices an anti-Zionist counter-culture, Palestinian and Mizrahi.

Jabali's trans-local project activated local and global networks, which he interpreted in a colonial fashion. While Tel Aviv looks up to Berlin's cultural trends, Jabali called to release Jaffa from the cultural ghetto, while exposing the impotence of multicultural secularism:

The Anna Loulou is a rational attempt to do something good outside the main-stream. Tel Aviv falls in love with Turkish Berliners but does not accept Arabs. The Muslim migration to Europe had a stronger impact on Tel Aviv than Israeli processes. There's a colonial process going on and everybody is talking about gentrification. Tel Aviv is an apartheid city: it closes its borders with Ramallah, but enjoys global trends – Africans in south Tel Aviv. It wants to be multicultural while maintaining its apartheid. I didn't see Jaffa as a deserted island. I knew what's happening in Haifa, in Ramallah, in South Tel Aviv.

Is Jabali's project post-national or Palestinian? He did not compromise for either ends, and provocatively suggested his vision for an open Arab space and a future city which "respects the rights of the Ashkenazi minority in the Middle East". His interest lies in "creating a post-colonial, cosmopolitan Arab culture", as opposed to "cosmopolitanism under Israeli hegemony". Nevertheless, Jabali's contribution to Anna Loulou's success should not be read solely against his radical politics or critical stance, but rather in relation to his musical practice and hipster groove which translated politics into a car-nival. Jabali synthesized between musical genres, high and low culture, going against commercial Arab mainstream and Israeli orientalism alike.

Moving between "pleasing the crowd" and his personal preferences, he created a rhythmic pastiche blending village beat, city vibe, and desert groove. He juggled between hip-hop, rural Dabke and Khaliji (Persian Gulf) tribal music in order to challenge both the conservative Jaffan tastes and the Jewish Orientalist fantasy. "Playing Dabke in the Loulou is both protest and release", he said. Through dancing, the music enables a sensual encoun-ter with other "exotic" cultures and adds an erotic dimension to the tensions seeking relief in Jaffa. These were highlighted in contrast to the "non-conflictual" Arab urbanism in Haifa, and its notion of "Palestinian dominance" (Karkabi 2018). "The catharsis is unique to Jaffa", he concluded by highlight-ing the virtues of agonistic urbanism.

In the peak of his success he confessed he "got stuck in the Loulou", and became over-identified with the place: "At the beginning you define the hit, and then it defines you", he quoted Tamer Nafar. Jabali's trademark line included some hits like the national Palestinian protest song "Wein 'a-Ramal-lah' portraying Palestinian refugees" political aspirations. These soon defined the bar's repertoire, which Jewish DJs had to adopt following audience demand. It seemed like the ironic inversion came full circle – the protest was replaced with sentimental neo-orientalism, but surprisingly by the Jewish audience. This paradox pushed Jabali to withdraw from his inclusive vision and stress rather Palestinian translocal entitlement:

I felt like saying to the Jews – this is not for you! This is not an oriental fantasy game. When I saw Jews embracing the song I wanted to tell them – stay on the Tel Aviv-Berlin line. You invaded enough to the East. I'm going to play a song and I'm not playing it for you.

"A party is a demonstration": Eyal Sagui Bizawe and the Levantine project

Eyal Sagui Bizawe, a Jew of Egyptian origin, is a researcher of Egyptian culture and cinema a documentary film director, a gay activist and a journalist. His critical stance rejects Western and Israeli unreflexive celebration of alternative culture, which fails to recognize Mizrahi and Arab history and identity. He positioned the meeting point between the political-identitarian field and the cultural space at the Loulou:

> I deejayed Arab music in great places and everyone had a blast – but there were no Arabs in the crowd. These are not places that invite Arabs in. Few places do … The Anna Loulou is distinctly THE place that does that … A space Arab identity is clearly a part of.

Sagui Bizawe described his attachment to Arab culture as a counter-reaction to the Israeli ethnoscape of the 1970s when he came of age. He considers himself as an Arab Jew (Shohat 2017; Shenhav 2006), which makes him immune to cultural appropriation allegations: "Arab culture is my culture. I don't need confirmation from 'real' Arabs. I am part of the Egyptian culture *and* the Israeli culture whether I like it or not". Yet, he does not regard his composite identity in essentialist terms, but rather as elastic and relational:

> in some contexts I am a Mizrahi, and in others I am an Arab Jew. This doesn't mean I can speak for the Palestinians living in Israel, because I don't share their experience. Just like the Levantine idea – it's always contextual.

In order to express the translocalism encapsulated in his hybrid identity, Eyal added his Egyptian family name – Bizawe, to Sagui – the Hebrew name his father registered when migrating to Israel. This addition symbolizes the fluid borders of his identity space, inspired by Jacqueline Kahanoff's Levantine writings (Kahanoff 2011a, 2011b; Monterescu 2011). Kahanoff wished to reclaim the negative labelling of the Levant, understanding Levantinization as a cultural hybridization. The fruitful synthesis of Western and Oriental legacies constitutes a new identity, which Kahanoff (2011b) qualified as a "much needed cultural mutation". Sagui Bizawe operates in the Levantine cultural space while reflexively juggling between the colonial European heritage and his Arab Jewish identity.[5]

As a DJ, he performed his identity politics through music. For him, music creates an emotional, sensory and immediate experience: "the emotions Mizrahi music evokes are totally different from the ones Arab music does. It connects to different parts in me, which sometimes overlap". While the identity play has intellectual and socio-political meaning, (Mizrahi) music engenders a new cultural category that can embrace such hybridity. On the DJ stand, Sagui Bizawe recreated childhood experiences and blended Mizrahi and Arab music. It is through music that he connected with the crowd's memories of oppression:

> Playing "'Ali al-kuffiyeh" ["Raise the Kuffiyeh" by Mohammad Assaf winner of Arab Idol], or Jacky Mekaiten'n "Judge Song" [an Israeli Mizrahi song] is a banal classic, but whenever I play even the corniest song – I have tears in my eyes. Because on a personal level I remember this was a cry out. There's rage in it, as well as emotional release.

Bizawe Sagui transformed his personal cultural and musical experience into a political statement against the Ashkenazi hegemony. The protest was skilfully and reflexively interwoven into his playlist, so much so that the tipsy crowd might have missed its subtleties. "Are things so evenly balanced outside that I am supposed to represent them as such?" he asked ironically, indicating that his musical line suggests an alternative by refusing to fabricate a balanced representation of the Jewish-Arab social mix.

Much like Bronstein and Gal, Bizawe Sagui was ambivalent about the kind of alternative space that Anna Loulou formed. For him the Loulou was a cultural carnival (Turner 1986), which accentuated the fault lines in Israeli society by creating "a political alternative through alcohol and music". Political Eros did not stand on its own, but represented a principal political partnership rising from within the open wound:

> For me, the Anna Loulou mirrors the abnormality outside. It creates an event from everyday partnerships. But one should not mistake it for a partnership between equals, because once you step outside it's not. It's a bubble, but it is important, because it does create an alternative. People need to see other models, and the Loulou is an alternative – because it presents a different model.

While Jabali's national aspirations called for de-colonizing and Arabizing space, Sagui Bizawe focussed on forming a binational community in Jaffa, and beyond. This approach was mediated through the concept of political Eros, which regards an alcohol-induced party as a protest, and as political participation in and of itself. For Sagui Bizawe a party is a radical political act as much as any other form of activism:

> One of the things I did I am most proud of is the Friday night parties during the war [Israel-Gaza 2014]. Once the war broke out, the immediate reflex was to cancel the party. When facing a tragedy, people tend to withdraw onto their own pain, their own national grief ... But I wanted to expose the predicament: I posted on Facebook that I will play that night, and that as far as I am concerned this is a demonstration. The reactions were amazing. The place was packed, people wanted to dance. It was surreal. Two girls were dancing and crying. People came back from a demonstration, put their signs aside and danced. It was the most political party I've ever seen.

In 2014 Sagui Bizawe decided to quit deejaying, but not forsake the Levantine project he launched in the Loulou. He proposed that Laissez-Passer group should take his place in the Friday night slot: "something in the traditional Ashkenazi-Palestinian alliance had to break. I thought it's important that more Mizrahis would come to the Loulou, and hoped Laissez-Passer would bring them along".

"Mizrahiyut without borders": Ophir Toubul and Jewish rootedness

"Laissez Passer: Music Without Borders" introduces the third facet of the political hipster, complementing Mediterranean Levantinization (Sagui Bizawe), and Palestinian translocalism (Jabali). The label by Ophir Toubul, Gal Kadan and Khen Elmaleh offered a unique music set, which combined World Music from around the Middle East, in Arabic, Hebrew, French and more.

Toubul grew up in Ashdod, a peripheral city in the south of Israel, where he became a "compulsive music collector". He was raised in traditional Mizrahi Jewish surroundings and relocated to Tel Aviv to study law. Moving from the periphery to the big city entailed rapid adoption of "Ashkenazi practices and culture". But he "sobered up", and shortly joined the Mizrahi struggle in the city. Combining all of these lifeworlds, he established "Café Gibraltar" cultural website, which aims to produce what Hakim Bey (2003) termed "Temporary Autonomous Zone" (T.A.Z).

His previous acquaintance with the owners led him to the Loulou. He proposed a Café Gibraltar weekly line, where each DJ would "give his worldview in the Loulou". These evenings attracted a special blend of Tel-Avivian, Palestinian and Mizrahi hipsters, the latter being underrepresented in the Loulou's clientele. Toubul attributed the Loulou's success to Jabali, without whom "the Loulou would be just another place owned by two Ashkenazi Tel Avivians. With Jabali on board the place became a hotspot for Arab hipsters".

As part as an ongoing dialogue with Jabali, Toubul's project aimed to "crack open geography" and juggle between cultural and spatial boundaries, creating "a continuous musical space from the Sahara to Sudan, through the Nuba Mountains, and up to Bedouin music in Israel's Negev desert". Exploring musical borders, rather than geographical frontiers, opened up an alternative cultural geography which rises above national conflicts, and challenged the political economy of the border as an institutionalized violent space. "Of course music is influenced by borders and politics", Toubul noted, "but through music geography can be differently understood and constructed". Reassembling the spatial dichotomy into a sensual experience enables borders to "function as material reality, as metaphor, as social practice, as structures of feeling and as embodied experience" (Belkind 2021, p. 5).

While Jabali and Sagui Bizawe aimed to reconnect the Palestinian and the Israeli in spatial terms, Toubul's cultural aspiration was to deconstruct the representation of the Jew as a European colonial settler, and reposition Jews as natives of the region. He responded to the Palestinian discourse of indigeneity with a Mizrahi claim to roots, which resonates with but also departs from the Ashkenazi Zioinist hegemonic discourse.

> When I play Maor Edri [Israeli Mizrahi singer] as part of my set – it is consequential. Jabali won't play him. So I expand on Jabali's position when I say – I am part of this space! You tell me I'm a foreigner, a European colonialist. I am no European. I have a political say in this space as much as you do.

Laissez Passer's distinction lay in its creative freedom and cultural subversion. Toubul's musical line-up, moving between "Indie-Mizrahi" and "pop hits", reflected his rejection of the dichotomy between high (Western/Ashkenazi) and low (Oriental/Mizrahi) culture. The differences between the geographical origins of Moroccan, Ethiopian and Caucasian music are blurred in front of their rhythmic coherence: "that was the idea – the musical set doesn't have to be genre-based – it should be based on feeling and rhythm".

Joining the Anna Loulou crew exposed Laissez Passer to new audiences, but also restricted them to the musical repertoire identified with the bar. Toubul addressed the difficulties of maintaining a weekly line by pointing out the frequent contradiction between his musical and ideological vision as a DJ, and the Loulou's demands. When he started the Friday nights line, he recalled, he got a list of hits the crowd expected: "I understood I should not disregard this repertoire, since it is a metaphoric home to people, and I should be respectful". But as a proud professional DJ, he found it hard to fit a predetermined format: "I didn't have the creative freedom to play what I wanted all of the time".

Like Jabali and Sagui Bizawe, Toubul too understood music as a form of political protest. His protest focussed on the Jewish-Mizrahi struggle, and he wished to create a new reality that gives voice to the oppressed Mizrahi culture, *alongside* the oppressed Palestinian one. In the Loulou, he claimed, Ashkenzi Jews were overrepresented, and dominant cultural power structures were not challenged: "My ideal was that both Mizrahi and Palestinian crowds would come to my Loulou line. It didn't happen and it's not happening there still. It is mostly Ashkenazis and Palestinians".

The dance floor holds a special opportunity for forming a Mizrahi-Palestinian alliance based on musical consciousness. Toubul recalled an evening in the Loulou, where a Jewish guy of Yemenite origin joined the Arab dancers who performed a Dabke dance. Toubul played an elegant musical transition which ended up with Jews and Palestinians dancing a traditional Yemenite dance, which is similar in rhythm and in move.

Laissez Passer's line lasted for a couple of months, but by the time the interview with Toubul was conducted, he already decided to quit playing the Friday line, and his partners Gal Kadan and Khen Elmaleh took over. What started as a great promise became increasingly conflictual since as a conservative Jew he did not wish to work on a Friday night. The meeting point between Eros and politics, which transformed the party into a political binational statement, posed a dilemma for Toubul. This dilemma had to do with the language barrier since Toubul is not bi-lingual (unlike Jabali and Sagui Bizawe). He felt uneasy playing songs in Arabic (especially Palestinian ones) which might represent political stances he does not share:

> The Friday line in the Loulou represents a conflict for me. There's a song by Mohammed Assaf which is played every Friday. At the beginning of the song he praises the *Shuhada* [Palestinian martyrs]. I don't speak Arabic and that's the way I understood it, it might be my wrong interpretation. It's a song with a strong national-Palestinian connotation. It was weird. If you don't find it weird you are detached. But once you played this song the crowd went crazy, the party really took off. So I played it every time – I wanted to, because I want to make the crowd go wild, even if it means playing the Hammas anthem! But that was problematic. Once I stepped off the DJ stand I was reflecting – 'today I played a song I don't understand the meaning of, it might say – let's bomb Ashdod … And he does mention the word Shahid at the beginning and the crowd applauds. It's not ideal and I am uncomfortable with it.

Toubul's ambivalence towards the musical line-up, which celebrates a Jewish-Palestinian "carnival" distinguishes him from others actors in two ways. For him, as an alternative space, the Loulou had the potential of creating a Mizrahi-Palestinian alliance (instead of the established Ashkenazi-Palestinian one), based on joint culture. Though he did not regard the Loulou as orientalist, or blamed it for commodifying the oriental experience, Toubul claimed a wide Mizrahi crowd was never present in the space. The overrepresentation of "Orientalist hipsters" in the Loulou, he suggested, distinguished it from other cultural initiatives that share a distinct Mizrahi orientation (Like Albi café, Achoti house or café Gibraltar). He refused to take part in the alternative cultural discourse since he regarded it as an "inner Ashkenazi discourse". Accordingly, the Anna Loulou advanced a false image of subversive culture, celebrated as "cultural capital", while "the real alternative scene" operates in "low culture spaces" which "blend Arab and Mizrahi audiences and cultures" (such as Tel Aviv café or the Flaka club). "Ultimately, it's a scene of good Ashkenazi kids", he concluded his Loulou experience, "I don't think the ISA (Israel Security Agency) is concerned".

Requiem for a dream: the political hipster in search of a new home

> During the damned year of 2015, I came back home to Jaffa after a whole week of demonstrations in the West Bank … In the very same evening, I went to the Loulou; a place that always felt right and natural, but in that evening just accentuated the dissonance of our lives … I understood that an alternative imagined reality is also an escape from reality. But even escapism became impossible. The Anna Loulou inevitably closes its doors now. Jaffa has changed, reality changed,

we've changed too. A lot can be said about how this place changed the space and how the space changed the place – for better and worse – and I'm sure much will be written on this.

(Hagar Shezaf, a Loulou regular, Facebook post 10.1.2019)

During the early 2000s, gentrification in Jaffa has reached a temporary balance between the ever-rising cost-of-living and its allure for radical gentrifiers: up-to-date young activists who struggle against the process they are part of (Monterescu 2015). Resonating with the "rent gap" in gentrification studies (Smith 1987), this "culture gap" fostered a unique alternative subcultural scene on the margins of the city. Consequently, a new social type emerged, one which embodies the tensions of the binational city on the periphery of the centre. These agents lament their anticipated defeat in the struggle against gentrification, but at the same time feed off the energies triggered by it, in order to sustain a subversive counter-culture.

The typical hipster, an urban reflexive consumer, transformed into what we called "the political hipster", positioned at the intersection between the artistic, political and consumerist fields. The paper outlined an ideal type not as a stereotype of fixed positions, but rather as defining the contours of a broad spectrum of positionalities, which operate as resources for identity-formation. Three symbolic types – Palestinianism, Levantinization, and Mizrahiyut – define the political hipster's repertoire of action, from cosmopolitanism to trans-localism. Arab and Mizrahi music provided a local answer to the search for authenticity, while romantic orientalism is replaced with self-orientalism. The bar's protagonists took an active part in shaping both the imaginative and the actual space, through a creative use of identity politics. The common hipster's aversion of politics was substituted by an active political engagement, on the dance floor or beyond.

The political hipster came to life in the conflictual yet safe space of the Anna Loulou: an alternative cultural institution that challenged the Israeli principle of ethnic separation and mirrored a myriad of national and gender identities. But the place, like the political economy that enabled it, was not sustainable. In 2016 Gal and Bronstein decided to close the bar, which resulted in eight of the bar regulars buying the place in order to keep its activity. Though the bar clients were relieved at first, as time went by they felt the transition blurred some of the bar's distinctiveness and avant-garde appeal. Gradually, the main players dispersed: Bronstein and Gal migrated to Berlin, Jabali moved to Haifa and then to Berlin, Sagui Bizawe moved on to other Levantine projects, and Toubul founded an organization supporting conservative, Jewish, Zionist Mizrahiyut.

Against all odds, the bar operated for three more years, becoming even more radical as a BDS safe space.[6] In 2019, the new owners announced laconically that the bar would be closed due to endless legal struggles with greedy neighbours and municipal planning authorities. In response, the Anna Loulou community filled the social media with sentimental memories, and shared their nostalgic gratitude. Khen Elmalech, of Laissez-Passer, eulogized the social community that prospered in the liminal space:

> The Loulou didn't exist in a vacuum, reality always permeated, but there was a conscious and reflective sense of escapism, that was directly dependent on the reality outside … The crowds I witnessed in the Loulou's wildest nights were of people who wanted to make a real difference. A happy dance floor is a political dance floor. But enough with the sentimental posts. Twenty years from now they will make a docu-series on us … It will be titled 'dancing Dabke with pearls [lit. Arabic for Loulou] in our eyes'. (Facebook post 31.1.2019)

The rise and fall of the Anna Loulou unravels the relationship between the artistic, political and consumerist fields in the neo-liberal city. Once the bar closed down, the political hipster lost its natural habitat, rendering her future unclear. Despite the fact that no other urban institution managed to replace Anna Loulou, the political hipster continues to operate in other cultural venues in the binational city and beyond, as part of the "urban tribe" (Maffesoli 1995) that came to life. In the lack of a "home" which could contain the political hipster's tripartite facets (Palestinianism, Mediterranean Levantinization, and Mizrahiyut), different venues and pop-up events try to offer shelter for "Loulou refugees", as they refer to themselves, who wish to keep alive the social, political and musical line the bar entertained.

In September 2019, in a side street in Jaffa, a group of thirty Loulou refugees met in a small pub for an "Arab party". Hassan and Hadar, a Palestinian and a Jew, DJs of the younger Loulou generation, made the sentimental crowd dance to Arab music with a European touch. For a split moment, it felt like there could be an heir to the Loulou after all. Close to midnight, as the party started to take off, the owners asked the DJs to lower the volume. "The neighbors are complaining", he explained. It seemed like the chronicle of a foretold struggle between bourgeois gentrification and alternative culture is repeating itself.

Is the existence of the political hipster confined to the conflictual setting in Israel/Palestine? Or is the political hipster a new global figure that can thrive elsewhere? The productive tensions between the political and the hip call for additional research on the potential reciprocation between progressive ideologies and charisma, creative practice and institutional urban setting, social action and the cool. Contested cities such as Haifa and Jerusalem but also Berlin, Bratislava and Budapest, as well as Beirut, Cairo, Istanbul and other cities in the Global South could provide fruitful sites for such emerging configurations. The relations between culture and politics are always context-specific and express vernacular grievances. But with the global rise of right-wing populism, which mobilizes xenophobic affect, the political hipster seems like a potential agent of social change. Reflecting the specific sensibilities of late Capitalism, this new form of political engagement may serve as an opportunity for the Left to regain its political Eros and reach out to a new generation of concerned citizens.

Notes

1. The term *Mizrahi* (Hebrew for Oriental) denotes the identity politics which emerged with the second and third generations of Israeli Jews of Middle Eastern and Sephardic descent. The identity category *Mizrahiyut* is set in opposition to Ashkenazi hegemony, led by Jews of Euro-American descent. In recent decades, some Mizrahi Jews self-identify as Arab-Jews, thus opposing the categoric violence of Israeli ethnic classification, which created a false antinomy between Jewishness and Arab identity. For an analysis of the relation between the Mizrahi and the Arab-Jew see Shenhav (2006) and Shohat (2017).
2. We thank an anonymous reviewer for pointing to the parallels between the contemporary political hipster we analyze and the cultural setting of the original late 30s and 40s American hipster. In pre-Beat Culture, the historical hipster was also culturally ambiguous, navigating in a special tolerant space – i.e. Afro-American/white-American environments centered on black music (Jazz) – riddled with tensions and yet racially open. This is where black culture first became hip and the hipster started as a black figure (Leland 2005).
3. According to Handelman (1991, 205–206), symbolic types are charismatic and captivating individuals that are "rare but potent molders of the realities of others". Their defining feature is that they "are engaged in the search for perfect praxis — the erasure of the distinction between the ideal and the real (and so their synthesis) through the projection of a complete, holistic state of being, however this is envisaged".
4. The ambivalent discourse about labelling and self-identifying as a hipster assumes a contested political meaning when it comes to hipsterism in Palestinian society. See Arad's journalist account (2013).
5. Sagui Bizawe explicitly endorses the Levantine framing of his project, rather than what is known as "the Mediterranean option", which has been criticized for normalizing Israel's colonial place in the region (Ohana 2011, 77). Kahanoff's notion of Levantinism is thus an attempt to represent the Mediterranean as a space of cross-cultural exchange intimately linked to its colonial history and conflictual present. In this regard, the Levantine option constitutes an objective possibility for a binational road not taken (Aharon-Gutman and Ram 2017).
6. The Boycott, Divestment, Sanctions (BDS) is a Palestinian-led movement promoting sanctions against Israel.

Acknowledgments

We wish to express our gratitude to the Anna Loulou community for creating an alternative reality and for letting us join the ride. We thank Niv Gal and Ilana Bronstein for openly discussing fantasies and failures alike. Special thanks are due to DJs Muhammad Jabali, Eyal Sagui Bezawe, Ophir Toubul and Gal Kadan for the political Eros they spun around them. We are grateful to all our interviewees and friends for sharing their time and thoughts with us. The responsibility for the analysis of these narratives and observations remain ours along with any errors and omissions. We are indebted to Tamir Sorek and the participants of the Culture and Conflict in Palestine/Israel conference at the University of Florida. Daniel thanks the Central European University and the Gerda Henkel Foundation Funding Programme Lost Cities for making this project possible. Merav thanks Avner de Shalit and the Minerva Centre for Human Rights at the Hebrew University of Jerusalem for their support. Lastly, we thank the Ethnic and Racial Studies editorial board and anonymous reviewers for their valuable comments and helpful insights.

Disclosure statement

No potential conflict of interest was reported by the author(s).

ORCID

Merav Kaddar ⓘ http://orcid.org/0000-0002-5774-468X
Daniel Monterescu ⓘ http://orcid.org/0000-0002-6731-3015

References

Aharon-Gutman, Meirav, and Moriel Ram. 2017. "Objective Possibility as Urban Possibility: Reading Max Weber in the City." *Journal of Urban Design* 23 (6): 803–822.

Alsayyad, Nezar. 2001. *Hybrid Urbanism: On the Identity Discourse and the Built Environment*. Westport: Praeger.

Arad, Roy. 2013. "The New Underground". *Haaretz*. https://www.haaretz.com/. premium-how-do-you-say-hipster-in-arabic-1.5295748.

Belkind, Nili. 2021. *Music in Conflict: Palestine, Israel and the Politics of Aesthetic Production*. London: Routledge.

Bey, Hakim. 2003. *T.A.Z: The Temporary Autonomous Zone*. New York: Autonomedia.

Bourdieu, Pierre. 1984. *Distinction: A Social Critique of the Judgement of Taste*. Cambridge: Harvard University Press.

Brickell, Katherine, and Ayona Datta. 2011. "Introduction: Translocal Geographies." In *Translocal Geographies: Spaces, Places, Connections*, edited by Katherine Brickell and Ayona Datta, 3–20. Farnham: Ashgate.

Cowen, Deborah. 2006. "Hipster Urbanism." *Realy* 13: 22–23.

DiMaggio, Paul. 1982. "Cultural Entrepreneurship in Nineteenth-Century Boston: The Creation of an Organizational Base for High Culture in America." *Media, Culture & Society* 4 (1): 33–50.

Geoffrey, Moss, Wildfeuer Rachel, and McIntosh Keith. 2019. *Contemporary Bohemia: A Case Study of an Artistic Community in Philadelphia*. New York: Springer.

Greif, Mark. 2010. "Positions." In *What Was the Hipster? A Sociological Investigation*, edited by Mark Greif, Kathleen Ross, and Dayna Tortorici, 4–13. New York: N+1 Foundation.

Handelman, Don. 1991. "Symbolic Types, the Body, and Circus." *Semiotica* 85 (3–4): 205–225.

Hebdige, Dick. 1979. *Subculture: The Meaning of Style*. London: Routledge.

Hubbard, Phil. 2016. "Hipsters on Our High Streets: Consuming the Gentrification Frontier." *Sociological Research Online* 21 (3): 106–111.

Kaddar, Merav. 2020. "Gentrifiers and Attitudes Towards Agency: A new Typology." *Urban Studies* 57 (6): 1243–1259.

Kahanoff, Jacqueline. 2011a. "What About Levantinization?" *Journal of Levantine Studies* 1: 13–22.

Kahanoff, Jacqueline. 2011b. *Mongrels or Marvels: The Levantine Writings of Jacqueline Shohet Kahanoff, ed. Deborah Starr and Sasson Someck*. Stanford: Stanford University Press.

Karkabi, Nadeem. 2018. "How and Why Haifa Has Become the 'Palestinian Cultural Capital' in Israel." *City & Community* 17: 1168–1188.

Kobayashi, Koji, Steven.J. Jackson, and Michael P Sam. 2019. "Globalization, Creative Alliance and Self-Orientalism." *International Journal of Cultural Studies* 22 (1): 157–174.

Leland, John. 2005. *Hip: the History*. New York: Harper Perennial.

Maffesoli, Michel. 1995. *The Time of the Tribes: The Decline of Individualism in Mass Society*. California: Sage.

Maly, Ico, and Varis Piia. 2016. "The Twenty-First-Century Hipster: On Micro-Populations in Times of Superdiversity." *European Journal of Cultural Studies* 19 (6): 637–653.

McDonald, David A. 2013. *My Voice Is My Weapon: Music, Nationalism, and the Poetics of Palestinian Resistance*. Durham: Duke University Press.

Michael, Janna. 2015. "It's Really not hip to be a Hipster: Negotiating Trends and Authenticity in the Cultural Field." *Journal of Consumer Culture* 15 (2): 163–182.

Monterescu, Daniel. 2009. "The Bridled Bride of Palestine: Orientalism, Zionism, and the Troubled Urban Imagination." *Identities* 16: 643–677.

Monterescu, Daniel. 2011. "Beyond the Sea of Formlessness: Jacqueline Kahanoff and the Levantine Generation." *Journal of Levantine Studies* 1: 23–40.

Monterescu, Daniel. 2015. *Jaffa Shared and Shattered: Contrived Coexistence in Israel/ Palestine*. Bloomington: Indiana University Press.

Moss, Geoffrey, Rachel Wildfeuer, and Keith McIntosh. 2019. *Contemporary Bohemia: A Case Study of an Artistic Community in Philadelphia*. New York: Springer.

Oakes, Tim, and Louisa Schein. 2006. *Translocal China*. London: Routledge.

Ohana, David. 2011. *Israel and Its Mediterranean Identity*. New York: Palgrave Macmillan.

Pratt, Mary Louise. 2017. "Arts of the Contact Zone." In *Ways of Reading*, edited by David Bartholomae, Anthony Petroksky, and Stacy Waite (pp. 512--532). New York: Bedford/St. Martin's.

Sagui Bezawe, Eyal. 2016. "The Jaffa Bar That Takes a Leap Beyond Coexistence". *Haaretz*. February 8.

Schiermer, Bjørn. 2013. "Late-Modern Hipsters: New Tendencies in Popular Culture." *Acta Sociologica* 57 (2): 167–181.

Shenhav, Yehouda. 2006. *The Arab Jews: A Postcolonial Reading of Nationalism, Religion, and Ethnicity*. Stanford: Stanford University Press.

Shohat, Ella. 2017. *On the Arab-Jew, Palestine, and Other Displacements*. London: Pluto Press.

Smith, Neil. 1987. "Gentrification and the Rent Gap." *Annals of the Association of American Geographers* 77 (3): 462–465.

Turner, Victor. 1986. *The Anthropology of Performance*. New York: PAJ Publications.

Wacquant, Loïc. 2008. *Urban Outcasts: A Comparative Sociology of Advanced Marginality*. Cambridge: Polity.

Wampole, Christy. 2012. "How to Live Without Irony". *The New York Times*. November 17.

Yiftachel, Oren, and Haim Yacobi. 2003. "Urban Ethnocracy: Ethnicization and the Production of Space in an Israeli 'Mixed City'." *Environment and Planning D: Society and Space* 21: 673–693.

Face control: everynight selection and "the other"

Yotam Hotam and Avihu Shoshana

ABSTRACT
The paper analyzes micro-inequality in Tel Aviv night clubs, relying upon Levinas's concept of *the face*. In-depth interviews with nightclub doormen, or "selectors", as they are called in Israel, revealed that the clients' faces comprise a critical component of their screening work. At the same time, they reported that customers' faces make it difficult for them to do their jobs and force them to engage in *evading faces* and *suspending* ethical judgments. The paper shows how in these face-to-face interactions, the face of the "Other" (the "dangerous" Mizrahi male client) is fully recognized and then suspended, enabling the selectors to affirm and then resist its ethical call. The paper's discussion points to some of the implications of the ability of the selectors to affirm and resist the ethical obligation that Levinas attributes to the face, including a focus on the selectors' justification of violence.

Introduction

In-depth interviews with Tel-Aviv nightclub *selectors*, as they are called in Israel (*doormen* and *bouncers* in the United States and the U.K.) (see also Amir and Shoshana 2018), revealed how they identify the "dangerous other" (Watt 2010). In general, the objects of their screening can be referred to as the potential clients' *habitus*, a collection of behaviours, habits, skills, inclinations, and preferences that individuals acquire during their lifetime, in Bourdieu's (1984) terms. The selectors seek out cues of members of a specific group that does not pass the nightclub selection: *Mizrahi* men – these are Jews whose origin or the origin of their family is in Arab or Muslim countries. The selectors refer to these men as "heavy *Mizrahim*", compared with *"lite Mizrahim"*, those Mizrahim who "pass" as non-Mizrahim or whose appearance does not match the Mizrahim stereotype in Israel. These individuals are identified as "other" in the internal Jewish-Zionist symbolic order in Israel due to their physical and cultural proximity to what is considered to be "Arab", the non-Jewish other, constructed as the national "enemy" (Shenhav 2006; Shohat 1999). Due to the Arabness of the "heavy Mizrahim", who are warded off from entering the nightclubs, they are stigmatized as "arsim".

Ars, whose literal meaning in Arabic is pimp, is a pejorative term for Mizrahim.[1] This derogatory term, or this social type, contributed to the boundary work between Mizrahim and Ashkenazim (Jews originating from European countries and North America). The term also had a role in the establishment and maintenance of the "new Jew" in Israel, which assisted in the process of nation-building in Israel. The category of the "new Jew" was achieved, inter alia, through the aggressive elimination of the Arab habitus or the Jewish habitus that is closely related to Arabness (Mizrahiness) (Shohat 1999).

As portrayed in the current study, these ethnic and national dynamics were utilized by the selectors themselves, in the screening work in "everynight" (Handelman 2005) selection. These selectors, being Mizrahim themselves, testify to the resemblance (in terms of phenotypic appearance and habitus)[2] between themselves and the "heavy Mizrahim", "the arsim", and "the Arabs", and the fact that they themselves would not pass selection for nightclubs. In this sense, the selectors do not only symbolically eliminate (or "kill" in terms of Rimon-Or 2002) the "Arab" (who does not even attempt to enter the nightclubs due to what the selectors call "pre-selection"), but also the Arabness within themselves, which in turn, reinforces the Zionist order in Israel.

A crucial component of the screening work is the customer's "face" (in Hebrew: panim). This screening process is based on status signals to determine who is a bona fide client and who will be barred from entering the night club. At the same time, as the selectors in our study related, the "faces" of customers can make it difficult for them to do their jobs or may undermine their worker evaluations. Quoting Niv, a selector in one of the most sought-after night clubs in Tel Aviv:

> You have to do quick *face control* [a term said in English] that includes a rapid scan of the face and body for half a second, but––and here is the big 'but'––you have to remember that the moment you look at his face for more than that half a second, boom, you've lost it. You can't go on working. The key part of the work here––that's what I tell new selectors––is not to look at their faces. Remember what I'm saying to you: If you want to be professional and do your job properly, then there's no face. Evasion is the name of the game. No face, no face. The moment you look at his face, you are done for. You must obliterate his face. You do not want to see the sadness in his face.

The centrality of the concept of the face in the practice of everynight selection, as described by Niv, is crucial. The face concept refers not only to the body part but to the *general appearance* of the client that includes, among other things, skin colour, clothing style, accessories, tone of voice, and features (such as hot-tempered, violent, noisy).

The term "evading faces" refers to the frequent avoidance of looking at the others' faces (especially the "dangerous" male client or anyone failing to pass the selection process) and showing indifference to the denied client. The selectors view this action as a confirmation of their ability to be "professionals". Professionalism means that the selectors are required to "scan" the clients, which means engaging in what they term "face control".

Such terminology indicates the role of the face and the face-to-face interaction in the technical context of the selectors' profession. However, can this terminology also denote the ethical dimension that accompanies the selectors' work in their own eyes? Could the controlled and scanned face present an ethical demand? The face may appear in such a way as to be more than just a physical organ. It may also stand as a testimony to something deeper: the *Other* as a human being. The selectors' reference to concepts and images of extermination, Auschwitz, the annihilation of the Other, and murder (as we shall see) may indeed support such a reading of the mechanisms of their work and invite an exploration of some of its implications.

Through the use of Immanuel Levinas's face concept, we would like to explore the possible ethical dimensions that accompany the selectors' work from their perspective and to discuss some of their implications. The concept of the face, central to the selectors' nightly routine, is largely identified with Levinas's moral legacy, and hence the significance of Levinas's philosophy to the theoretical discussion in this paper.[3] Moreover, Levinas's face ethic touches upon images such as extermination, murder, and Auschwitz, and invites a possible, even if speculative, connection between the theoretical discussion and the selectors' work. Our aim, however, is not to compare Levinas's discussion of the face with the selectors' work, or to question the validity of his philosophy in the face of everynight practice. Rather, we seek to present an in-depth analysis of the everynight selection, for which Levinas's philosophy is highly relevant and, we suggest, fruitful.

Levinas's face concept seems to us to be more pertinent to our study than is Goffman's celebrated *face work* (1967). The preference of Levinas's concept lies in the fact that Goffman's theory, as Raffel (2002) argued persuasively, shows a lack of concern for morality, which is central to Levinas's work as much as it is to our examination (see also Pearl 2017). Against this background, our article posits two primary questions: What is the "face control" that nightclub selectors identify as critical to their professionalism? How can Levinas's conceptualization of the face facilitate an examination of nightly face control?

On this theoretical basis, we argue that the selectors' practice of refusing to look at the face of the other is due to their acknowledging and then suspending this action's ethical demand. The selectors thus refuse to look at faces, after, and perhaps because of, their acknowledging them for what they ethically represent. This refusal to look at the face does not emanate from not acknowledging the face. It is a refusal that stems from recognizing the face's "command", as Levinas (1961) put it. A refusal that takes shape after having acknowledged the face also differs from the unfamiliarity with the imperative of the face, of which Levinas (1961) speaks. In Levinas's face ethics, the face, once recognized, makes it impossible to kill. As we would like to demonstrate, in the context of the selectors' work, the face does not necessarily constitute such a difficulty, because it can be recognized and immediately deferred.

The face and "the other" in Levinas's philosophy

The concept of "the Other" (l'Autre) is central to Levinas's philosophy. The origin of this philosophy lies in the phenomenology of Husserl and Heidegger, the historical circumstances of post-1945 Europe, the experiences of Levinas as a prisoner of war, and the shock left by Auschwitz. Levinas sought, from an ontological point of view, to formulate human existence and define it as a total surrender to otherness (Davis 1996).

Levinas's *Time and the Other* (1947) can illustrate this matter. In this text, Levinas's ontological quest sought to show how "time is not the achievement of an isolated and lone subject, but that it is the very relationship of the subject with the Other" (1947, 39). The crux of the matter here lies in the departure from the subject's isolation by introducing the relationship to "the Other" as its basis. This move, then, can be considered as a turn from "solitude" to "relation".[4] Contrary to the assumption of the philosophical tradition extending from Parmenides to Heidegger that "the subject is alone because it is one", Levinas suggested that the basis of being is found in the "relationship with the Other" (Levinas 1947, 54). This relationship assumes "duality" rather than solitude at the root of human existence, and this duality assumes the otherness of "the Other" (represented here mainly by the notion of death) as wholly external to the human experience.

Levinas's concept of the "face" embodies the meaning of an ontology in our relations with others, in the social, ethical, and to a large extent, political spheres. If *Time and the Other* was an expression of Levinas's ontology, *Totality and Infinity* (1961) can serve as an illustration of the role of the face in his ethic, as it developed in the first decades following World War II.

Levinas's *Totality and Infinity* presents the face of the concrete other individual as comprising two primary characteristics: an expression of the absolute Other in the relationship with others and an ethical demand. As an expression of absolute otherness, the face is primarily (though not solely) a concretization of the subject's relationship with the idea of infinity. This idea gives expression to what remains wholly external and foreign to the subject, and in this sense, cannot be grasped or contained by the subject in any way. Thus, "The Other remains infinitely transcendent, infinitely foreign" (Levinas 1961, 194).

Infinity gives expression to absolute otherness in relation to the subject. It represents what remains wholly external to the subject (Levinas 1961). Thus, infinity may indicate something of an endless openness, or better, an *open endlessness*, beyond any grasp, standing over and against a "metaphysical closure" that Levinas associated with totality. The face obtains its fundamental meaning here. The revelation ("epiphany") of the face of the other manifests the infinite that cannot be contained, interpreted, identified, or merged with the subject, thus remaining completely "foreign". The face expresses the fact that the infinite otherness cannot be seen in an ordinary sense, as forms, because it is outside all "seeing forms". At the same time, it cannot be accessible to conceptualization. It can thus be revealed to the subject only as a "face", a concept that describes a presence that cannot be contained within the framework of language, vision, understanding, and comprehension of the subject. The presence of the face in this manner means standing "in the face" of the subject (Levinas 1961, 160).

If the face is an expression of absolute otherness, it also makes an ethical claim. This ethical claim relies upon the precedence of the Other over the subject. The term "welcoming the Other" expresses this ethical interpretation of the face's status, namely, the fact that "the epiphany of the face is ethical" (Levinas 1961, 199). This ethic seeks to discern a subject that is not a closed entity within itself, identical to itself, and exists or does not exist in relation to other entities, which are also closed within themselves. The subject is an entity dependent upon the otherness that comprises it, and, by extension, on the existence of other entities, referred to by this original otherness. Our identity is not a matter of being identical to ourselves, but rather of the prior condition of being with others. Our ethical obligation to others derives from this notion.

As it is inaccessible to the subject, the infinity of the face resists the power exerted by the subject's ego. However, this is an "ethical resistance". Levinas's "ethical resistance" to the face underscores a demand for responsibility, which the subject cannot resist. The inability to resist the face's demand is substantial. Because of this structure of ethical requirement, contrary to the urge to eradicate, the subject encounters a primary, inescapable claim encapsulated in the commandment, "Thou shalt not kill" (Levinas 1961, 199).

The revelation of the face, as an imperative not to kill, lay for Levinas at the heart of recognizing the other's concrete face, as well as at the heart of one's social life (Levinas 1961, 207). Society should represent a collective response to this commitment. Such a community for Levinas is a "fraternal community", based on the "welcoming of the Other" (Levinas 1961, 176). By employing the concept of "fraternal community", Levinas was not unaware of the theological language from which he sought to dissociate. Our aim, however, is to show how Levinas sought to establish the "original fact of fraternity" (Levinas 1961, 214) based on his face ethics. Here, the ethical precedence of the other over me is concretely embodied as "my position as brother", that is, in the way it assumes my responsibility toward others. (Levinas 1961, 176). In this way, relations with others and social relations in general are based upon the "wonder" of inner revelation – a revelation of the completely external Other and unknown and that of the self as comprising such an Other.

Study design

The findings is base on ethnogrpahies in two popular Tel Aviv nightclubs. These clubs are for heterosexual clients. The study includes several data sources: ethnographies of waiting in the lines to enter the clubs on the weekends, from October 2012 to October 2016; ethnographies of conversations between the selectors and customers in situ, that is, just before entering the club; interviews with clients who were denied access or gained entrance to clubs; and interviews with selectors and club owners (see also Amir and Shoshana 2018).

A total of 24 in-depth interviews were conducted with selectors who had worked from 1 to 4 years in popular Tel Aviv nightclubs (22 men and two women). Most of the selectors were in their late twenties. Twenty of the twenty-four selectors were Mizrahim, born in Israel (their parents or grandparents were born in Arab countries in Asia and Africa) and grew up in the socioeconomic periphery. The remaining four were Jews of Russian descent, born in the Former Soviet Union and raised in a socioeconomic class similar to that of the Mizrahi selectors. The findings of this article are based on interviews with Mizrahi selectors only. The interviews lasted between one and a half and three hours and were conducted in coffee shops or the interviewees' homes.

The interview comprised seven main sections: a description of the job; the basic decision-making process in accepting or denying a customer's entry to a club; a description of the ideal customer type that is admitted without issue; a depiction of three clients recently rejected by the selector; differences in selection policies regarding gender; the degree of interviewees' familiarity with the legal aspects of discrimination at clubs; and interviewees' social critique regarding selection for clubs.

All observations and interviews were analyzed using the methodological processes proposed by grounded theory (Strauss and Corbin 1998). Following open readings, focused readings were conducted (description of the job characteristics and fundamental difficulties encountered; characterization of customer types; identifying status cues; characterization of a typical rejected client; characterization of a typical admitted customer; and delineating ethnicity factors in selection). During these readings, several unanticipated themes were emerged from the data (the face concept; face evasion and strategies for implementing it; the face control concept; failing to evade faces; discernment between types of Mizrahim such as "heavy" and "lite" "Mizrahim").

Status signals, marked customers, and bona fide customers

Status signals adopted to assess the worth of other people (Berger et al. 1977; May and Chaplin 2008; May and Goldsmith 2018; Rivera 2010) are central at the entrance to night clubs in Tel Aviv. Based on these cues, members of an ethnic group regularly were denied access – Mizrahi men and especially those characterized by the selectors as *arsim* or as "heavy Mizrahim". Thus, as in other locales worldwide (May and Chaplin 2008; May and Goldsmith 2018; Rivera 2010), marked ethnic group members are those enduring selection at the entrance to nightclubs. In their study on discrimination in urban night-life, based on experimental audit methods, May and Goldsmith (2018) found that although whites, blacks, and Latinos dressed similarly, the doormen assessed them differently. Moreover, their research, like Rivera's (2010) study, based on ethnographies in an elite nightclub, as well as our research, shows that it is the doormen's responsibility to assess and determine which of the patrons will enter the club and who will be denied entry. It is noteworthy that, differing from these studies, the selectors in Tel Aviv make an explicit distinction within the members of the marked ethnic group ("heavy Mizrahim" vs. "lite Mizrahim") to facilitate their selection work.

The *arsim* (or "heavy Mizrahim") are described by the selectors as "violent", "barbarians", "human waste", and those who "diminish the quality and prestige of the place". The definition of "heavy Mizrahim" or "arsim" was suggested by several selectors as closely related to the word and the derogatory term "Arab", common in everyday Hebrew. This is how Lior described it:

> Heavy Mizrahi or ars is also called 'Arabic' or 'our cousin'[5] in our [selectors'] slang. This is also why Arabs do not come here altogether. There is a preselection process. A heavy Mizrahi is one with Arab's appearance, taste, and Arabic behavior.

Interviewer:	What is Arabic taste?
Lior:	Dressing very elegantly, as if they came to their sister's wedding in the village. And everyone is dressed the same, too. You can't tell them apart. They're all similar. Most importantly [laughs] – the cologne. They sprinkle half a bottle on themselves. They even use the same kind of cologne as Arabs.
Interviewer:	And what is Arabic behavior?
Lior:	The attire, the violence, the horniness, and they arrive in groups of just men. Arsim cannot come in here because, within twenty

minutes, they are drunk, become violent and look at the girls like Arabs look at Jewish women at the beach. As if they had never seen a girl in their life. They also use their Arabic language: my life (hayati), my eyes (ayuni), my friend [habibi].

Noteworthy are several characteristics in Lior's description. Lior alludes to "Arabic habitus" in terms of style of dress, language, and recreation characteristics; Lior uses the word Arabic as a derogatory term or curse, similar to common phrases in Hebrew (such as "Arabic taste" to describe the lack of an aesthetic sense); Arab partygoers do not come to the nightclubs in Tel Aviv, which makes them Jewish spaces; as part of the Zionist meta-narrative, Lior indicates the "Arab" as other, and to Jews originating from Arab countries (Mizrahim) as an additional other, within the Jewish group, who are required to conform to the ideal Israeli habitus that is "free" of Mizrahi status cues.

Analysis of the interviews facilitates the identification of nine status cues – attesting to Levinas' (1961) claim that "ethics is an optics" – which are identified by the selectors: skin colour ("Blacks are a kind of 'suspicious object' before they even open their mouths. They are less likely to pass selection".); place of residence ("development towns" – those communities in Israel's periphery with a high concentration of Mizrahim); style of dress ("Adidas suit"[6]; "button-down shirts and Tommy Hilfiger or Armani or Versace cigar pants and elegant black shoes … What is important is that some of the top buttons are undone, and their shaved chest peeks out".); haircut style ("a soccer player haircut": "cropped hair with a shaved stripe on the side, a so-called mohawk on the side, and sometimes even one shaved eyebrow"); types of cologne ("They spray a strong cologne you can smell from miles and they have a few kinds of them"); language ("cheap language, street language, inarticulate, heavy Mizrahi, grammatical mistakes. They use words like 'my eyes',[7] 'God is blessed'"); tone of speech ("The clumsy talk of drugged people who draw out the words and sentences as if they are snorting now"); walking style ("clumsy walking, a bit like a monkey, exposed arms on the right and left"); accessories (gold necklace, star of David pendant, gold necklace with the name of his girlfriend, a gold chain linked bracelet, a large ring with a black stone in the middle of it, what is called an "Eyal Golan ring"[8]).

Unlike the prevailing studies concerning selection bases and status cues in nightclubs, which emphasize race, skin colour, clothing style, and accessories (May and Chaplin 2008; May and Goldsmith 2018; Rivera 2010), the selectors in Tel Aviv also refer to unique status cues such as scent (and specific cologne brands), walking style, and speaking style. The broad ethnographies have revealed how some of the customers who know from experience that they do not pass selection try to "correct" their appearance (see Amir and Shoshana 2018). In this way, they try to pass.[9] The most common "corrective" passing practices are closing the upper shirt buttons, putting their cigarettes in their pocketand speaking in a low voice.[10] The identification of status cues by the selectors transform the cusemers into an object of the "problematic" or "dangerous" customers, or as Levinas (1961, 85–86) put it:

> you turn yourself toward the Other as toward an object when you see a nose, eyes, a forehead, a chin, and you can describe them ... .The relation with the face can surely be dominated by perception, but what is specifically the face is what cannot be reduced to that.

Selection work in everynight life

Face control

Among the interviewees, the concept of the face and its various uses frequently appeared in this context and particularly in response to questions about the decision-making process regarding admitting or rejecting customers to the club. The preoccupation with the face concept arose when we asked, "What is the most difficult thing for you at work?" ["The face. Where you can see the pain"], "What makes your work easier?" ["Not looking at the face"] or "What tip would you give to a new selector?" ["Do not ever look at the (denied-entry) customer's face".] Analyzing the explicit use of the term "face" points to two main steps in the selection process: face control and face evasion.

In response to the question, "How do you decide who enters and who does not enter the club", Maor replied:

Maor:	We do what selectors call *face control* ... a quick scan of the face and the body. Two seconds and you already know who will be admitted and who is an *ars*. There is no playing games here, you know right away. Face control is a fast 'whish' over the person in front of you. You cannot be too wrong.
Interviewer:	You never get it wrong?
Maor:	Rarely. If at all. And if I'm hesitant, I ask for an identity card and solve it.
Interviewer:	How?
Maor:	If his family name is "Azzarzer,"[11] and he lives in Netanya. I understand that I was not wrong.
Interviewer:	About what?
Maor:	..with there being a 'suspicious object' before you [laughs] ... I mean, an *ars*.
Interviewer:	Have you ever been wrong?
Maor:	There have been only a few cases where I was wrong. I've been working in this business for a long time. I'm proficient at face control. Face control is like a *gay-dar*. We have Omer here, a gay bartender, who has radar in his head. He takes a half-second look at a man and knows if he's gay or straight. His *gay-dar* never lies. I'm the same with face control on *arsim* [laughs] ... You immediately recognize them, and the fact that

we have devices, such as *gay-dar* and face control, helps us impose order.

It is interesting to note that Maor, like all the other selectors, did not refer only to the "face" itself when using the concept of "face control", but rather to a whole-body scan to identify the status of a controlled person. Like in Levinas's (1961) concept of the face, the selectors' concept refers not only to specific facial features, but to the kind of person standing in front of the selector, the person's character or worth in the eyes of the selector. Against this backdrop, however, Maor referred to face control, like *gay-dar*, as an instrument with a low probability of error for the detection of socially marked populations.

Other selectors presented similar confidence in their "face control". Their engagement in sorting and scanning relates to being in control, particularly regarding the connection between concrete faces and the worth of the person behind the face (from their perspective), central to Levinas' theory, as well. In just a few seconds, they construct a preliminary impression of the person in front of them (see also Rivera 2010).[12] At this stage, the selector identifies the face and what it ostensibly represents.

Face evasion

The expression face evasion was introduced by Yarin as a response to the question, "What happens after the face control?"

> Face evasion. From this point on, the whole story is to evade the face of someone who does not pass selection, that is, not to look at his face. ... and to look in other directions or to find other solutions, and especially to understand that he is not an ordinary client ... That he is big trouble, or an *ars* that is going to ruin your evening. Stick to the understanding that he is an *ars*, a criminal, a problem, another person, not the ordinary people that come out to enjoy themselves ... He is a negative, dangerous person that lowers the level.

Face evasion means not looking at the face of a customer who has been denied entry or defined in the nightclub scene as "someone who doesn't pass selection" (Amir and Shoshana 2018). But somehow echoing a Levinasian conceptualization of the other's humanity under the concept of the face, the selectors evade looking at the other person as a person. After the selection decision, it becomes difficult to look at the other's face because of what it represents, namely the other's humanity. The selector sees himself as someone who operates *face-to-face*, in Levinas's terms, and he encounters the difficulty involved with the other being denied access. The intimacy compels him to search for "other solutions". Yarin hints at one of the solutions, to be discussed below, "clinging to the understanding that he [the denied client] is an *ars*".

Analyzing the selectors' accounts reveals three key tactics for face evasion. It is important to emphasize that these face evasion tactics are undertaken when the denied-entry customer lingers at the site and when the selector fails at "not looking him in the face".

Face-evasion techniques: stereotypes, "mug", and eliminating otherness

When Eliraz related a client's insistence on entering the nightclub, even after being informed that he could not enter ("You are not on the guest list") and had to leave, he proceeded to the following tactic:

> He was insistent, and it started to be difficult because he was not a bad person, he was just an *ars*. So, I switched to the tactic of not looking him in the face and seeing him as a "mug." Mug (*partzuf*, in Hebrew) is a slang term adopted by selectors for a stereotypic *ars*, from head to toe. That makes the job easier because then he becomes just another one of the masses, anonymous.

Later, when we asked why it was easier, Eliraz replied:

> Because then, you don't really see a person before you, but some kind of icon, a cheap stereotype, it looks like a joke on *'Eretz Nehederet'* [a popular satire program in Israel] about *arsim*. You move it from just a human face to a mug.

Eliraz's attempts not to see the "problematic" customer's face can indicate, as Levinas (1961) suggested, that the face is a reminder not to exhibit violence toward the other. Encountering the face of the other, Levinas emphasizes, carries moral significance. In this sense, Levinas does not perceive the face as a particular depiction or appearance, but as a moral reminder: Do not exhibit violence toward the other. At the same time, Eliraz was trying to overcome the *ethical stimuli* (in Levinas's terms). As Eliraz stated, "It started to be difficult because he was not a bad person".

The transformation of the human client into an extreme stereotype by "shifting" the customer from the status of "face" to the status of "mug" helps create cognitive and behavioural shortcuts. Moreover, this transformation helps shift him from a "persona" to a non-singular, thus dehumanizing him, which in turn, makes the selection process easier for the selector. Earlier in this paper, we underlined Levinas's emphasis on the intimate relations between recognizing the face and humanizing the other, and here we encounter a somewhat parallel, albeit opposite, association between eschewing the face and dehumanizing the other. Moreover, the transformation of a person into a stereotype generates the emotional distance required of selectors. In other words, the subject's transformation from being a "face" to being "faceless" is done by perceiving him as a stereotype and hence placing him under the category of the "masses". Switching the rejected client's "face" to the status of a "mug" defers a moral dilemma, thus enabling a potentially violent response. In other words, this tactic does not ignore the face of the other person, but defers it, by turning it into a "mug", following the recognition of his face.

The materiality of status, voice, and body cues

When Liran also noted that transforming the rebuffed customer into a stereo-typic image did not always work for him, mainly because the client repeatedly insisted on entering by what he calls "pleading, that touches you a bit", we asked him how he deals with it:

> I do guided imagery [laughs]; I pretend to close my eyes and hear only his voice or even stare only at his *ars* bracelet … The moment you hear only his voice, you get tougher, and then it's easier for you to stand up to his supplications and do your work … because it's literally the voice of an *ars*.

The selection work described by Liran, therefore, includes a special kind of emotional work (Hochschild 1983): guided imagery, which calls for a pro-longed focus on status cues (voice, accessories). Dor also describes this focus:

> This focus on his rings, his voice, and his body produce 'immersion in his *arsi-ness*' [laughs], meaning you are overwhelmed by his *arsiness* and realize that he cannot enter [Laughs]. It's too much. Experience the *arsiness* in this immer-sion, and it's enough for you [laughs].

Dor, like other selectors, noted the long gaze at the physical status cues of the social types that do not pass selection. He also described how the prolonged gaze or the "immersion in *arsines*" makes selection easier, mainly because of the "overload" experience. The selector "places himself" into a few seconds of "intense *arsines*" or "overload" of *arsiness*, and then experiences a physical and emotional experience of "danger" and "threat" associated with the social construction work of "dangerous individuals" (Foucault 1977) and "*arsim*" in Israel.

"What happens when all the tactics are exhausted?"

When we asked the selectors, "What happens when all the tactics are exhausted?" we received a collective response, accompanied by some dis-comfort, embarrassment, and an apology for the poor taste of its black humour: "The Final Solution". Twenty out of 24 selectors used this term. The embarrassment associated with this term is related to the memory of the Holocaust in Nazi Germany to which the term refers, even if it is used as black humour. When we asked Ofek, our first interviewee, "What do you mean by *final solution*?" he replied:

Ofek: Wow, I feel really uncomfortable now; you will think I'm a Nazi, but remember that this is just an expression used by club

	selectors here. Besides, you promised me that everything will remain anonymous [laughs]. The 'Final Solution' is that after you have exhausted all the tactics used to ignore the problematic customer and get rid of him, you send him to the 'Holocaust corner' [laughs]. There is a joke among us [the selectors]: He's better off leaving before we put him in the 'Holocaust corner' … It's black humor … Have you heard of it?
Interviewer:	No.
Ofek:	The Holocaust corner is a small area near the entrance to the club where we put the customers that have no chance of getting in, the heavy *arsim*, just to have them wait and give up. The humiliation puts them in a corner [laughs], and they leave in the end.
Interviewer:	And if they don't give up?
Ofek:	No way. It is done with the assurance that they will give up. That's the whole point. They leave in the end just from the embarrassment. It's a kind of punishment. Only the problematic ones are there on display [laughs].

The above depictions show that the term "final solution", which is well known to the selectors as relating to the fate of Jews under the Nazi regime, is recycled by them as an emblem for public exposure and punishment. The very term "selectors", as it is used in the Israeli context of gatekeeping, points to the same collective memory. One may recall how Levinas's face ethics was redolent of the Holocaust and the memory of Auschwitz. Notwithstanding the colossally different social political and cultural context, selectors fall back on the same collective memory. Thus, the final solution is a concept used by selectors when the "problematic" client, following a long argument with the selector, is firmly requested by the selector to move to a space reserved for the "deviants". The public visibility and the social stigma accompanying it comprise a punitive measure that not only puts the "deviant" on public display (in the "city square"), but also establishes, through increased self-awareness, feelings of social inferiority, such as shame, embarrassment, and humiliation (Shott 1979).

While the selectors may adopt a Holocaust-related lexicon for its slang factor, the current article presents it also as a mechanism that allows evasion of the subject that is portrayed by such terminology. It enables the continuation of abusive acts toward a targeted group of clients. Put otherwise, the use of black humour, as Kidron (2010) shows, for example, works against the burdens of "heavy" meanings and "serious" interpretations. Black humour, in this sense, seems to give the selectors cultural (and personal) authorization to commit what they acknowledge are acts of violence.

Cultural similarity and face evasion

The selectors in our research were mostly Mizrahim, who testified to having "a heavy Mizrahi appearance" themselves, thus resembling in many ways those potential customers to whom they are entrusted to bar entry. Thus, the selectors are the gatekeepers who assess and sort culturally similar individuals or whose "faces" are similar to their "faces".

This last point appears critical. The most common finding in the research literature on sorting out face-to-face interactions (e.g. job interviews) points to a "similar-to-me bias" (Rivera 2015). This bias means that cultural similarity between gatekeepers and candidates enhance their chances for acceptance. However, the selectors in our study showed the opposite inclination. Unlike other studies on evaluation and sorting (Lamont 2009; Rivera 2015), not only do they not make it easier for others like them to obtain material and symbolic rewards (i.e. admission to the club or positive regard), they make it more difficult for them. Sixteen of the 24 interviewees explicitly referred to issues of cultural similarity and "self-reflection" as answers to the question about their efforts to evade faces. Noam, for example, had to stop himself three times as he recalled:

> And as you see, I am also a kind of an *ars*. I'm a black Mizrahi who would not pass selection myself … and in general, some of the people I do not allow entry look exactly like me, like my brothers … Sometimes they [people] get confused and think that I am an Arab. It happens to a lot of heavy Mizrahim. They even talk to me in Arabic sometimes. That's the reason we don't pass selection in Tel Aviv [laughs]. I am sure that in nightclubs in Gaza, we will easily pass selection [laughs]. Maybe we need to move to Gaza [laughs]. … [Who is 'we'?] … Heavy Mizrahim … The Ashkenazim here think we're Arabs anyway, so let's end it that way, and that's that [laughs].

Noam, as did other interviewees, used his appearance as proof that the selection story was not personal, but social. Eliav articulated this perspective:

> My heavy Mizrahi appearance and the fact that I myself would not pass selection is proof that you do not have to take it personally. It's a social matter. We need to keep customers safe.

What is interesting in the accounts of the selectors in this context is that they used their "heavy Mizrahi appearance" and their cultural similarity to customers whose entry was denied (adopting the term "brothers") to normalize the selection.

Discussion: face, face evasion, resistance, and ethics

How are we to understand the selectors' refusal to look the denied other in the face and the range of mechanisms associated with this refusal? Here, we wish to bring Levinas's (1961) conceptualization of the face, discussed in the first section of this paper, to more closely bear on the "face control" of selectors in Israeli nightclubs. Specifically, we suggest that applying Levinas's conceptualization to the selectors' work facilitates an understanding

of their ability to resist the ethical duty that Levinas attributes to the face following its recognition. Thus it seems, that the selectors acknowledge (rather
than ignore) the face and only then suspend its ethical demand.

In this context, three points can be asserted. First, the face is an explicit
element of the selectors' workplace ethics. It lies at the core of their everynight selection, which is the identification process used by the selectors,
determining entry to the club. Second, for the selectors, the face comprises
a broad term, signifying an essence of the other. Thus, the face appears as
more than just a particular physical organ. It also stands as a testimony to
the other as a human being. The critical point relates to how Levinas's
ethics may underscore the work strategies of the selectors. When selectors
refer to the face, they allude to what, for them, is the value of the human
being facing them. Following this conceptualization of the face, the selectors
repeatedly include not only the context of the concrete face, but all that per-
tains to its meaning as a representation of the character of the other, their
qualities, and their value as a human being. In Levinas's (1961) terms, it
could be contended that the human qua human presents itself in the face
of the denied other. By claiming this, we do not ignore the pragmatic and
technical dimensions of the selectors' identification work that addresses
social and cultural issues in a concrete Israeli context of young people's nightlife. However, the selectors themselves allude to ethical meanings that stem
from the face of the other, and from what this face represents to them:
namely, a confrontation with their own humanity as evoked by the face of
the other and, in this sense, by its predominance.

For the third point, we recall that despite the intimidation experienced by
encountering the other's face, the selectors continue to use violence against
the other (i.e. the customer) or, to use the Levinasian term, "to kill" the customer. Given our discussion of Levinas, how are we understand this action taken
by the selectors? We suggest the following: Upon being confronted by ethical
demand, as they repeatedly noted, they suspend it. Indeed, suspending the
ethical demand, fully acknowledged by the selectors, enables them to sur-
mount it. Even once the ethical demand of the face is fully revealed to the
selectors, in applying a range of techniques, they suspend and resist its "call".

Face control, or the refusal to look at the face, is one technique that does
not emanate from not recognizing the face. It is an evasion that stems from
recognizing the face's "command" in Levinas's (1961) terms. The point to
note, then, is that face evasion does not relate to conscious or deliberate
acts, even if so articulated, but instead marks an inescapable consequence
of encountering the face and responding instinctively to its command. Suspending a reaction after acknowledging the face differs from the lack of familiarity with the imperative of the face, as addressed by Levinas.

Here, Levinas's reiteration of the command, "Thou shalt not kill", is central.
This call ethically binds those who acknowledge the face of the other and

serves as a command that cannot be ignored or denied. The selectors' face control, however, signifies their capacity to resist this ethical duty despite its acknowledgment. In the context of the selectors' work, the face can be recognized and deferred, a conclusion that might suggest how the other is concurrently recognized and rejected.

This last point appears to be critical, since the selectors in our study were not participants who were unaware or denied the threat of the other or the "murder" (in Levinas's terms) that they carried out, and yet, they continued to discharge their duties. Consider, for example, how selectors adopted specific strategies of face evasion to carry on in their jobs. Under this strategy, we can understand how face control involves identifying and recognizing the face in its full ethical sense. Unlike a situation where the individual is unable to recognize the other's face or ignores it, the situation under study involves recognizing the other's face and then turning away from it. Arguably, then, the individual is cognizant of the strong ethical demand before suspending it. This dialectic of acknowledgment and suspension enables the continuation of violence.

Exploring the selectors' work in light of Levinas's ethics enables us to further suggest three main strategies for the persistence of violence, despite the recognition of the face and its ethical imperative. First, turning the face into a "mug" reframes the other as a stereotype that obliterates the person's otherness and reclassifies them into a stigmatized public category (i.e. the "masses"). The second strategy was engaging a long deferral (which a selector called "guided imagery") with concrete cues (i.e. voice and body) increases the selector's experience of threat and moral panic and highlights the dangerous resemblance to the other. The third strategy involved physically placing the other in a stigmatized public arena to induce their shame and embarrassment (also termed *emotions of social control*; Shott 1979). This public humiliation and self-regulation push the other's face aside and eventually away from the scene.

Finally, an additional mechanism that provides justification for violence and operates to suspend the face should be noted: the role of cultural similarity. This tactic seem to be especially valuable in view of Levinas's discussion of "fraternal community" and the "welcoming of the Other". Thus, we suggest that the selectors do not only recognize the face, in the Levinasian sense, but even recognize "brotherhood", within their victims. This feeling of "fraternal" resemblance compels them to recognize that they, too, would not pass selection ("We look like brothers ... I wouldn't pass selection either"). The selectors, nonetheless, continue to "kill" the brotherly other or at least resist the ethical call entailed in the recognized face. Thus, at the heart of this fraternal identification lies not the "welcoming" of their brother, but his rejection.

This complexity, related to the screening that Mizrahi selectors administer on the Jewish "other" – i.e. Mizrahim – in the hegemonic Zionist order deserves focused research attention. It could be argued that the marking and exclusion of the heavy Mizrahi (arsim) from a space of entertainment also means the exclusion of the selectors from their own Mizrahiness or the symbolic death of the embodied Arab habitus within them (Rimon-Or 2002). At the same time, in contrast to Mizrahim who have attained socioeconomic mobility and prefer to dissociate from their ethnic-Mizrahi identity (Shoshana 2016), the selectors, who are characterized by a low socioeconomic background, do not express phenomenological or practical dissociation from their (heavy) Mizrahism in their everyday lives. The selectors described this symbolic death of Mizrahism and Arabism phenomenologically as an ad-hoc practice, as their source of livelihood. The Mizrahi selectors identify as Jews and Mizrahim, rather than as Israelis, such as Mizrahim who executed mobility (Shoshana 2016) or as Arab-Jews, such as Mizrahi intellectuals (Shoshana 2014).

Moreover, the selectors, aware of their proximity to the Arab habitus and their social perception as "arsim", internalized the social construction of heavy Mizrahism as threatening to the social order. At the same time, they reported the "naturalness" of their heavy Mizrahiness and their sense of comfort with it. Indeed, they did not admit to maintaining a distance from Mizrahiness, nor view Mizrahi identity as sabotaging acquisition of symbolic cultural capital as mobile Mizrahim claim.

All of this exists alongside a strong emphasis by the selectors on their Jewish (and not Arab-Jewish) identity. Perhaps this ambivalence can be explained in terms of how spaces intersect with individuals' personal identities (Gieryn 2000). The selectors live and work in Mizrahi spaces (development towns and working-class jobs) that allow them to maintain Mizrahi identity as it is constructed in the hegemonic Zionist order (emphasis on the Jewish component and symbolic elimination of Arabness). On the other hand, however, mobile Mizrahim, who live and work in Ashkenazi spaces (prestigious neighbourhoods and professional jobs), prefer dissociation from Mizrahiness because it is associated with a low cultural and symbolic capital under neoliberal discourse and the meritocratic ethos (Shoshana 2016).

Bringing together these complexities in the context of ethnic relations and the Levinasian concept of the face in a specific arena of popular culture in Israel may stimulate further research into additional cultural and social spaces. In particular, there is a need to continue to theoretically and empirically contemplate the ambivalent and elusive positions of various ethnic subjects as they relate to hegemonic orders, in those situations in which they simply and unavoidably stand face-to-face with their "other".

Notes

1. Despite all our many attempts we have not been able to find an academic paper on the genealogy of the term *"ars"*.

2. The interviews with the club managers and the selectors themselves revealed that the selectors were chosen, inter alia, because of their resemblance to Mizrahi customers who do not pass selection. The appearance of "Heavy Mizrahism" is described as "threatening" and as someone having the power to deal with "problematic" customers.

3. Levinas' (1961) face concept that refers to the bodily organ as well as to the other's being, evokes the Hebrew association between face (*panim*), and inner content (*pnim*). This conceptual approximation appears in the Jewish textual tradition in a variety of contexts relating to God and to others, and it reappears in the cogitation of Franz Rosenzweig, to which Levinas relates.

4. We thank Cedric Cohen Skalli for his pointing to this possible reading of Levinas.

5. "our cousins" is a slang term commonly used by Israeli Jews in relation to Arabs.

6. It is interesting to compare these sartorial practices to descriptions in Arkin's (2009) study of the construction of identity among young North African Jews in France, using the distinctions of young North African Muslims in France, through fashion. These distinctions help young Jews dissociate from the cultural and physical resemblance to young Muslims. These young Jews, for example, do not wear the *Adidas* brand because it is identified with Muslim Arab clothing and is considered "cheap".

7. My eyes (*eynaim sheli*) is the Hebrew literal translation of the Arabic *Ayuni*, which relates to an intimately precious close person, such as a child or a beloved subject.

8. Eyal Golan is a popular Mizrahi music singer in Israel, described by many selectors as an example of a person who would not pass selection because of being an *ars*.

9. Harel's (2019) auto-ethnographic article offers an interesting engagement in sartorial practices in another context – in Jewish settlements – by wearing and removing the yarmulke that is on his head. Through sartorial politics, Harel describes dynamics of visibility, belonging, respectability, and control over social identity.

10. For passing techniques in another context see Kelly's (2006) article on identity documents at military checkpoints in the Palestinian territories. The article describes how Palestinians use passing techniques to cross the checkpoints and avoid being detained by Israeli soldiers. These passing techniques include carrying a foreign passport, an Israeli identity card, or a yellow (not green) Israeli license plate; driving luxury vehicles (like a Volvo); physical appearances by young men; haircut style, manner of appearance and dress style, speaking the Hebrew slang of Israeli teenagers, and playing hip-hop music on the car radio.

11. Azzarzer is a common family name in the Jewish community of immigrants from Morocco.

12. For research on how rabbis in conversion institutes in Israel take a quick look to decide whether the potential convert can be admitted into the "Jewish club", see Kravel-Tovi (2017).

Disclosure statement

No potential conflict of interest was reported by the author(s).

Funding

This work was supported by Israel Science Foundation: [Grant number 1598/12].

References

Amir, D., and A. Shoshana. 2018. "'My Body Spoke to Me': 'Marginal' Organs, Metonymic Somatization, and the Pain of Social Selection." *Journal for the Theory of Social Behaviour* 48 (4): 475–491. doi:10.1111/jtsb.12185.

Arkin, K. 2009. "Rhinestone Aesthetics and Religious Essence: Looking Jewish in Paris." *American Ethnologist* 36 (4): 722–734. doi:10.1111/j.1548-1425.2009.01206.x.

Berger, J., F. Fisek, R. Norman, and M. Zelditch. 1977. *Status Characteristics and Social Interaction: An Expectation States Approach.* New York: Elsevier.

Bourdieu, P. 1984. *Distinction: A Social Critique of the Judgment of the Taste.* Cambridge: Harvard University Press.

Davis, C. 1996. *Levinas: An Introduction.* Malden, MA: Polity Press.

Foucault, M. 1977. *Discipline and Punish: The Birth of the Prison.* New York: Vintage Books.

Gieryn, T. 2000. "A Space for Place in Sociology." *Annual Review of Sociology* 26: 463–496. doi:10.1146/annurev.soc.26.1.1463.

Goffman, E. 1967. "On Face Work." In *Interaction Ritual: Essays on Face-to-Face Behavior,* edited by E. Goffman, 5–33. New York: Doubleday Anchor.

Handelman, D. 2005. "Dark Soundings: Towards a Phenomenology of Night." *Paideuma* 51: 247–261.

Harel, A. 2019. "Under the Cover of the *Kippah*: on Jewish Settlers, Performance, and Belonging in Israel/Palestine." *Journal of the Royal Anthropological Institute* 25 (4): 760–777. doi:10.1111/1467-9655.13130.

Hochschild, A. 1983. *The Managed Heart: Commercialization of Human Feeling.* Berkeley: University of California Press.

Kelly, T. 2006. "Documented Lives: Fear and the Uncertainties of Law During the Second Palestinian Intifada." *Journal of the Royal Anthropological Institute* 12 (1): 89–107. doi:10.1111/j.1467-9655.2006.00282.x.

Kidron, C. 2010. "Embracing the Lived Memory of Genocide: Holocaust Survivor and Descendant Renegade Memory Work at the House of Being." *American Ethnologist* 37 (3): 429–451. doi:10.1111/j.1548-1425.2010.01264.x.

Kravel-Tovi, M. 2017. *When the State Winks: The Performance of Jewish Conversion in Israel.* New York: Columbia University Press.

Lamont, M. 2009. *How Professors Think: Inside the Curious World of Academic Judgment.* Cambridge: Harvard University Press.

Levinas, E. 1947. *Time and the Other.* Pittsburg: Duquesne University Press.

Levinas, E. 1961. *Totality and Infinity.* Boston: Martinus Nijhoff Publishers.

May, R., and K. Chaplin. 2008. "Cracking the Code: Race, Class and Access to Nightclubs in Urban America." *Qualitative Sociology* 31 (1): 57–72. doi:10.1007/s11133-007-9084-7.

May, R., and P. Goldsmith. 2018. "Dress Codes and Racial Discrimination in Urban Nightclubs." *Sociology of Race and Ethnicity* 4 (4): 555–566. doi:10.1177/2332649217743772.

Pearl, S. 2017. *Face/On: Face Transplants and the Ethics of the Other.* Chicago: University of Chicago Press.

Raffel, S. 2002. "If Goffman Had Read Levinas." *Journal of Classical Sociology* 2 (2): 179–202. doi:10.1177/1468795X02002002222.

Rimon-Or, A. 2002. "From the Death of the Arab to 'the Death of the Arabs'." *Theory and Criticism* 20: 23–56. [Hebrew].

Rivera, L. 2010. "Status Distinctions in Interaction: Social Selection and Exclusion at an Elite Nightclub." *Qualitative Sociology* 33 (3): 229–255. doi:10.1007/s11133-010-9152-2

Rivera, L. 2015. *Pedigree: How Elite Students Get Elite Jobs*. Princeton: Princeton University Press.

Shenhav, Y. 2006. *The Arab Jews: A Postcolonial Reading of Nationalism, Religion, and Ethnicity*. Palo Alto, CA: Stanford University Press.

Shohat, E. 1999. "The Invention of the Mizrahim." *Journal of Palestine Studies* 29 (1): 1317–1334. doi:10.2307/2676427.

Shoshana, A. 2014. "Discursive Alliances and Discursive Clashes in Everyday Life." *Sociological Spectrum* 34 (2): 99–113. doi:10.1080/02732173.2014.877308.

Shoshana, A. 2016. "'Ethnicity without Ethnicity': Reeducation and (new) Ethnic Identity." *Social Identities* 22 (5): 487–501. doi:10.1080/13504630.2016.1145584.

Shott, S. 1979. "Emotion and Social Life: A Symbolic Interactionist Analysis." *American Journal of Sociology* 84 (6): 1317–1334. doi:10.1086/226936.

Strauss, A., and J. Corbin. 1998. *Basics of Qualitative Research*. Thousand Oaks: Sage Publication.

Watt, H. 2010. "Muslims, Fundamentalists, and the Fear of the Dangerous Other in American Culture." *Journal of Religion and Society* 12: 1–14. http://hdl.handle.net/10504/64591.

The impossible quest of Nasreen Qadri to claim colonial privilege in Israel

Nadeem Karkabi ⓘ

ABSTRACT
Nasreen Qadri is an Israeli pop singer of Palestinian-Arab origin whose professional achievements came in return for her loyalty to Israel. Successfully crossing cultural lines, Qadri claims Mizrahi identity, challenges the Ashkenazi-Zionist definition of Jews and Arabs as antagonistic ethnonational binaries, and helps Mizrahim reclaim their Judeo-Arabic heritage. However, following her controversial attempts to convert to Judaism, she fell short of crossing into religious-national privilege in Israel-Palestine. Qadri's failure to overcome colonial segregation testifies to how Israeli racism is based on a perceived religious blood community, which is anchored in state laws and to which non-Jewish women are mostly exposed. Qadri's case demonstrates how racialized politics of conversion are related to demographic considerations that show the fragility of the Zionist settler-colonial project. Finally, this article suggests that Palestinians in Israel may face elimination, if they seek racial and religious equality with Jews based on a shared Arab culture with Mizrahim.

Nasreen Qadri is the only Palestinian citizen of Israel who has reached stardom in Israeli mainstream music. From small taverns in the Mizrahi (Oriental) periphery of Israel inhabited by Jewish immigrants from Arab and Muslim countries, she emerged into the wider Israeli public after winning Eyal Golan's televised singing competition in 2012. Under the wing of Golan, a prominent Mizrahi singer, she made a name for herself by singing Mizrahi pop music in Hebrew and accompanying different Israeli ensembles in performing classics of *tarab* music in Arabic. Qadri's uncompromising support of the Israeli state, the IDF, and Zionist ideology paved the way to the largest stages of Israeli national ceremonies, endless plays on leading Israeli radio stations, and appearances in musicals and reality TV shows.

Qadri's personal life has also pushed the boundaries, including a turbulent romantic relationship of over a decade with a Jewish Mizrahi man. She even began the process of an orthodox *giyur* (conversion to Judaism), only to find out that devout Jewish women are not permitted to sing before mixed-gender audiences. Despite the failure of this interreligious relationship, widely documented by the Israeli media, Qadri recently announced that she had converted to Judaism after all. However, her conversion is not recognized by Israel's Chief (Orthodox) Rabbinate or Ministry of Interior, because it was supervised by a Reform rabbi, leaving her a Muslim on official state documents.

Qadri offers a unique example of an indigenous Arab willing to do whatever it takes to be accepted into Jewish Israeli society, including crossing lingual, ideological, and even religious-national boundaries. In her pursuit of recognition, she has become a subversive figure who is not simply willing to give up her Palestinian identity and accept "second class citizenship" in Israel (Tatour 2019). Rather, she has attempted to cross into the privileged Jewish collective. In terms of anticolonial scholarship, she has not been satisfied with being a "good Arab" (Cohen 2010; Kanaaneh 2008), the Israeli equivalent of what Malcolm X referred to as a "house negro." Instead, she challenges the rules of colonial segregation by trying to break through the glass ceiling into the master's upper floors.

This article demonstrates how culture and politics meet in the making of an Israeli pop icon who not only serves to demarcate the boundaries of Jewish collective but also challenges the official state laws that safeguard its privileges. Colonial segregation in Palestine-Israel is not based simply on ethnic grounds, but on complex religious-national racism that has distinctly gendered implications. Religious racism in Israel has been on the rise with the global expansion of the neoliberal economy and migration (Gorski et al. 2012). In many of these cases, race, religion, and gender intersect in ultranationalist right-wing politics, resulting in a misogynist public discourse and legislative acts that negatively influence women's rights (Graff, Kapur, and Walters 2019). However, engrained in the very foundation of the Israeli settler colonial state, religion is a mediating racial category for both national and inner cultural segregation. In this sense, religion in Israel determines racial privilege in the form of access to land and allocation of resources between Palestinian Arabs and Jews, and also internally between Jewish groups. Although embraced by Israeli society as a marginalized woman in a patriarchal Arab society, Qadri's failure to officially cross the religious lines into Jewish-national privilege is a testimony to how Israeli racism is anchored in state laws, to which non-Jewish women are mostly exposed. However, her relationship with an observant Jewish Mizrahi man and her attempt at religious conversion also challenge the racist colonial structure in Israel.

This article is based on analysis of interviews and coverage of Qadri in the Israeli Hebrew media. Interested in examining her reception in Israeli society, I have surveyed over eighty items in twenty-two online news platforms, from 2012 to 2019. These provide a wide variety of sources, ranging from mainstream media and specific media directed at religious Jews, to tabloids reporting on celebrities. Protected as Qadri is, by producers and managers, I was unable to reach her for an interview. However, the numerous interviews and extensive reporting on her life by the media provide sufficient resources to trace her public biography and image.

Qadri is a unique "single case-study" in three ways (Flyvbjerg 2006). First, her story is "extremely" uncommon, exposing general features of Israeli society with regard to the scarcity of interreligious marriages between Palestinian Arab women and Jewish Israeli men, as well as the rarity of Palestinian conversions to Judaism in Israel. Second, Qadri offers a "critical" case-study, in that she challenges familiar Palestinian acts of complacency with, and dissent from, Israeli social structures, shedding light on the general relations of Palestinian citizens with state institutions and Jewish society. Finally, even though abnormal, this case study is "paradigmatic," as it elaborates on interconnections between race, religion, gender, language, and nationalism in settler-colonial theory, in the context of Palestine-Israel. Qadri's case is therefore not presented to draw conclusive generalizations, but rather to expand the range of critical interpretations available in the given context (Donmoyer 2000).

In what follows, I begin by disentangling the colonial categories of religious cultural racialization in Israel that define the binaries of Jews/Arabs, Mizrahi/Ashkenazi Jews, and Mizrahi Jews/non-Jewish Arabs, according to a continuously reproducible Zionist ideology. I then continue to unpack the Israeli colonial category of the "good Arab," showing how this historical construct is reproduced today, mostly among Arab women in public culture, through the promise of individual privileges in return for loyalty. Following this, I narrate Qadri's attempt to pass into Jewish Israeli society in three sections – which consecutively focus on her lingual-cultural, ideological, and religious-national crossings – to discuss the complex reasons for and implications of her successes and failures in passing.

"Ethnicity" in Israel: the entanglement of race, religion, and culture

Qadri's unusual attempt to pass into the heart of the Israeli national collective through the prism of religion should be understood in light of the earlier transformation of Arab-Jews into Mizrahi Jews. However, the racialized distinction of both Mizrahi Jews (Mizrahim) and Palestinian citizens of Israel, as Jews or Arabs, heavily relies on religion, though in two different ways

(Lentin 2018; Wolfe 2016). In this section, I revisit the construction of the Miz-rahim in Israel to clarify Qadri's ambiguous cultural association with this group. To unpack colonial stratification in Israel, special attention is given to the twofold discursive uses of "ethnicity"; first, as a racialized religious cat-egorization that differentiates between Jews and Arabs, and as racialized cul-tural categorization that internally distinguishes between Mizrahi and Ashkenazi Jews.

Although originally a secular national movement, influenced largely by modern European thought, Zionism had to embed Jewish religion as insepar-able from Jewish nationality (Peled and Peled 2019). Religion was important for Zionism, both to cohesively define its diverse target population and to legitimize its colonial project in Palestine (Massad 2006). In this sense, "there can be no secular Judaism which is not anchored in the Jewish tra-dition and there is no Jewish tradition that denies its religious roots" (Liebman 1998, 43). This ambiguous connection to religion urged the leading Zionist secular party Mapai to strike a "historic partnership" in 1935 with religious, mostly Ashkenazi Orthodox, Zionist movements, in return for a compromise over the observance of Shabbat and kashrut. Furthermore, in 1947 Mapai assured Agudat Yisrael, the Ashkenazi ultra-Orthodox move-ment arriving from Europe, that it would observe Jewish religion in the future state's public life, adding to the Orthodox rabbinical courts the exclu-sive juridical authority over marriage and divorce of Jews, and later on the conception of "who is a Jew," as a blood community based on racialized reli-gious grounds (Abu El-Haj 2012; Peled and Peled 2019; Sand 2009).

The Zionist racialization of "Jews," based on primordial religious grounds, came along with a similar racialized definition of "Arabs" (and "Palestinians," see Goldberg 2008). While in Israel Arab identity became uniquely defined by the state according as an "ethnic" (read racial) category, elsewhere in the Arab world it has been constructed according to cultural affiliation, primarily based on language (even when speaking about nationality, *qawmiyya*, in the sense of Pan-Arabism: Alshaer 2012; Hammond 2007).[1] Indeed, Palestinians devel-oped an established sense of particularized Arab national identity vis-à-vis the British and Zionist colonial identities, which took form in the first half of the twentieth century (Sorek 2015). However, the newly established State of Israel granted Israeli citizenship in 1952 to Palestinians who remained within its borders, aiming to integrate them by denationalization. Simul-taneously, the "ethnicization" of these Palestinians as "Israeli Arab" kept them inferior and excluded in a state defined as Jewish (Robinson 2013; Tatour 2019). Furthermore, the Israeli state fragmented its "Arab" citizens into religious and cultural sub-minorities, such as Muslims, Christians, Druze, and Bedouins (Kanaaneh 2008; Peteet 2005).

While religion has been a tool for defining an indigenous inferiority based on racial grounds, it also served in the 1950s and 1960s as a mediator to accommodate Jewish immigrants from Arab countries into the privileged colonial collective in Israel. Looking like Arabs and speaking Arabic, Arab-Jews were de-Arabized upon arrival in Israel and nationally "ethnicized" (read racialized) as Jews on the basis of religion. Mostly secular or *masorati* (traditional), a less observant form of Judaism that sees religion as a cultural construct based on traditions, these Jews ended up adopting more observant forms of Judaism so as to qualify as a legitimate part of the Jewish Israeli national blood community (Leon 2008; Shenhav 2006).

However, "ethnicity" in Israel has also been used as a racialized construct of *eda* (congregation), through which an internal hierarchy between Ashkenazi and Sephardi Jews was created based on Orientalist categories of cultural *motza* (origin) and religiosity (Lentin 2018, 80; Shenhav 2006, 193). To distinguish between "modern" European colonizers of higher class and *masorati* Oriental colonizers of lower class, ethnicity as a construct of cultural racialization was translated into class. Thus, the twofold use of ethnicity in Israel was shaped by a colonial rationale to both contain Jewish immigrants from Arab countries and justify their racialized cultural inferiority to Ashkenazi Israelis, secular and Orthodox, and to redistribute state resources accordingly. With the Israeli cultural policy of the "melting pot" (Cooper and Danet 1980), it is not surprising that most Arab-Jews, turned Mizahim in Israel (Shohat 1988), gave up much of their original Arabic culture and language – unless used in the service of the Israeli security apparatus (Mendel 2014) – instead, adopting Hebrew so as to integrate into Israeli culture.

This cultural transformation was prominent in the field of music. Many Jewish Arab musicians arrived in Israel having already established careers in their countries of origin, and many among them had to switch to performing in Hebrew or abandon their profession altogether; others confined themselves to small cultural enclaves (Perlson 2006). In the 1970s and 1980s, the new hybrid pop genre of "Mizrahi music" flourished on the margins of Israel's Ashkenazi-dominated mainstream culture (Regev and Seroussi 2004). Developed by the second generation of Arab-Jews turned Mizrahim, this genre drew on Arabic, Greek, and Turkish popular music styles with rock instrumentation and arrangements, but was sung mostly in Hebrew.

Mizrahi audiences listened to Arabic music at home, and musicians often performed songs in Arabic, or their remakes in Hebrew. Appreciation of Arab authenticity also paved entry for a few "Israeli Arab" singers, such as Samir Shukri and Sharif "The Druze Boy," into the Mizrahi music scene in the early 1990s. Although both performed mainly original songs in Hebrew, they were praised when singing covers of Arabic music. Neither, however, gained success in Israeli mainstream music, because Mizrahi music was still considered "low culture" (Shoshana 2013).

Mizrahi identity politics became widely resonant following the famous 1977 elections for the Israeli Knesset, where they were the main force behind the success of the right-wing Likud Party over the long-ruling Mapai party (Chetrit 2000). The positioning of Mizrahim on the political right consolidated both their enmity toward Palestinian Arabs and their Israeli belonging (ibid.). Considering it a vote against Ashkenazi "leftist" elitism, Mizrahi political activists – especially with the founding of the Mizrahi Democratic Rainbow in 1996 (ibid.) – gradually began emphasizing their Middle Eastern and Arab cultural heritage, though mostly by using regional terms such as Yemenite Jews, Iraqi Jews, Moroccan Jews, and so on.

In tandem, the hegemony of Ashkenazi European-based popular music styles sung in Hebrew began to decline in Israel toward the late 1980s. This came with the global influence of non-Western popular genres marketed as "world music" or "ethnic music" (Taylor 1997), which inspired the diversification of idioms and languages in Israeli music. In addition, the Oslo Accords (1993) and Israel's peace treaty with Jordan (1994) precipitated a host of ensembles singing in both Hebrew and Arabic under the cloak of peace performances. This facilitated the exposure of some Mizrahi singers to diverse regional Arab audiences (Swedenburg 1997), including Zehava Ben, who performed in Arabic for audiences in the West Bank and Jordan (Horowitz 2005). Although such cross-Arab initiatives came to a complete halt with the outbreak of the Second Intifada in 2000, Mizrahi music gained mainstream acceptance in Israel as repackaged "Mediterranean music" (Horowitz 2010). Moreover, these developments led many third-generation Mizrahim to further emphasize their regional Arab heritage through cultural production (Erez and Karkabi 2019; Levy 2017). However, the restoration of bridges between young Mizrahim and Arab culture faces great challenges, especially because of the decline in their command of the Arabic language (Karkabi 2019; Shenhav et al. 2015).

Although this movement was initially organized from the bottom up, and often counter to state policies, ministers in Netanyahu's right-wing governments, especially former Minister of Culture Miri Regev, have recently endorsed Judeo-Arab heritage while simultaneously rejecting Palestinian culture and political rights (Lynfield 2015). This is most vividly seen in the 2018 issuing of the Basic Law: Israel as the Nation State of the Jewish People, which lowered the official status of the Arabic language, among the violation of other rights of non-Jewish citizens of Israel. This position joins a new Zionist ideology led by Mizrahi identity politics (such as that of the Tor Ha-Zahav [The Golden Age] movement, Galili 2016), which claims indigeneity as opposed to accepting foreign, European Ashkenazi hegemony. Although promoting connection to Middle Eastern cultural heritage, such politics eclipse Palestinian indigenous national identity by diluting it to a mere regional Arab cultural identity. Moreover, with the blur of cultural boundaries between "Israeli Arabs" and Mizrahi Jews, this new Mizrahi Zionist discourse maintains racial difference based on religious difference vis-à-vis Palestinians (Karkabi 2019). This fits the general shift of Israeli politics toward religious nationalism, especially since the conquest of the additional Palestinian population in 1967 (Peled and Peled 2019), because the Zionist project could proceed only by sustaining the Jewish religion as the common colonial denominator against indigenous non-Jews (Wolfe 2016, 261).

Though there are voices emphasizing political connections between Mizrahim and Palestinians (Shohat 2003), most Mizrahim focus on overcoming the cultural and class inequality with Ashkenazim, while failing to bridge the colonial gap with Palestinians (Lavie 2011). In this reality, Qadri is an authentic voice helping Mizrahim reclaim their Judeo-Arab cultural heritage. She is also endorsed as an exemplary "Israeli Arab" when she expresses her national loyalty to Israel. However, she falls short of crossing religious demarcations between colonizers and colonized.

The "Good Arabs": from loyalty to crossing

Defeated and dispossessed of their lands after the Nakba (catastrophe) in 1948, Palestinians who became Israeli citizens had, until 1966, to face military rule that restricted their movement, political organization, and access to means of livelihood (Robinson 2013). They were subjected to the biopolitics of Israeli governmentality (Foucault 1977) through denationalization, racialization, and fragmentation into religious sub-minorities. They were also divided into binary distinctions in line with their political orientation to the state, such as friend/enemy, loyal/hostile, complicit/resistant, and most reductively, "good Arabs"/"bad Arabs," to be governed with "care" or "punishment," accordingly (ibid.).

Under these conditions, some Palestinians complied with Israel's demand for loyalty and collaborated with Israeli security services in return for individual privileges and financial benefits (Cohen 2010). Israeli state authorities fostered these "good Arabs," to "reshape Arab consciousness and identity in accordance with the hegemonic Israeli worldview by controlling the society's political discourse" (Cohen 2010, 3). This meant promotion of the Zionist narrative, erasure of Palestinian national identity, and distinction between religious communities. Many "good Arabs" were among local and national political leaders, such as the mukhtars (village representatives) (Cohen 2010). Others came from the ranks of the education system (Rabinowitz 1998) and state media in Arabic (Jamal 2013), or were ethno-religiously classified through the compulsory drafting of Druze and Bedouins into the Israeli military (Kanaaneh 2008). Whether led by fear or privileges, some of the "good Arabs" internalized their inferiority through perceptions of modern Israeli Jewish culture as being advanced.

While the racialization of Palestinians as "Arabs" led to quick success, their denationalization was more complicated. Since non-Jews cannot become equal Israeli citizens, Palestinians turned "Israeli Arabs" could not become fully part of the Israeli nationality (Tatour 2019). This ambiguous *in-exclusion* of "Israeli Arabs" preserved Palestinian national identity among many during Israeli military rule. However, after the 1967 war, and despite the reconnection with other Palestinians from the West Bank and Gaza Strip, Palestinian citizens of Israel became vividly differentiated from the rest of the Palestinian nation, owing to the political and economic privileges their Israeli citizenship allowed (Ghanim 2008). This led many Palestinian citizens to adopt an integrative civil rights discourse in Israel, which peaked with the Oslo Accords during the 1990s, as they were excluded from the negotiations over the establishment of a Palestinian state based on the 1948 armistice Green Line. Contrary to past perceptions of "good Arabs" as anti-national traitors, personal achievements of individual Palestinian citizens became an optimistic indication of civil equality, allegedly conditioned on proving their loyalty to the state. Internalization of inferiority, along with the hope for individual acceptance, brought many Palestinian citizens in the 1990s to believe that a memetic crossing was possible, if only they changed their performance to look more like Israeli Jews and less like Palestinians in the territories occupied in 1967 (ibid.).

This reality was shattered with the second intifada (2000-2004) and the failure of peace negations over a future Palestinian state. Many Palestinian citizens joined the protests in solidarity with their national counterparts, which led to a political rift with the Israeli state and its Jewish citizens (Zreik 2003). In reaction, right-wing Israeli governments issued a series of undemocratic laws, including "the cultural loyalty law" drafted by Miri Regev,[2] to underline the demand for loyalty from the Palestinian citizens in return for civil rights and personal privileges (Adalah 2017). With racial discrimination rooted in state structures, the estrangement of many Palestinian citizens grew. Others, however, insisted on integrative efforts toward civil equality, in light of the impasse in Palestinian national politics.

Before the selection of Rana Raslan as Miss Israel in 1999 (Ghanim 2008), almost all of the "good Arabs" operating in the Israeli public sphere were men. Stark as it is, this fact has never been pointed out, yet it could be understood through the gendered assumption of Israeli authorities that Palestinian women are socially inferior to men in their own communities (Abdo 2013; Lentin 2018; Shalhoub-Kevorkian and Daher-Nashif 2013), and are therefore less valuable to co-opt as potent public figures. Lately, Arab woman such as Lucy Aharish and Mira Awad have appeared in the Israeli public sphere, especially in the highly visible fields of media and culture, to represent Israel as a liberal democracy that respects women's individual rights, as opposed to Arab (and especially Muslim) patriarchal society. Although some Palestinians in the West Bank and East Jerusalem are still recruited to collaborate with Israeli security services (Dudai and Cohen 2007), the co-opta-tion of Palestinian women has nevertheless become urgent, to externally legit-imize Israel as a liberal democracy amidst growing international BDS (Boycott, Divestment and Sanctions) campaigns. Assuming the internationally per-formed role as liberated "Israeli Arab" women, their criticism of "ethnic" inequality in Israel is tolerated to confirm Israel as a democracy, as long as they operate within the domestic(ated) framework of citizenship rights. Thus, instead of using their public exposure to draw awareness, these women become a voice that obscures Israeli violations of Palestinian collective rights.

Nasreen Qadri did not, however, stop at adopting Israeli Hebrew culture, nor at proving her loyalty as a "good Arab," in return for professional oppor-tunities: she became the first Arab public persona in Israel to attempt full crossing into the privileged Jewish national collective based on a religious transformation. While converts from majority religions to minority religions are treated with great suspicion and marked as a security threat, conversions from minority religions to that of the majority are usually celebrated (Özyürek 2009). In fact, conversion has been massively used by imperial and colonial powers to assimilate internal minorities and produce complicit subjects in distant territories (Comaroff and Comaroff 1991). However, even when volun-tary, conversion is a radical political event that affects the cohesion of the departed as well as the receiving communities (Viswanathan 1998). As reli-gion often relates to racialized and gendered national boundaries, interracial marriages and métissage subjects, like colonized converts to Christianity, have caused different levels of alert and severity of divisive policies among colonial authorities, who wanted to safeguard colonial privileges (Stoler 1992). As I elaborate in the final section, the politics of conversion and race in Israel are also related to demographic considerations.

In the following I narrate Qadri's life story in accordance with her different crossings into Israeli society, thus demonstrating the complex categorical intersections that include and exclude her. Although religion, like language, is supposed to be an adoptable cultural construct, I show how her attempt to convert to Judaism exposes the racial ideology at the heart of the Israeli settler-colonial state, when state laws are enacted to preserve both demo-graphic superiority and purity of the Jewish nation. Qadri's case demonstrates also Israel's failure to live up to its liberal promise to protect the civil rights of its Palestinian female citizens in the fields of matrimony and reproduction, which are quintessential elements of women's equality.

Lingual crossing: an "Israeli Arab" in the Mizrahi music scene

Nasreen Qadri was born in 1986 to a working class Muslim Arab family in the "mixed city" of al-Lidd (Lod, in Hebrew), whose original Palestinian population was almost entirely expulsed and replaced by Jewish immigrants. The family moved to Haifa, where her father worked as a taxi driver and her mother, owing to illness, lost her ability to work as a nurse, which meant that Qadri grew up with her sister and brother amidst financial hardship (Ben Dayan 2014). With the elementary experience of singing at school celebrations, she first went on stage at the age of fifteen, after being discovered by an Israeli music agent of Moroccan Jewish origin who was looking for a female musician to sing Arabic classics in an authentic accent (ibid.). He offered her employment at *khammarot* (small taverns) located in Mizrahi "development towns" in the southern periphery of Israel. Working long nights away from home at venues populated mainly with men, Qadri admits: "I turned from an innocent girl to a woman who experienced a lot [… but] my refuge from all I went through in life was on the stage" (Shalev 2016). Her parents were not happy about it, but her income was too valuable for the household to give up. A few years later, she formed a band that performed Arabic songs, ranging from *tarab* classics to contemporary Egyptian and Lebanese pop, and whose percussionist, Aviezer Ben Moha, later became her boyfriend (ibid.).

In 2012, at the age of twenty-five, Qadri emerged into the wider public after winning the music reality show *Eyal Golan is Calling You*, which was screened on Israeli commercial television. The show was produced by Golan, one of Israel's main celebrity singers and an important figure in the breakthrough of Mizrahi music into the Israeli mainstream, by transforming a strand of this style into what became known as "Mediterranean music" (Horowitz 2010). On the show, Qadri not only sang for the first time in Hebrew but also created her first public controversy by performing Sarit Haddad's "Kshe-ha-lev Boche" (When the heart cries). This song being sung by a Muslim was astonishing to the Israeli audience, as it includes the phrase beginning "*Shma' Yisrael*," which appears in the daily morning and evening prayers and is part of a biblical verse perceived as a statement of Jewish faith. This only encouraged Golan to coronate Qadri as a rising talent and legitimize her entry into Israeli music as an "Arab." He soon took her into the spotlight by giving her a chance to warm up his own shows on the largest stages in Israel, performing Mizrahi hits in Hebrew combined with Arabic classical music. Qadri was eventually declared the new star of Israeli music and compared to Zehava Ben and Sarit Haddad (Uzan 2014), who share the story of the Israeli Cinderella, having arrived in Tel Aviv from the Mizrahi periphery (Horowitz 2005).

In 2014, Qadri released her eponymous debut album with Liam Productions, Golan's music label. To market her to the Israeli audience, Hagai Uzan, appointed Qadri's producer, wrote all of the album's songs in Hebrew, leaving minimal space for Arabic to be heard in the chorus of two songs and in Qadri's accent. The fact that an Israeli Arab, whose mother tongue is Arabic, released her first album in Hebrew while a growing number of Mizrahi singers are reclaiming Arabic in their music, raised eye-brows among Israeli music critics: "Qadri manages to jump over the hurdles of religion, sex, and prejudice. It is a shame that she didn't also cross the barrier of language and sing a little more in her mother tongue – Arabic" (Shalev 2014).

For Qadri to culturally pass as Mizrahi, she had to cross to the Hebrew language. Two years later she released her second album, *Banadik* (I call you, in Arabic). Despite the Arabic title, and the critique, most of the songs were written in Hebrew. Qadri increased the performance of classical and popular covers in Arabic in her shows, which opened the door to occasional cooperation with the Jerusalem East–West Orchestra and Firqat al-Noor, Israeli ensembles dedicated to music from the Arab and Muslim world. However, Qadri's language crossing was comprehensive in both her music and her life. After moving to Tel Aviv, she became so accustomed to using Hebrew off stage that even on her family visits to Haifa, she admits: "I can't speak Arabic at home today, or it is hard for me. My mother curses me for this: *Yil'an abuki 'ars* [damn your chav father, in Arabic], you became a Jew? What is this, speak Arabic" (Shalev 2016). Interestingly, Qadri's mother was already concerned about her daughter's categorical crossing from Arab to Jew (not Israeli) when she replaced Arabic language with Hebrew. However, Qadri has not downplayed her Arab identity at any stage of her career. On the contrary, it was her main trademark and challenge as a singer, especially when she declared early on that "Israel is ready for an Arab singer" (Uzan 2014).

"National" crossing: an Arab performing Zionism

In 2015, Qadri was invited to sing in her first ceremonial state performance before Israel's president, Rubi Rivlin (Nevo 2015). Later that year, she performed "Shir la-Shalom" (Song for peace) before 50,000 people at an event commemorating twenty years since the assassination of then Israeli Prime Minister Yitzhak Rabin (Eldar 2017). As Qadri's career reached new heights, the acclaimed British band Radiohead was scheduled to play in Tel Aviv in the summer of 2017. Pro-Palestinian organizations and music celebrities called on the band to cancel the show and adhere to the international BDS campaign (Barrows-Friedman 2017). The band refused and selected Dudu Tassa as the opening act for their US tour and their later show in Tel Aviv. Although an Israeli rock musician, Tassa has been invested in reintroducing the music of Saleh and Dahoud al-Kuwaiti, his grandfather and granduncle, whose prestigious career in Iraq severely declined after their immigration to Israel in the 1950s. Tassa, who does not speak Arabic, performed the Kuwaitis' material well enough for Israeli audiences, despite the inaccuracies of accent and diction. For his major international appearance with Radiohead, he invited Qadri to join as lead singer. Initially, Qadri received the news nonchalantly, as she was unacquainted with Radiohead. However, as a perfect political choice to counter pro-Palestinian calls to boycott the show, her controversial collaboration with Radiohead and Tassa was proof of her loyalty to Israel (Ilnai 2017).

While still on tour in the US, she was invited by Miri Regev, who saw in her an exemplary Israeli Arab, to sing at both official state ceremonies on Yom ha-Zikaron (Remembrance Day, for fallen soldiers) and then at Israel's Independence Day. Qadri's welcome "as a quintessentially Israeli singer" was complete after her performance at the Israel Festival that year, where she sang in Hebrew and Arabic to represent Israeli multiculturalism (Eldar 2017). Qadri's celebration as being "quintessentially Israeli" was, however, a deceptive statement, since entry to the Israeli national collective is open only to Jews. It is therefore more accurate to describe this performance of loyalty as an ideological crossing to Zionism. This was indeed what concerned the Israeli Channel 2 interviewer, after Qadri's Independence Day performance, who remarked, "You are very Zionist." Qadri answered, "Of course, this is my home. I am not ashamed. On the contrary, I am proud of it."[3] Like other "good Arabs" before her, being Zionist, and not formally an Israeli by citizenship, is what qualified her as a quintessentially loyal subject.

Although she lost the support of many Palestinians (Kan'an 2018), Qadri's public appearances at Israeli national ceremonies as a declared Zionist led to her commercial success. The two singles she released that summer reached a phenomenal number of plays on YouTube: "Tomru Li" (Tell me) had over 5 million plays, and "Lomedet La-lechet" (Learning to walk) reached over 15 million. This came in preparation for the release of her third album in September 2018, the same month in which Israeli media announced Qadri's conversion to Judaism.

Religious crossing: the limits for an indigenous Arab in the Jewish state

Qadri met Aviezer Ben Moha, a percussionist in her early-career band, in 2004. A Jewish Israeli of Moroccan origin, Ben Moha, then sixteen years old, is two years younger than Qadri (Shir 2017). This did not stop them from entering into a long, turbulent relationship. Two years later, Ben Moha was reluctant to join the military because his family relied on his income. However, Qadri proudly convinced him to go "to the army for both of us, so that we will have a better future" (ibid.). Ben Moha began his service but soon dropped out, which according to Qadri led to their first breakup: "He disappointed me. I also began feeling uncomfortable with lying to his parents [about their relationship]" (ibid.).

After Qadri won Golan's reality show in 2012, the couple resumed their relationship and moved in together. However, uncomfortable with keeping their interreligious romance a secret, they decided to marry. Given that marriage in Israel is conducted only by religious courts, interreligious couples usually opt for a civil marriage abroad, which is legally recognized in Israel (Burton 2015; Hacker 2009). For Ben Moha, a *masorati*, mildly observant Jew, this was not enough (Mirkin 2017), so Qadri began the process of conversion to Judaism. Following the instructions of the Orthodox rabbinate, she changed her manner of dress, began keeping kosher, and abstained from performing on Shabbat (Shir 2017). However, Qadri stopped her *giyur* after the rabbi requested that she stop performing before mixed-gender audiences, which for her meant "not to perform at all" (ibid.). She also broke up with Ben Moha, who sided with the rabbi, and went on to pursue her music career (ibid.).

A few years later, immediately after her successful tour with Tassa and Radiohead, Israeli media reported Ben Moha and Qadri's surprising engagement (NRG 2017). It is assumed that Ben Moha compromised on a civil marriage. In preparation for the wedding, the couple lived together again (Mirkin 2017). Bentzi Gopstein, the head of racist Israeli organization Lehava, approached Ben Moha in a video, asking him to reconsider his marriage to Qadri. Although Lehava usually targets Jewish women involved with non-Jewish Arab men in Israel, to prevent assimilation (Burton 2015), this case was more extreme, as Gopstein explained to Ben Moha:

> Nasreen already said that she doesn't want to go through a *giyur*. [...] So do you want, as a son of a family that preserved Judaism for so many years, for your children to be *goyim* [gentiles]?[4]

Qadri's match with a Jewish man was an even greater problem than her religion. If Qadri and Ben Moha married in a civil ceremony abroad, and each maintained their religion, their offspring would grow up as religious bastards. They would be neither Muslim nor Jewish, since according to Orthodox Judaism the child's religion is determined by the mother's religion, whereas in Islam it is determined by the father's. This explains why in Jewish exogamic marriages in Israel, non-Jewish female spouses experience stronger pressure to convert than non-Jewish male spouses (Hacker 2009). Had Qadri been a Muslim man and Ben Moha a Jewish woman, they would likely have opted for a civil marriage, and their children could later have chosen their religion (Burton 2015), even embodying the anomalous category of Arab-Jews. Moreover, a male singer converting to Judaism would not have been required to follow restrictions on singing before mixed-gender crowds. Indeed, of the already small number of such interreligious marriages, Arab women are less likely to marry Jewish men (Karkabi-Sabbah 2017). However, social class also plays a large role in such marriages. Secular Arab women with higher education usually marry secular Ashkenazi men in a civil ceremony, whereas working-class Arab women, such as Qadri, are more likely to marry Mizrahi men, such as Ben Moha (ibid.). The cultural proximity of Palestinians and Mizrahim also explains why Ben Moha had to maintain his Jewish religion, or else he, and more importantly his future children, might have been regarded as crossing the line in the other direction. A month later, media reports revealed that the wedding had been cancelled, and the breakup was final.

Amidst these events, Qadri was selected for her first acting role in *Solika*, a musical based on the true story of Sol (Solika) Hatchuel (or Hatuel), a Jewish Moroccan girl who was involved in a mid-nineteenth-century religious controversy. Muslims claimed that Hatchuel had converted to Islam but wished to return to Judaism out of regret; Jews claimed that she had never actually converted to Islam and was forced to do so (Vance 2011). Either way, Hatchuel was sent to the sultan in Fez to face trial. The crown prince fell in love with her and tried to convince her to stay in, or convert to, Islam and marry him. Hatchuel stubbornly refused and was eventually decapitated under the sultan's order. She is considered a saint who died for her faith at the age of seventeen, and her grave in Fez became a pilgrimage site for Moroccan Jews and Muslims (ibid.).

The musical focuses on the love story between Hatchuel and the prince. Qadri was ironically recruited to play Hurra, a fictional Muslim neighbour who advises Hatchuel on how to choose between love and faith. Aware of the enactment of the dilemmas reflected in her personal life, Qadri admits: "There are many conflicts in the play that we also fight in our reality today." The play's success, according to its playwright, Tair Siboni, is in its underlying message: "the value of the right to choose, so that we would be able to accept others even if we disagree with them" (Mish'ali 2018).

This theatrical message was soon tested in Qadri's real life. In September 2018, the Israeli public awoke to the surprising news that Qadri had completed a *giyur* process and changed her first name to Bracha (Kuma 2018). Supervised by a Mizrahi Reform rabbi from the U.S., her conversion was marked on her thirty-second birthday with "a trip to the Western Wall, a ritual bath in a *mikvah* and a celebratory meal at a (kosher) restaurant in Jerusalem" (ibid.). Although Solika and Qadri made opposite religious choices, Solika's right to choose was celebrated, while Qadri right was disapproved. Since an automatic claim for Israeli citizenship can be made by Jews, only the strict Orthodox rabbinical authority can decide such demographic matters in Israel. Backed by the state, this institutionalized power limits the acceptance of foreign, non-Israeli converts not simply to Judaism, but more importantly into the Israeli national collective (Hacker 2009). Qadri, however, already a citizen, tragically fell in between Jewish religious authorities, since her Reform conversion, which is more lenient than the Orthodox equivalent, was not recognized by Israel's Chief Rabbinate or the Ministry of Interior. This meant that even though according to the Reform interpretation of halacha (Jewish law) Qadri is Jewish, the State of Israel does not recognize her conversion and continues to refer to her officially as Muslim (Haleli-Avraham 2018).

To answer why Qadri decided to convert after breaking up with Ben Moha, the tabloids reported the next day that she was apparently dating the Jewish keyboardist in her band and wanted to finally overcome her old problems (Cohen 2018). Such gossip is not needed to assume that, having lingually, ideologically, and socially crossed from Arab society into Jewish society, Qadri had been dating mainly Jewish men, with whom religious identity problems continued to surface. Although living in Jewish Reform and *masorati* circles, Qadri had not found a life partner, and she bitterly admitted that her unrecognized conversion was badly received in wider Israeli society, among both Jews and Palestinians: "On the Jewish side they say that I did it [converted] to gain more exposure, on the Arab side [they call me] – a traitor" (Brazilayi 2019). This, however, did not stop her from becoming a celebrity who gains from Israeli tabloids reporting on the "Israeli Arab" who observes halacha (Kipa 2019). Stuck between pursuing her musical career and wanting to find a life partner, Qadri's final crossing fell short before the legal structures in Israel, in which racial, religious, and gendered discrimination intersect, forcing her to pay a painful price for her choices. The refusal to recognize Qadri's conversion speaks to the racial underpinning of colonial nationalism in Israel, in which the Jewish people are seen as a blood community, closed to indigenous subjects. According to this logic, a "good Arab" should be loyal to the Israeli state, but also loyal to her religious affiliation, which secures her racial inferiority.

Co-opted to Sustain superiority

Conversion is a radically "unsettling political event" as it alters "the demographic equation within a society and produces numerical imbalances" (Viswanathan 1998, xi). Demographic considerations explain both the celebration of converts from minority religions to the religion of the majority and the anxiety around conversions from the majority's religion to that of a minority (Özyürek 2009). Jewish diasporic communities' long-standing suspicion toward converts to Judaism, supported by historically strict criteria, shows that demographic anxiety also exists among receiving minority communities. However, the anxiety of Israeli authorities, both secular and religious, around the conversion of Palestinian Muslims and Christians to Judaism is somewhat surprising, especially in light of relentless Israeli efforts to maintain a Jewish majority. It can be argued that this anxiety around conversion in Israel is a remnant of diasporic Jewish culture, yet one should look at the larger picture to understand this matter demographically. If counting Palestinians in the adjacent West Bank and Gaza Strip, the numbers of Palestinians under de facto Israeli control is almost even to Israeli Jews. Palestinian conversion to Judaism, even if only in a far-fetched imagination, challenges not only the religious doctrines and moral claims of Israeli Jews but also the safeguarding of colonial privilege. In this sense, the severe anxiety around Palestinian conversion may be an indication that the Zionist settler-colonial project is far from being accomplished.

The normalization of Mizrahim in Israel as racially Jewish allows many, like Miri Regev or Dudu Tassa, to feel more comfortable reclaiming their Middle Eastern or Judeo-Arab cultural heritage and challenge their lower classification in Israel vis-à-vis the Ashkenazim. Likewise, coming from a lower social class, Nasreen Qadri wholeheartedly crosses the lingual and even the ideological lines as a Mizrahi. Sharing the same cultural heritage with Mizrahim of Arab origin, she capitalizes on the rising appreciation of her Arab cultural background in mainstream Israeli culture.

Despite the growing Mizrahi urge to locate their Jewish identity as part of their Arab cultural heritage, religion persists as a primary racial category unifying the Jewish blood community as a nation, distinguished from the non-Jewish Palestinian indigenous population. So, while Qadri is welcome in Israeli society when she speaks Hebrew and publicly praises the IDF and Zionist ideology, thus abandoning her Palestinian national identity, her religious crossing caused anxiety owing to the blurring of the last frontier of racial distinction in Israel, that between colonizers claiming indigeneity and the dispossessed indigenous population. The Mizrahi reclaim of Middle Eastern or Arab culture as native, while having difficulty accepting non-Jewish indigenous Arabs as equals, enables the integration of "Israeli Arabs" while eclipsing their inferiority based on racialized religious difference. Moreover, the inclusive discourse of "Arabs" and their culture enables Israel to present itself as a multicultural, liberal democracy (Karkabi 2019), by recruiting "Israeli Arab" public figures for the mission, such as Qadri. However, these non-Jewish Arabs tragically cannot attain civil equality in a racialized Jewish state, even when they attempt a conversion to Judaism.

Qadri's impossible relationship with Ben Moha was not so much about a cultural mismatch between two individuals of Arab background who attempted to bridge their religious differences; rather, gender incompatibilities became an obstacle when translated to secure the reproduction of settler colonial structural segregation based on racialized religious categories. Instead of protecting individual rights of an "Arab Israeli" woman who left her patriarchal society, the Israeli state failed Qadri where it hurt most, as legal structures of matrimony and reproduction, so central to women's rights, become the main locus for sustaining racial difference in Israel. Even though Qadri paid a heavy social price for her controversial conversion, she still unintentionality challenged Jewish privilege by publicly unmasking the racialized, gendered colonial boundaries in Israel.

While material subordination may lead the colonized toward complacency and collaboration with the colonizer, the internalization of inferiority can lead to a relentless quest for recognition, which the colonized seek from their colonizers. Fanon (2008 [1952]) has long observed that in this destructive dynamic the colonized face dispossession of not only their material resources but also their distinct collective culture.

Although early twentieth-century Ashkenazi halutzim (pioneers), evidently foreign and white in the Palestinian context, appropriated elements of indigenous culture, their acts of mimicry did not pose enough danger to its dispossession. However, the recent Mizrahi demand to recognize Middle Eastern and Arab heritage as equal in Israel is justified by claiming Jewish regional indigeneity. Emphasis on cultural ties between indigenous Arabs and Mizrahim claiming indigeneity, with a rooted history in the Middle East, enables the symbolic elimination of Palestinians by framing their Arab culture also as regional affiliation. While skin colour evidently prevented Black subjects from crossing the colonial line of race, a shared Arab culture between Mizrahim and "Israeli Arabs" gives a false impression of racial equality, while obscuring the gradual loss of claiming a unique cultural and national identity. This is so, especially in light of the detachment from the everyday practice of the Arabic language, not only among Mizrahim, but gradually also among "Israeli Arabs" (Mari 2013) such as Qadri, who stopped speaking Arabic at home even though she performs it on stage. With the declining ability to raise resistance based on unified indigenous affiliation, the dispossessed and fragmented Palestinian population in Israel is being led toward an eternal political subordination as non-Jewish Others, literally defined as a racialized religious negation.

Notes

1. The word "ethnicity" does not have an equivalent cognate in Arabic.
2. Although the law did not pass in the Knesset, Regev has de facto been implementing it during her ministerial post.
3. Snippet video from that interview: https://www.youtube.com/watch?v=gQWN3VQJ4Jw
4. Retrieved from Lehava's website: https://www.leava.co.il/%D7%A4%D7%A0%D7%99%D7%94-%D7%A9%D7%9C-%D7%91%D7%A0%D7%A6%D7%99-%D7%92%D7%95%D7%A4%D7%98%D7%99%D7%99%D7%9F-%D7%9C%D7%90%D7%91%D7%99%D7%A2%D7%96%D7%A8-%D7%91%D7%9F-%D7%9E%D7%95%D7%97%D7%90-%D7%90/

Acknowledgments

I am grateful to Lana Tatur, Avihu Shoshana, and Tamir Sorek for reading and commenting on earlier drafts of this article.

Disclosure statement

No potential conflict of interest was reported by the author(s).

ORCID

Nadeem Karkabi ⓘ http://orcid.org/0000-0002-4440-1047

References

Abdo, Nahla. 2013. *Women in Israel: Race, Gender and Citizenship*. New York: Zed Books.

Abu El-Haj, Nadia. 2012. *The Genealogical Science: The Search for Jewish Origins and the Politics of Epistemology*. Chicago: University of Chicago Press.

Adalah. 2017. "The Discriminatory Laws Database." *Adalah*, September 25. https://www.adalah.org/en/content/view/7771.

Alshaer, Atef. 2012. "Language as Culture: The Question of Arabic." In *Arab Cultural Studies: Mapping the Field*, edited by T. Sabry, 275–296. London: I.B. Tauris.

Barrows-Friedman, Nora. 2017. "Radiohead May Never Live Down Tel Aviv Show, Says Ken Loach." *Electronic Intifada*, July 7. https://electronicintifada.net/blogs/nora-barrows-friedman/radiohead-may-never-live-down-tel-aviv-show-says-ken-loach.

Ben Dayan, Ortal. 2014. "The Singing of Hope." [in Hebrew]. *At*, October 28. https://www.atmag.co.il/%D7%A9%D7%99%D7%A8%D7%AA-%D7%94%D7%AA%D7%A7%D7%95%D7%95%D7%94/.

Brazilayi, Reut. 2019. "Blessing and Success: The Journey of Nasreen Qadri – from the Night Clubs to Caesarea." [in Hebrew]. *Mako*, December 22. https://www.mako.co.il/news-entertainment/2019_q4/Article-9c4898b566a2f61027.htm.

Burton, Elise. 2015. "An Assimilating Majority?: Israeli Marriage Law and Identity in the Jewish State." *Journal of Jewish Identities* 8 (1): 73–94.

Chetrit, Sami S. 2000. "Mizrahi Politics in Israel: Between Integration and Alternative." *Journal of Palestine Studies* 29 (4): 51–65.

Cohen, Hillel. 2010. *Good Arabs: The Israeli Security Agencies and the Israeli Arabs, 1948–1967*. Berkeley: University of California Press.

Cohen, Gilad. 2018. "The Rabbinate Will Not Recognize the Giyur of the Singer Nasreen Qadri. [in Hebrew]. *Kipa*, September 3. https://www.kipa.co.il/%D7%91%D7%A8%D7%A0%D7%96%D7%94/%D7%94%D7%A8%D7%91%D7%A0%D7%95%D7%AA-%D7%9C%D7%90-%D7%AA%D7%9B%D7%99%D7%A8-%D7%91%D7%92%D7%99%D7%95%D7%A8-%D7%A9%D7%9C-%D7%94%D7%96%D7%9E%D7%A8%D7%AA-%D7%A0%D7%A1%D7%A8%D7%99%D7%9F-%D7%A7%D7%93%D7%A8%D7%99/.

Comaroff, Jean, and John Comaroff. 1991. *Of Revelation and Revolution: Christianity, Colonialism, and Consciousness in South Africa*. Vol. 1. Chicago: University of Chicago Press.

Cooper, Robert L., and Brenda Danet. 1980. "Language in the Melting Pot: The Sociolinguistic Context for Language Planning in Israel." *Language Problems and Language Planning* 4 (1): 1–28.

Donmoyer, Robert. 2000. "Generalizability and the Single-Case Study." In *Case Study Method: Key Issues, Key Texts*, edited by Roger Gomm, Martyn Hammersley, and Peter Foster, 45–68. London: Sage Publications.

Dudai, Ron, and Hillel Cohen. 2007. "Triangle of Betrayal: Collaborators and Transitional Justice in the Israeli-Palestinian Conflict." *Journal of Human Rights* 6 (1): 37–58.

Eldar, Shlomi. 2017. "Israeli-Arab 'Diva of Middle Eastern Music' Empowers Coexistence." Al-Monitor, May 29. http://www.al-monitor.com/pulse/originals/2017/05/arab-israeli-singer-highlights-coexistence.html#ixzz51WpfQC00.

Erez, Oded, and Nadeem Karkabi. 2019. "Sounding Arabic: Postvernacular Modes of Performing the Arabic Language in Popular Music by Israeli Jews." Popular Music 38 (2): 298–316.

Fanon, Frantz. 2008 [1952]. Black Skin, White Masks. New York: Grove Press.

Flyvbjerg, Bent. 2006. "Five Misunderstandings about Case-Study Research." Qualitative Inquiry 12 (2): 219–245.

Foucault, Michel. 1977. Discipline and Punish: The Birth of the Prison. New York: Vintage.

Galili, Lily. 2016. "Meet the Israelis Calling for a New Golden Age." I24 News, February 24. https://www.i24news.tv/en/news/israel/society/104107-160225-meet-the-israelis-calling-for-a-new-golden-age.

Ghanim, Honaida. 2008. "What is the Color of the Arab? A Critical Look on Color Games." [in Hebrew]. In Racism in Israel, edited by Yehuda Shenhav, and Yossi Yonah, 76–92. Jerusalem: Van Leer Institute.

Goldberg, David T. 2008. "Racial Palestinianization." In Thinking Palestine, edited by Ronit Lentin, 25–45. London: Zed Books.

Gorski, Philip, David Kim, John Torpey, and Jonathan Van Antwerpe, eds. 2012. The Post-Secular in Question: Religion in Contemporary Society. New York: New York University Press.

Graff, Agnieszka, Ratna Kapur, and Suzanna Walters. 2019. "Introduction: Gender and the Rise of the Global Right." Signs: Journal of Women in Culture and Society 44 (3): 541–560.

Hacker, Daphna. 2009. "Inter-Religious Marriages in Israel: Gendered Implications for Conversion, Children, and Citizenship." Israel Studies 14 (2): 178–197.

Haleli-Avraham, Yiphat. 2018. "Nasreen Qadri Went Through a Giyur – but Will Not Be Recognized by the Rabbinate." [in Hebrew]. Mako, September 3. https://www.mako.co.il/entertainment-celebs/local-2018/Article-f8f848ee11e9561006.htm.

Hammond, Andrew. 2007. Popular Culture in the Arab World: Arts, Politics, and the Media. Cairo: American University in Cairo Press.

Horowitz, Amy. 2005. "Dueling Nativities: Zehava Ben Sings Umm Kulthum." In Palestine, Israel, and the Politics of Popular Culture, edited by R. L. Stein, and T. Swedenburg, 202–230. Durham, NC: Duke University Press.

Horowitz, Amy. 2010. Mediterranean Israeli Music and the Politics of the Aesthetic. Detroit: Wayne State University Press.

Ilnai, Itai. 2017. "To Perform at Independence Day for Me Is to Belong." [in Hebrew]. Yediot Aharonot, April 19. https://www.yediot.co.il/articles/0,7340,L-4951051,00.html.

Jamal, Amal. 2013. "Manufacturing 'Quiet Arabs' in Israel: Ethnicity, Media Frames and Soft Power." Government and Opposition 48 (2): 245–264.

Kanaaneh, Rhoda A. 2008. Surrounded: Palestinian Soldiers in the Israeli Military. Stanford, CA: Stanford University Press.

Kanʿan, Nadeen. 2018. "Nasreen Qasri the 'Star' of the Israeli Sewer." [in Arabic]. Al-Akhbar, February 20. https://al-akhbar.com/Last_Page/244969.

Karkabi, Nadeem. 2019. "Arabic Language among Jews in Israel and the New Mizrahi Zionism: Between Active Knowledge and Performance." Journal of Levantine Studies 9 (2): 81–106.

Karkabi-Sabbah, Maha. 2017. "Ethnoreligious Mixed Marriages among Palestinian Women and Jewish Men in Israel: Negotiating the Breaking of Barriers." Journal of Israeli History 36 (2): 189–211.

Kipa. 2019. "Nasreen Qadri Observes Shabbat." [in Hebrew]. *Kipa*, May 13. https://www.kipa.co.il/%D7%99%D7%97%D7%A1%D7%99%D7%9D/%D7%A0%D7%A9%D7%99%D7%9D/940713-/.

Kuma, Tzachi. 2018. "Raise a Prayer: Nasreen Qadri Went through a Giyur." [in Hebrew]. *Ynet*, September 3. https://pplus.ynet.co.il/articles/0,7340,L-5340100,00.html.

Lavie, Smadar. 2011. "Mizrahi Feminism and the Question of Palestine." *Journal of Middle East Women's Studies* 7 (2): 56–88.

Lentin, Ronit. 2018. *Traces of Racial Exception: Racializing Israeli Settler Colonialism*. London: Bloomsbury Publishing.

Leon, Nissim. 2008. "The Secular Origins of Mizrahi Traditionalism." *Israel Studies* 13 (3): 22–42.

Levy, Lital. 2017. "The Arab Jew Debates: Media, Culture, Politics, History." *Journal of Levantine Studies* 7 (1): 79–103.

Liebman, Charles S. 1998. "Secular Judaism and Its Prospects." *Israel Affairs* 4 (3-4): 29–48.

Lynfield, Ben. 2015. "Israel's Minister of Culture Miri Regev Vows to Withhold Funds from Artists Who 'Defame' the State." *The Independent*, June 19. https://www.independent.co.uk/news/world/middle-east/israels-minister-of-culture-miri-regev-vows-to-withhold-funds-from-artists-who-defame-the-state-10333262.html.

Mari, Abed el-Rahman. 2013. *Walla Beseder: The Linguistic Profile of the Arabs in Israel*. [in Hebrew]. Jerusalem: Keter.

Massad, Joseph. 2006. *The Persistence of the Palestinian Question: Essays on Zionism and the Palestinians*. London: Routledge.

Mendel, Yonatan. 2014. *The Creation of Israeli Arabic: Security and Politics in Arabic Studies in Israel*. London: Palgrave Macmillan.

Mirkin, Orli. 2017. "If God Did Not Want This to Happen It Would Not Have Happened." [in Hebrew]. *Mako*, August 8. https://www.mako.co.il/tv-people/articles/Article-5b8504c94c0cd51006.htm?partner=tagit&Partner=interlink.

Mish'ali, Linoy. 2018. "Solika: Coexistence in a Play Full of Faith and Self-Sacrifice." *Srugim*, January 10. https://www.srugim.co.il/232822-%D7%A1%D7%95%D7%9C%D7%99%D7%A7%D7%90-%D7%9C%D7%A4%D7%90%D7%A8-%D7%90%D7%AA-%D7%A2%D7%93%D7%95%D7%AA-%D7%94%D7%9E%D7%96%D7%A8D7%97-%D7%9C%D7%91%D7%A8-%D7%A2%D7%9C-%D7%A7%D7%99%D7%A4%D7%95%D7%97.

Nevo, Asaf. 2015. "The Peace Dove: Nasreen Qadri Connects All the Edges." [in Hebrew]. *Mako*, January 25. https://www.mako.co.il/music-news/local-taverna/Article-81af8f36f212b41006.htm.

NRG. 2017. "The Singer Nasreen Qadri Got Engaged to Her Jewish Partner." [in Hebrew]. *NRG*, July 17. https://www.makorrishon.co.il/nrg/online/7/ART2/886/896.html.

Özyürek, Esra. 2009. "Convert Alert: German Muslims and Turkish Christians as Threats to Security in the New Europe." *Comparative Studies in Society and History* 51 (1): 91–116.

Peled, Yoav, and Horit Herman Peled. 2019. *The Religionization of Israeli Society*. New York: Routledge.

Perlson, Inbal. 2006. *Great Joy Tonight: Arab-Jewish Music and Mizrahi Identity*. [in Hebrew]. Tel-Aviv: Resling.

Peteet, Julie. 2005. "Words as Interventions: Naming in the Palestine–Israel Conflict." *Third World Quarterly* 26 (1): 153–172.

Rabinowitz, Dan. 1998. "National Identity on the Frontier: Palestinians in the Israeli Education System." In *Border Identities: Nation and State at International Frontiers*, edited by Thomas M. Wilson, and Hastings Donnan, 142–161. Cambridge: Cambridge University Press.

Regev, Motti, and Edwin Seroussi. 2004. *Popular Music and National Culture in Israel*. Berkeley, CA: University of California Press.

Robinson, Shira N. 2013. *Citizen Strangers: Palestinians and the Birth of Israel's Liberal Settler State*. Stanford, CA: Stanford University Press.

Sand, Shlomo. 2009. *The Invention of the Jewish People*. London: Verso.

Shalev, Ben. 2014. "Where Did the Arabic Disappear from the Debut Album of Nasreen Qadri?" [in Hebrew]. *Haaretz*, October 11. https://www.haaretz.co.il/gallery/music/musicreview/.premium-1.2452488.

Shalev, Ben. 2016. "At the Tavern in Nablus or in Front of 'La-Familia': Nasreen Qadri Only Wants to Be Allowed to Sing." [in Hebrew]. *Haaretz*, April 7. https://www.haaretz.co.il/gallery/music/EXT.premium-EXT-MAGAZINE-1.2905717.

Shalhoub-Kevorkian, Nadera, and Suhad Daher-Nashif. 2013. "Femicide and Colonization: Between the Politics of Exclusion and the Culture of Control." *Violence Against Women* 19 (3): 295–315.

Shenhav, Yehouda. 2006. *The Arab Jews: A Postcolonial Reading of Nationalism, Religion, and Ethnicity*. Stanford: Stanford University Press.

Shenhav, Yehuda, Maisaloon Dallashi, Rami Avnimelech, Nissim Mizrachi, and Yonatan Mendel. 2015. *Command of Arabic among Israeli Jews*. [in Hebrew]. Jerusalem: Van Leer Institute.

Shir, Smadar. 2017. "I Told Him: If You Love Me, Take Me as I Am, as a Muslim Arab." [in Hebrew]. *Yediot Acharonot*, September 18. https://www.yediot.co.il/articles/0,7340,L-5018047,00.html.

Shohat, Ella. 1988. "Sephardim in Israel: Zionism from the Standpoint of Its Jewish Victims." *Social Text* 19 (20): 1–35.

Shohat, Ella. 2003. "Rupture and Return: Zionist Discourse and the Study of Arab Jews." *Social Text* 21 (2): 49–74.

Shoshana, Avihu. 2013. "Minor Language and Major Responses in the Field of Popular Music in Israel." *Poetics* 41 (5): 481–500.

Sorek, Tamir. 2015. *Palestinian Commemoration in Israel: Calendars, Monuments, and Martyrs*. Stanford, CA: Stanford University Press.

Stoler, Ann. 1992. "Sexual Affronts and Racial Frontiers: European Identities and the Cultural Politics of Exclusion in Colonial Southeast Asia." *Comparative Studies in Society and History* 34 (3): 514–551.

Swedenburg, Ted. 1997. "Saida Sultan/Danna International: Transgender Pop and the Polysemiotics of Sex, Nation, and Ethnicity on the Israeli-Egyptian Border." *Musical Quarterly* 81 (1): 81–108.

Tatour, Lana. 2019. "Citizenship as Domination: Settled Colonialism and the Making of Palestinian Citizenship in Israel." *Arab Studies Journal* 27 (2): 8–39.

Taylor, Timothy D. 1997. *Global Pop: World Music, World Markets*. New York: Routledge.

Uzan, Hagai. 2014. "Israel Is Ready for an Arab Singer." [in Hebrew]. *Walla*, January 8. https://e.walla.co.il/item/2708432.

Vance, Sharon. 2011. *The Martyrdom of a Moroccan Jewish Saint*. Leiden: Brill.

Viswanathan, Gauri. 1998. *Outside the Fold: Conversion, Modernity, and Belief*. Princeton, NJ: Princeton University Press.

Wolfe, Patrick. 2016. *Traces of History: Elementary Structures of Race*. London: Verso Books.

Zreik, Raef. 2003. "The Palestinian Question: Themes of Justice and Power. Part II: The Palestinians in Israel." *Journal of Palestine Studies* 33 (1): 42–54.

Mediterraneanism in conflict: development and settlement of Palestinian refugees and Jewish immigrants in Gaza and Yamit

Fatina Abreek-Zubiedat ⓘ and Alona Nitzan-Shiftan

ABSTRACT
This article examines Israeli development in the Gaza Strip and Northern Sinai from 1972 to 1982 from the perspective of architectural history. We argue that the prime objective of the Israeli occupation in this decade was economic development, not elimination; its guiding logic saw humanitarian aid as the preferred way to "resolve" the Palestinian refugee crisis. We follow how the pro-development, humanist "know how" of the architects and urban planners wrote themselves onto Gaza's politics of space. Their scientific approach embodied in Mediterranean architecture was the solution of choice to hit two birds with one stone: end the refugee crisis by assimilating them into the Gaza strip cities, and ensure dependence on Israel by a new development plan with Yamit city at its epicentre. Mediterranean architecture expressed the gradations of vernacularity in the Israeli policy, and helped fashion a unique ideology of development based on exclusion and ethnic separation.

The children who will be born here and walk the city streets will think that the commercial center has been planted here in ancient times, just like we used to think that Allenby Street [in Tel Aviv] was built with the coastline. Whoever would like to tell these children, in twenty years' time, that he knew Yamit when it was all sands and dunes and that he had missed the opportunity of a lifetime to buy a lot in Yamit, for almost nothing, must make haste.

Arch. Yehuda Drexler, Ministry of Housing, 1974[1]

Planning a brand new city in an environment deeply committed to its own national history is a challenge Architect Yehuda Drexler knows something about. Together with few colleagues, Drexler was charged to plan a new city in the occupied Sinai desert after the 1967 War. Yamit (derived from the Hebrew world "Yam" – sea), a new port city in the Rafah Salient or North-ern Sinai area, stood on the border between the Gaza Strip and Egypt. That Yamit, slated to become the region's new economic centre and a strategically important Israeli settlement, had managed to attract settlers was no small feat. Drexler, the leading professional figure in the undertaking, understood the need to ignite the project by infusing it with a sense of historicity while also promising settlers a bright future of sound investment and contri-bution to the building of the Jewish national home.

Strategically, Yamit was part of broader Israeli attempt to establish control in the Gaza Strip through a two-pronged approach of economic development and civic modernization. This strategy was laid out in detail in the *Gaza Strip and Northern Sinai Masterplan* (GSNS). The GSNS encapsulates Israeli policy-makers' ideas about the usefulness of economic development to ensure Israeli interests in the Strip, and specifically the centrality of "resolving" the Palestinian refugees to ensuring long-term prosperity. Practically, the deal offered to refugees was straightforward: the Israeli government would replace their refugee camps with permeant houses in the strip's cities and recognize them as permanent and equal residents of those cities. In return, Israeli planners hoped, refugees would abandon the Palestinian national demand of the right of return to their 1948 homes.

Scholars such as Roy (1995), Gordon (2008) and Weizman (2007) have made inroads in examining the civilizing mission's manifestation as develop-ment policy as part of a broader structural logic of settler colonialism. They join other scholars in critically discussing the modalities of settler colonialism, whose ultimate goal is the eventual "elimination" of native Palestinians (Lustick 1993; Wolfe 2006; Veracini 2006; Gorenberg 2007; Azoulay and Ophir 2008), through a gradual process of economic "de-development" (Roy 1995, 128). Although we do not deny that Gaza has long been an arena of wanton violence – state or otherwise – we argue that we must rethink the settler-colonial process through production of space as "discur-sively meaningful" (Said 1978).

Once we decentre military violence from the analysis of the Israeli occu-pation of Gaza, the primacy of economic development to Israeli policy in Gaza emerges. This article examines the history of Israeli development in the Gaza Strip, and the GSNS masterplan in particular, from the prism of developmental architecture, that is, we read it as a mode of cultural pro-duction that historically emerged after W.W.II. Israeli development ended abruptly in 1982 with the Egypt-Israel peace treaty, a watershed date that paved the way to the current state of de-development in the Gaza Strip. Our discussion of this particular time frame follows the call of Kim Dovey (2009; quoted in Jones 2011, 1), to scholars to focus on *how* – rather than *whether* – architecture stabilizes meanings in this complicated reality.

The first part of the paper demonstrates how the dispossessory dynamics take multiple forms. It shows how architectural conventions were used to approach politically charged issues with a casual problem-solving attitude that offered "politically neutral" professional "solutions" to solve those "problems" (Crinson 1996; Dovey 1999; Jones 2011). The second part of the article discusses the GSNS masterplan and its bungled attempt to leverage promises of humanitarian aid and economic and political enfranchisement to further the Israeli settler-colonial project. This part focuses particularly on the incompatible political objectives Israeli planners pursued of enrooting Palestinian refugees by eliminating the possibility of their return, while legitimizing the settler project by attracting Jewish immigrants in Yamit. It argues that, under a settler colonial conditions, dispossessory dynamic can be stitched into architectural aesthetic. In our case, Meditteraneaism materialized the colonial urban everyday, and therefore it needed to be explored in order to reveal the subordination dynamics. This has been casted by a heuristic adoption of main protagonists – architects, planners and engineers – whose actions are reconstructed through hitherto unpublished private and archival materials.

Development and Israeli settler colonialism

After the Israeli occupation in 1967, the Gaza Strip loomed increasingly large as *the* central challenge to the triumphant Zionist project of controlling, developing and ethnicizing the territory under its authority (Lustick 1993; Yiftachel 2006). The geopolitical narrative of a zero-sum confrontation between Zionist settler and Palestinian indigenes, however, overlooks an array of attendant mechanisms of inclusion and assimilation, or of exclusion and difference, that developed as part of settler colonial relationship (Rouhana and Areej 2014; Tatour 2019). These mechanisms are indispensable the formation of the threat of eliminating the native (Veracini 2006; Wolfe 2006). Accordingly, the dynamics of power and violence have been privileged when critical scholars examined Palestinian cities (Bollens 2000; Pullan 2011; Porter and Yiftachel 2019). Yiftachel (2010), for example, discusses displacement, erasure and destruction of the indigenous as a constant to Israeli policy, while Cohen and Gordon (2018, 200) argue that erasure mechanisms and Jewish resettlement programmes were deployed side by side to racialize the occupied space in a "biospatial from".

A classically colonial dual mechanism emerged in Israeli governmental practice designed to boost prosperity in the occupied Palestinian territories. Labour exploitation joined with mass expropriation of Palestinian natural resources to wreak havoc on the Palestinian economy and de-develop it (Roy 1995; Gordon 2008). The Israeli economic appeasement, as Roy clearly demonstrates, created ties of dependence that would promote Israeli's

economic interests and ensure their safety. Eliminating of any and every competition gave the Israeli government complete control over the Strip's
resources; dependence on it for employment and material advancement
diminished the Palestinian nationalist aspiration. Jabary Salamanca has
extended Roy's argument on the intimate relationship between the settler
colonialism and development in post-Oslo era. He argued that the development logic embodied in building infrastructures became a mechanism to
manage the short-term "humanitarian" needs of Palestinians to ensure the
long-term of occupation. He has additionally claimed that the humanitarian
logic provided by the material and symbolic sinews of development is
another way to conceal violence (Jabary Salamanca 2016). We therefore
agree about the ultimate objectives of Israeli policy in the Gaza Strip, but
differ about the historical framing of the developmental logic.

Roy, Jabary Salamanca and other researchers base their analysis of Israeli
development within the structural logic imposed by a settler colonial
dynamic whose violence continues to exact heavy prices in life and property
to this very day. Our approach treats the development different manner. It
focuses on the external front of the existing historical paradigm of the
settler colonialism and development within the historical logic between
1972 and 1982. Our focus on the developmental logic of the Gaza's masterplan thus sheds a new light on neglected aspects of settler colonialism.
The GSNS, we point out, can and should be juxtaposed with and examined
vis-à-vis French architecture in North Africa that treated the region as a frontier of experimental modernism, inspired by development logic (Wright 1991;
Fuller 2006; Crane 2011). The materialization of the GSNS has been linked
with the development of the Southern Israel-Palestine area that became
impacted by spatial ideals and shaped by colonial powers operating in
Africa. The immediacy in creating facts in the southern district reveals the
encounter between the scientific and cultural objectives adapted by architects, planners and the radical undermining of this goal. The development
objectives become a mean of ethnic separation and racial segregation,
because of the planning techniques and cultural biases of the professionals
as also the interests of the Israeli government, such as in the case of
Afridar in Ashkelon- northern to Gaza (Levin 2019), or in the planning of
the Lakish Region (Sharon 2017). However, both cases approach the settler
colonial project from demographic objectives of state building following
the 1948. In our case, the GSNS demonstrates the way settler colonialism
was achieved to ensure the demographic factor.

The GSNS situated with postcolonial development projects which were
inspired by the "Truman doctrine". They offered "a fair deal" in which the
renamed "developed world" was made responsible to solve the "problems"
of the newly minted "developing world". Any political or racial hues from
the colonial era were purged, knowledge was rebranded as relevant to

development, and the endeavour was clothed with the language of universal of progress and the trappings of international multilateralism between sovereign states (Ferguson 1990; Sachs 1992; Escobar 1995). In this new postcolonial world, the developer wielded much power to direct and control the developed not as an inferior but rather as a subject temporarily contained within the dynamic of tutelage. Post-WWII development missions continued to be deeply rooted in the exploitative and civilizing logic of colonial urban planning (Comaroff 1997; Yacobi 2003; Robinson 2006; Legg and McFarlane 2008). "Development" as an object of inquiry, however, was to emerge in the post-WWII world due to the hegemony of the scientific discourse and its concomitant beliefs in the universality of the West, in which the colonizer of yesteryear turned to expertise and professionalism, to use the tools of social engineering to uplift peoples in the name of progress (Wright 1991; King 2004; Bissell 2011).

Rulers of newly independent post-colonial nation-states subscribed to the development agenda because it legitimated their rule as states providing their citizens with the fruits of progress through. But this global project was not necessarily compatible with nation-states' desire to distinguish themselves as unique national communities whose shared identities entitle them to particular bounded territories and closed-ended cultures. This task was entrusted in part to architects and planners, whose job it was to articulate the unique visions of national ideas in space, material and form (Vale 1992; Crinson 1996; Bozdoğan 2001; Prakash 2002; Nitzan-Shiftan 2017), and to mediate these ideas through daily practices (Markus 1993).

Scott (1998, 6) explored how such disciplinary knowledge allied itself with state power in pursuit of legibility and simplification. Hegemonic planning strengthened the imperialism of high-modernism and branded local knowledge as inessential to managing societies and economies. But if national identity is manifested through mutual engagement between the sovereign and architects (Vale 1992, 4), and if architects use modes and forms of knowledge as means to arrange population and stabilized social order, what, then, is the role of visualized power in directing our notions of the entangled relationship between architecture and politics?

To deconstruct the linkages between culture and power, one needs to know, as Said (1978, 49) reminds us, that power relations are representations of an "imaginative category". Understanding the power behind the legitimization of the modernizers' hegemony, to be both modern and culturally pure for claiming historical patrimony, one should stand on the historical and social processes devastated the colonized subjects and their way of life (Canclini 2005). Architecture actively participate in this effort because it can mediate power and can address and affect the ways in which people identify with their place (Jones 2015; Yaneva 2017).

Architecture and development are thus inextricably bound within an ever-evolving dynamic of power. According to Dovey, such architectural "languages of representation are primary tools in the practices of power" (Dovey 1999, 5): the largely passive and subconscious everyday consumption of the built environment renders the power relationship it embodies immutable. Once taken for granted, it is legitimated as a "natural" extension of the place (Jones 2011). This naturalization of particular power structures through the aesthetics and arrangements of the built environment was often exploited by idealistic architects and planners who wished to articulate a vision of collective identity by drawing on certain motifs.

The Israeli planners and architects use their power to articulate and carry to fruition a vision of the future for settler colonialism.

Economic development in conditions of uncertainty

In the few years immediately following the 1967 war, leading experts from Israel's academic and scientific communities, career administrators and influential public figures engaged in discussions about the future of the Palestinian territories occupied during the war. Unimpeded by political calculations or intrigues, specialists were invited to project their visions on this new *tabula rasa*. High on the agenda was guaranteeing Israel's financial and industrial sectors' interests through a development scheme tailored to their needs, and a new national masterplan that would effectively terminate the 1948 refugee problem.[2] Two main propositions were brought forth. The Settlement department of the Jewish Agency for Israel (JAI), headed by the agronomist Raanan Weitz, proposed agricultural regional development planning as a preferred means to implement control over Gaza. Clusters of permanent Jewish settlement "blocs" would serve as a buffer between the Strip and Sinai.[3] An new Arab cluster, near 'el-Arish, would rehabilitate the refugees of the Gaza Strip.[4]

Contrary to Weitz's tried-and-tested Zionist policy of expansion through Jewish-only agricultural settlement, the economic scientists headed by Michael Bruno proposed that long-term Israeli control over the territories may only be secured by means of a broader itinerary of integrated economic development. Comprehensive development, for them, was the best way for Israel to establish its control over the land and the populace while avoiding heavy government expenditure.[5] Bruno's taskforce argued that Weitz's suggestion would lead to a scenario of mass unemployment among the occupied Palestinians, which would be extremely dangerous, especially given the government's reluctance to extend Israeli citizenship rights to the newly occupied population.[6]

Bruno's team insisted that the wisest way was to adopt a strategy of control guided by the policy of involvement. Involvement, they wrote, would "convert politically charged issues into problem-solving daily issues".[7] They believed that the highly charged refugee problem could be solved by a short term extension of humanitarian aid, while an incentive-based policy of industrialization and modern urban planning was drawn up to effectively eliminate the problem once and for all. Refugee camps could be gradually emptied through by incentivizing emigration and providing attractive government loans for housing projects in new urban areas that conform to Israeli settlement interests.[8] Preliminary data supporting of their suggestions was based on a report submitted to Bruno's team through one of its members – the economist Yoram ben Porath, who collaborated with academic advisory that comprised of the sociologist-anthropologist Emmanuel Marx and the historian Shimon Shamir. All three worked together in investigating the recommendations in favour of an overall plan of involvement.[9]

Many of Bruno's proposals were eventually adopted alongside some of Weitz's agriculture-based initiatives. In this spirit, the Israeli government published the *Gaza Strip and Northern Sinai* (GSNS) masterplan in 1972 (Figure 1). The GSNS masterplan stipulated that 1948 refugees would be absorbed into the Strips' existing cities, and that they would be made dependent on an all-Jewish city that would become the new economic hub of the area for their livelihoods.[10] Building a Jewish city would allow the exploitation of Gaza's labour while preserving the principle of ethnic segregation between Jews

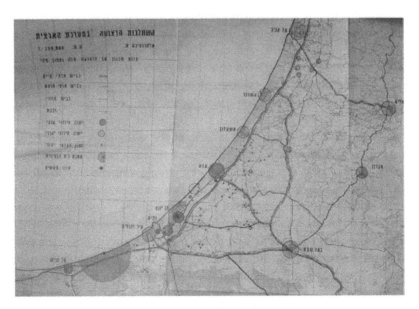

Figure 1. The "Gaza Strip and Northern Sinai" Master Plan, Ministry of Defense, 1972. The red colour describes Arab urban areas and the yellow one is for Jewish settlements (ISA-moch-moch-000poug,).

and Palestinians. The GSNS masterplan was not simply designed to eliminate the Palestinian population. It was also meant to forge relationships that resembled exploitation colonialism, rooted in dependence in employment and segregation in housing that Sorek called "integrative enclaves" (2003), and built on a limited accommodation of Palestinians within the process of development. Clearly, the primary goal of the plan was to cement Israeli colonial hold over the Strip. Israeli planners believed that by modernizing the Strip they would be able to settle the territory with Jews and submit Palestinians there to Israeli rule with minimal military intervention.

The "dark side" of development through planning (Yiftachel 1994; Yiftachel and Yacobi 2003) required that not only economists, but also architects and planners, rationalize these naked power relations "scientifically". The GSNS masterplan was a product of collaboration between representatives from the Ministry of Defense, some among whom had economic expertise, and a team from the Ministry of Housing headed by the architect Yehouda Drexler. The team delegated the planning work to the architectural "Engineering Services in Israel, LtD.", a corporate office that encompassed numerous private outfits and professionals from different disciplines.

The Israeli planning team emphasized the Sinai desert's strategic location as a land bridge between the Mediterranean and the Red Sea and argued it was important to permanently settle the area with Jews. Drexler was convinced that the best way to that was the tried-and-tested Zionist policy of creating facts on the ground first, in the hopes that these would eventually be recognized by the international community.[11] There was also something of the professional allure of the colonial laboratory about this, too. Perhaps Drexler himself put it best: "if there is a place where you can create *ex nihilo*, it is in this place [...] here you can accomplish Zionism in its purest form".[12] He considered urban settlements to be the best way to achieve economic prosperity and endure territorial control over the broad swathes of Sinai's desert. As he pointed out, "if a territorial continuity would exist between the Strip and Egypt, the people of the Gaza Strip would become the spearhead of aggression against Israel. If no such territorial connection existed, all their prospects for livelihood would depend on Israel, and would make them act more measuredly: A Strip without territorial continuity with an Arabic country is a peaceful one", in his words.[13] Drexler was cognizant, then, of his role as a servant of Israeli settler-colonialism. This wholehearted enlistment on the part of Israeli architects and planners from the private-sector to direct government settlement policy is representative of a broader phenomenon of enlisted professionalism among Israel's top practitioners.

A Jewish city named Yamit was the plan's linchpin. Placed several kilometres to the west of Rafah, it would sever the Strip from the rest of the Sinai Peninsula and serve as the area's new economic hub, becoming a major modern port town that would marginalize the historical port city of Gaza. The distance between Yamit and Port Said, Israeli planners found, was similar to that between Beirut and Haifa. A major port was therefore financially viable.[14] The plan also stipulated regional parallel continuums of Jewish and Arabic settlements that would be constructed along the shoreline up until the southern end of the Strip, where Yamit would be built. Yamit was to be a central port town of 250,000 residents, the forth in a string of Israeli port cities alongside the eastern Mediterranean seaboard.[15]

Soon enough, Egypt found out that Israel was planning a port called Yamit. Muhammad Hassanein Heikal, the influential editor of Egypt's leading newspaper, *Al-Ahram*, wrote in early 1974:

> Yamit", as Israel wished to call the port [...] meant war, at least for Egypt [...]." Israel must decide whether it wants to be part of the Middle East or remain a bridgehead on the Mediterranean coast. Israelis must adapt [and decide] whether they want to remain forever an alien implant within the Middle East rejected by the body or adjust to the reality of the Arab world of the Middle east, because then it would be accepted and become part of the entire body.[16]

Such vocal Arabic and international expressions of opposition to the project led some of the Israeli planners to worry that such a large development project in Gaza would backfire, and be taken as an Israeli attempt to de-facto annex the territories. The committee thus resolved to expressly focus its language on secondary objective of economically rehabilitating the 1948 refugees, and make the case that Israel was making an earnest attempt to resolve a humanitarian crisis whose urgency was universally recognized.[17] The humanitarian justifications for rehabilitating the Palestinian refugees, Israeli spokespersons claimed, would also render the costly UNRWA redundant – that same body that Israel long argued before the international community that was counterproductive and only deepened Palestinians' economic dependency and inflexible nationalist politics.

To dismantle the camps, the proposal spoke of Israeli-funded housing and economic development schemes for the refugees, who would acquire home-ownership and consume "the right to the city" as equal residents of the Strip's Palestinian towns (Abreek-Zubiedat and Nitzan-Shiftan 2018). Yitzhak Pundak, the civil governor of the Gaza strip and northern Sinai appointed by Israel in 1971, stressed the right of the refugees to turn into ordinary city inhabitants and enjoyed the services from the municipality rather from UNRWA: "I had to redefine who the real landlord in the Strip is. Only then could we end the refugees' dependency on UNRWA, control the daily space and eradicate the resistance, as the refugee becomes a citizen of the city".[18] The act of leveraging competing values of equality, and of inscribing power onto the practices of daily lives (Dovey 1999) was how Israeli planners sought to end the Palestinian refugees' right of return. "Eradicating the resistance" went hand in hand with "redefining who the real landlord is": both would be achieved by "anchoring" the refugees to their new place.

Mediterraneanism belongs to the refugees

The Israeli idea that the 1948 Palestinian refugees could be made to stay permanently in the Gaza Strip through a housing scheme was hardly new. In the surveys conducted by the plan's collaborators in the engineering services in Israel, LtD, the surveyors emphasized:

> If we seek to anchor the refugee to his place of residence and keep him occupied there, we must construct things so that eventually they will become his home. [...] the more his home is dearer to him, the more he is anchored to the place and the more attached to the place he is, the less interest he takes in factors which might require him to move once again. [19]

The surveying architects approached the relocation of the refugees project as a rural housing project in a developing country undergoing urbanization, and proposed a "traditional Gazan" inner courtyard house. As its name implies, this housing type was characteristic to many residents in Gaza who were mostly former Fellaheen or lower-income urban families. Israeli planners saw their responsibility as providing a basic initial structure that, through individual initiative, the refugee would make into his home. This, to them, would achieve the goal that the refugee would become an active agent in the development of his own home, and make him invested in his new home rather than "housed" by a governmental agency.

The urgency in resettling the refugees led architects to hastily oversee rehabilitation projects of refugees from Jabalia and then to Khan Younis and Rafah (Abreek-Zubiedat and Nitzan-Shiftan 2018). In a later stage, due to scathing criticism against the aesthetic alienation and poor construction standards in these projects, the Israeli government invested more in building the neighbourhood of Sheikh Radwan in the outskirts of Gaza city, a sub-urban neighbourhood for refugees planned, designed and built by the Israeli Public Words Department's (PWD).

The PWD's appearance in the scene is not coincidental. Apart from the fact that the PWD was one of the few Israeli contractors who had the capacity to execute such large-scale projects efficiently, its then main architect, Morde-chai Shoshani, actively sought to expand the PWD from a professional department that dealt primarily with technical design to one that also specialized in architectural design, especially in its more technological aspects. Shoshani searched for an architecture expression to that would place man at the centre, preferring "good technical work over art" as the best way to meet daily needs.[20] Pouncing on the opportunity to work in Gaza, he believed that here was an opportunity to experiment with the regional style of the

Mediterranean architecture: "this is a great opportunity for the PWD to plan Mediterranean housing for refugees" (Shoshani 1973).

The cultural aesthetic values of the Mediterranean basin of the climate and natural conditions reflected in and built environment was inscribed in the architects' imaginations. Light and shadow, simplicity of feeling, structural suitability, natural forms and practical design of structures around shared courtyards, bright colours and harmonious effects emerged from organic development, all loosely defined Mediterranean architecture. As a distinct style, Mediterranean architecture was developed mainly in north Africa's (post)colonial cities, where architecture was commissioned to "conquer the hearts of the natives" (Wright 1991, 1) and legitimize the colonial power (Fuller 2006; McLaren 2006; Crane 2011). Mediterranean architecture was believed capable of grounding a sense of community and belonging by creating a sense of "home" to counter the threat of vulnerability and temporality (Goldhagen and Legault 2000; Avermaete 2010; Van der Heuvel 2015). One basic premise to this colonial style was the belief that the "other" could be Westernized and assimilated (Crinson 1996) through an appropriate built environment that nevertheless appeared authentic. To a large degree, Mediterranean architecture was rooted in nineteenth century imperial orientalism and stood in the context for the heritage of the Roman Empire. As a distinctly modern style, however, it "acknowledged" the debt that the twentieth century modernist architecture owed to extant vernacular traditions from the Mediterranean basin, in which modern architecture was adorned with motifs and styles gleaned from vernacular architecture (Lejeune and Sabatino 2010, 6). Mediterraneanism (Herzfeld 2005) became a favourite way for architects to integrate European modernity with native traditionalism and claim timelessness and universality through the resulting hybrid aesthetic forms. Architects such Bernard Rudofsky, ATBAT-Afrique and Team 10 found in vernacular architecture ontological definitions of place, of being at home in the world, to the point of reclaiming it as "already Italian" (Fuller 2006; McLaren 2006) or "already French" (Crane 2011).

In the Zionist context, Mediterraneanism was hailed as a convenient non-Arabic and non-Islamic architectural vernacular by which belonging to the region was asserted, mainly through references to Greek and Italian aesthetics. For Zionist architects subscribing to what has been called "cultural Zionism", Mediterranean architecture undoubtedly belonged to the Middle East, and helped them articulate an architecture for the Zionist utopia that was at once modern and part of a region they sometimes imagined as an open Semitic Commonwealth (Heinze-Greenberg 2010, 191). Like most of the "cultural Zionist" movement, this proposition was marginalized by the main-stream of political Zionism, but had re-emerged a generation later, among Israeli-born architects. Their criticism of the rationalism and functionalism of the modernist movement in architecture, and their desire to better situate their architecture in the vernacular was inspired by a reappreciation of Palestinian construction styles that they hailed as the true local architectural expression of nativity. After 1967, Mediterraneanism was adopted as an umbrella term describing this wishful thinking that local architecture could also provide Zionist Israelis with a historical anchor and a sense of home in the region, and expressed, perhaps paradoxically, the global trend of enthusiasm with "regional architecture" after WWII. In the Israeli context, it inspired low-rise, hierarchical architectural forms, simulations of narrow alleyways, terraced building and clusters of varied apartment sizes around common courtyards (Nitzan-Shiftan 2017).

The large scale experiment with Mediterranean architecture attracted the engineer Dov Eizenbreg, who was authorized by Shoshani to design and built Shiekh Radwan, for the refugee living in the nearby Shati camp. Eizenberg – an executive in Solel Boneh – was amongst several experts that were send during the 1960s to civilizing mission' in Ethiopia (Yacobi 2015; Levin 2016), to serve as the PWD's chief engineer.[21] By the time Eizenberg was commissioned to work in Gaza over a decade later, he had already a proposed housing model, the "Growing house", to take centerstage in the rehabilitation of the refugees.

Eizenberg's "Growing house" model expressed the Mediterraneanism by the incorporation of certain elements of vernacular aesthetics and a hazy attempt to cater to a particularly local way of life. He has offered an idea of growing houses based on a modular approach that ranges in size $42m^2$ to $85m^2$ (Figure 2). The design was characterized by abstract symbolic forms that allowed the development of geometric patterns through of modular scale unite. This fitted Eizenberg's strategy of "building construction in self-

Figure 2. "Growing House"- Residential building in Sheikh Radwan, designed and executed by Dov Eizenberg (IAA archive).

management while enhancing productivity".[22] The modular, industrial and monotonous "box" served as the basic structure upon which subsequent independent expansion would take place. Eizenberg calculated that this would save as much as 50% in construction time and estimated costs (Shoshani 1973). The benefits of the "Growing house" were not only in cost and time efficiency – Eizenberg believed they allowed residents to quickly and seamlessly populate the neighbourhood and expand it according to their own needs (Ministry of Labor 1973).

The type that was eventually chosen, a 42 m^2 seminal unit at the front and a walled back-yard, combined the "traditional Gazan" inner courtyard house with the self-built housing model. The initial "core unit" provided the refugees with a crude shelter and anchored them to their places by encouraging them to "make it theirs" by initiating subsequent expansions and complete the construction themselves. Eizenberg chose to place the houses at the front of the plots, so that they formed a continuous façade towards the street and residents enjoyed a degree of domestic privacy in line with the Arab traditions. The back yards were partitioned by low walls and enabled the residents to develop their own living environment in accordance with the socioeconomic means of their owners (Ministry of Labor 1973). Thus, in replacing Gaza's refugee camps, the Mediterranean "Growing house" provided the PWD with a model that was both economic and encouraging of self-assimilation and a sense of belonging. Vernacular designs or Mediterranean styles, as one could observe, were linguistic detergents emptied of cultural content once they reinterpreted by technocratic professionals as an expedient answer to the state's immediate needs.

To the Israeli-Jewish settlers of Yamit, a more lavish variant of Mediterranean architecture would help instil a sense of settling on solid ground despite the shifting political sands of Israel's settlement project in the area.

Mediterraneanism as a means of belonging

The relationship between development and settlement had to be fostered by crafting a sense of belonging for the Jewish settlers who were settling in a region long considered hostile. As we mentioned before, the chief architect of GSNS masterplan, Drexler, was convinced that development epitomizes Zionism's praxis, and that it can be best realized in the colonial *terra nullius*. Yamit was to be constructed after levelling the area and forcibly evacuating all 20,000 Bedouins (Gorenberg 2007, 222) who lived in Southern Sinai. For his part, Drexler understood that a major challenge would be to instil a sense of home in the future settlers of Yamit that would overcome the incertitude and precariousness of settling the peripheral frontier outpost. These challenges required a planned city that would consciously try to provide its residents with a sense of homeliness.

To a settler society whose national identity asserted an organic connection to the national space, Mediterraneanism was an expression of an Israeli vernacular. For the architects of Yamit, the Mediterranean vernacular, played out in a different and even wider geopolitical landscape than the Middle East. Drawing inspiration from the Mediterranean urban values in the Greek and Southern Italian villages, Yamit's architects built the city as a European-Middle Eastern and distinctly Mediterranean hybrid.

Ze'ev Druckman, a young graduate of the Faculty of Architecture and Town Planning at the Technion, was invited by Drexler to join the work. Druckman later testified how "Yamit was a universal and cultural effort [...] a Mediterranean city worthy of the name".[23] Its residential area was inspired form architects such as Doxiads and Herzberger who were involved in planning many of the Greek cities.

Yamit's residential neighbourhoods were planned and built in stages. The first stage was planned by Drexler and Druckman, whose primary concern was to dispel feelings of temporariness and inauthenticity through an architecture inspired by timelessness and vernacularity. The planning itself addressed two major typological strands: terraced multi-story apartment buildings where each apartment had its own open-aired terrace on the roof of the one beneath it and overlooked the sea, just across a palm-treed boulevard, and low-rise housing unit of up to three stories tall, designed to provide maximum privacy. The spirit of Mediterraneanism was also expressed in street layouts and shared public areas designed to encourage on community life and to instil settlers with a sense of individual stake and pride of residence, which, Drexler hoped, would "enable them to overcome the dichotomy between a *house* with roof of family to *home* with roof to society".[24] The immediate expression for both was the provision of outdoor yards, or, as both architects described it,

> City life revolves, in fact, around the yards. Starting with the internal courtyards of the houses, through the larger yards of the neighborhood and until the square in front of the commercial center – on whose steps one can hold debates just like they do on Sundays in London's Hyde park.[25]

Houses were generally plastered white, but "many hues of white covered the city, in a kind of homage to the Greek village"[26] (Figure 3).

The theme of Mediterraneanism was taken up in later neighbourhoods, too, designed by architects Shmuel Shaked, Haim Ketzef and Yehouda Kirschner. Instead of replicating the kinds of housing units built in the first stage, Shaked, Ketzef and Kirschner opted for recurring clusters of closely built neighbourhoods around a shared internal yard intended to act as a place of communal gathering.[27] The architects of the latter neighbourhoods claimed that the clusters were "an architectural attempt to integrate into the area and assimilate the cultural heritage of the Mediterranean [...] the

Figure 3. View of one of the courtyards inYamit, 1977 (Harlap (ed)., Israel Builds, 1977).

yards bring people together and foster inward communication based on freedom and equality, rather than separation and domination".[28] The construction of second and third residential stages ended in 1977, and they started to prepare for the fourth stage.

These values of civic freedom, achieved in vernacular design as an expression of regionalism, formed, for example, the design of Avraham Avinu in Hebron old city . Its architects believed that clusters and courtyards could fit the urban fabric of the city as well as the settlers' living alongside Palestinians by granting privacy through separation. At the end, the contribution of the design to a hostile and violent form of segregation after its occupation by the settlers (Shoked 2020) launched political realities against the architects' prior conceptions. In Yamit, however, it is harder to evaluate how architecture influenced the politics of the everyday. Yamit's development was abruptly stalled in March 1979, when a peace treaty was signed with Egypt. Israeli settlements throughout Sinai evacuated, with the largest town, Yamit, being demolished at the end of a three year period, leaving no hope for the settlers to return or for Palestinians to resettle the emptied town. From March 1979, With it, too, came the effective demise of the masterplan of the Gaza Strip and Northern Sinai.

Summary and conclusions

The continuous humanitarian crisis haunting the residents of the Gaza Strip has drawn significant scholarly attention, that had produced a body of work mostly framed by military confrontation, humanitarian siege and cross-factional violence. Such a state of emergency calls upon scholars to decipher the Israeli mechanisms of settler colonialism that accelerated and perpetuated this crisis, and steered it to its current form. While drawing on this scholarship, this study departs from it by arguing that the Israeli settler colonial project gave rise to variegated and less conspicuous forms of state power and violence. Such is the practice of architecture and urban planning that we discuss as cultural politics that underlay the lived built environment and is similarly crucial to our understanding of settler colonialism.

The article unravels a key document, The *Gaza Strip and Northern Sinai* masterplan, that prescribed for the area a project economic development between 1972 and 1982. The study examines the plan in the context of developmental modernism that flourished after W.W.II in economically driven projects, particularly in the developing world. The knowledge these architects invested in the plan reveal their participation in critical aspects of the Israeli settler colonialism, and at the same time convey their architectural discourse as a complicated and varied rather than instrumental endeavour.

The article focused on two strikingly different groups that the master plan engaged. It treated the enormously loaded issues of the 1948 refugee problem and their right of return, and the settlement of Jewish-only immigrants in occupied Palestinian territories with a belief that the professional tools of urban development and architecture could improve the situation and that finding a sensible middle ground was essentially a-political. These two contrasting forms of spatial production goes beyond the limited bounds of a zero-sum game, where Jewish spatial production entails Palestinian spatial destruction. But why did they simultaneously apply the Mediterranean style of architecture to address their two different, but essentially compatible, political objectives in Gaza and in Yamit?

Mediterranean architecture embodied long-percolating Zionist ideals of belonging to a de-Arabized Middle East, and was carried out in accordance to overarching structures of an exclusive national citizenship structure and a physical reality of separation along ethnic lines. Mediterranean architecture was posited by Israeli architects and engineers in Gaza as a way to transform the conditions of refugees and make them ordinary urban citizens. In Yamit, Mediterraneanism was used to instil a sense of community and safety to a Jewish settler population in recently occupied territory and exclusively surrounded by Palestinian Arabic neighbours.

The development project that this paper reviewed slowed down in 1979, following initial talks that led to the signing of a peace treaty between Israel and Egypt in 1982. In keeping with its side of the deal, Israel withdrew from North Sinai and demolished Yamit, the major port city that was supposed to anchor Israeli power in the region. Without economic incentives to develop the Strip, Israeli presence was reduced to land-holding agricultural settlements and securing military borders. The Israeli disengagement from the

Gaza Strip in 2005 lead to ever tightening restrictions on movement, employment and essential supplies. Israel continued to exert control over key areas
of Gazan life in the name of the first and most constant of Zionist imperatives
– security.

Notes

1. Arch. Yehuda Drexler in an interview with **Davar** daily journalist Yossi Beilin,
   1974 (materials provided by Arch. Ze'ev Druckman).
2. ISA, "Refugee issues and more, 7/1967 to 9/1968", SA-Privatecollections-
   MichaelBruno- 000o7u9
3. ISA, "Plans for refugee rehabilitation and water desaliniation center", ISA-PMO-
   MinistersdeputyMinister-000cgx9
4. ISA, "Fundamentals of the proposition to settle refugees in 'el-Arish-1969", ISA-
   Privatecollections-MichaelBruno-000lb2k
5. ISA, "Refugee issues and more". SA-Privatecollections-MichaelBruno- 000o7u9
6. ISA, "Developing the held territories – examinations of alternatives". ISA-Priva-
   tecollections-MichaelBruno- 000o7u9.
7. ISA, Michael Bruno collection – public activities, "Rehovot Group in the Weitz-
   man Science Institute", 1969-1970. ISA-Privatecollections-MichaelBruno-
   000lb2k, working plans and memoranda of the "Rehovot Group" regarding
   the refugee problem and proposals for their rehabilitation.
8. ISA, "Rehovot Group" Plan on the refugee question. ISA-mfa-UNInterOrg2-000.
9. ISA, "Refugee issues and more". SA-Privatecollections-MichaelBruno- 000o7u9.
   By early 1968, Ben- Portath, Marx and Shamir produced a policy-oriented
   report on Jalazone camp: *A Refugee Camp in the West Bank, a Provisional
   Report*, Jerusalem [in Hebrew]
10. ISA, Michel Bruno Collection– public activity, articles on the held territories'
    economy et cetera. 1972-1973, "Background materials for work group of
    deputy committee for territories' affairs", ISA-Privatecollections-MichaelBruno-
    000ln1r.
11. "Yehouda Drexler: The Architects Are Not Active in Shaping the Image and
    Essence of the state", *AA – The Architects' Monthly Publication – The Architects'
    and Engineers' Society in Israel* 3 (1974): 3-4, 19.
12. Yehouda Drexler in an interview with Yossi Beilin, "Yamit emerges from the
    sands", **Davar**, 21 Mars 1975.
13. Yehouda Drexler in an interview with Yossi Beilin.
14. Yehouda Drexler in an interview with Yossi Beilin.
15. Correspondence between planners from the Ministry of Interior and Security
    officials at the South Command Centre, 6 February 1972. ISA-MOIN-Interior-
    Plans-0003vyl. See also his later letter, from 4 September 1972 and 25
    January 1973. ISA-MOIN-InteriorPlans-0003j3s.
16. An interview given by Muhammad Hassanein Heikal to Der Spiegel, "Sadat did
    not intend to occupy all Sinai", *Davar*, January 22, 1974.
17. Pinchas Eliav, 17 June 1969. ISA, "Rehovot Group" Plan on the Refugee Question
    . ISA-mfa-UNInterOrg2-000ah1y.
18. Interview with Yitzhak Pundak, Kfar Yona, Israel, December 2015.
19. Gaza Strip and Northern Sinai command center, the masterplan taskforce, plan-
    ning teams – Engineering Services in Israel LtD, **Plan for family residential unit**

in the Gaza Strip, The Avie and Sarah Arenson Built Heritage Research Center Archive, the Faculty of Architecture and Town Planning, the Technion, 1971.
20. ISA, Ministry of Economy and Industry, 1967-1970, "PWD execution policy – November 1968", ISA-moital-moital-0010r08.
21. See Dov Eizenberg's online blog: https://sites.google.com/site/doveizenberg/ (Retrieved: 03/10/2019).
    Eizenberg has been mainly influenced by Israeli architect Zalman Enav who worked closely with Emperor Haile Selassie. Enav expertise in tropical architecture. For further discussion see Levin (2016) and Yacobi (2015).
22. Yair Kotler, "Untitled." *Haaretz (suppl.)*, December 19, 1975; Eisenberg Blog
23. Interview with Ze'ev Druckman, Tel-Aviv, 14 May 2012.
24. Yehuda Drexler speech, quoted in: "Technical committee meeting of A.A.A.I on 14 March, 1974, hosting Avraham Ofer", *AA – The Architects' Monthly Publication – The Architects' and Engineers' Society in Israel* 4 (April 1974), 22.
25. "Yamit Emerges from the Sands", **Davar**, 21 March 1975.
26. Interview with Ze'ev Druckman, Tel-Aviv, 14 May 2012.
27. The definition of their work was also influenced by Alison and Peter Smithson, "Cluster City: A New Shape for the Community", The Architectural Review, 122, no. 730 (Nov. 1957): 333–336.
28. Interview with Rita Donsky, Ramat Gan, January 2013. Donsky was the chief architect for Shmuel Shaked's office, later becoming a name partner in the office. Similar architectural *mio credo*s arose in an interview with Haim Ketzef, Ramat Hasharon, 7 September 2015.

Acknowledgement (if any)

We are grateful for the reviewers for their insightful comments on the manuscript, and for the valuable discussions and remarks of Tamir Sorik. Our special thanks to Dr. Zvi Elhyani and the IAA Archive.

Disclosure statement

No potential conflict of interest was reported by the author(s).

Funding information (if any)

N/A

ORCID

Fatina Abreek-Zubiedat 🅘 http://orcid.org/0000-0002-6985-3373

References

Abreek-Zubiedat, Fatina, and Alona Nitzan-Shiftan. 2018. "'De-Camping' Through Development: The Palestinian Refugee Camps in Gaza, 1967–1982." In *Camps Revisited: Multifaceted Spatialities of a Modern Political Technology*, edited by Irit Katz, Diana Martin, and Claudio Minca, 137–157. New York: Rowman & Littlefield Publishers.

Avermaete, Tom. 2010. "Nomadic Experts and Travelling Perspectives." In *Colonial Modern: Aesthetics of the Past, Rebellions for the Future*, edited by Tom Avermaete, Serhat Karakayali, and Marion von Osten, 130–149. London, U.K: Black Dog.

Azoulay, Ariella, and Adi Ophir. 2008. *This Multiple Regime: Occupation and Democracy Between Sea and the River (1967–)*. Tel Aviv: Resling. [in Hebrew].

Bissell, William. 2011. *Urban Design, Chaos, and Colonial Power in Zanzibar*. Bloomington: Indiana University Press.

Bollens, Scott A. 2000. *On Narrow Ground: Urban Policy and Ethnic Conflict in Jerusalem and Belfast*. Albany, GA: State University of New York Press.

Bozdoğan, Sibel. 2001. *Modernism and Nation Building: Turkish Architectural Culture in the Early Republic*. Seattle: University of Washington Press.

Canclini, Néstor G. 2005. *Hybrid Cultures Strategies For Entering And Leaving Modernity, Trans. Christopher L. Chiappari and Silvia L. Lopez*. Minneapolis: University of Minnesota Press.

Cohen, Yinon, and Neve Gordon. 2018. "Israel's Biospatial Politics: Territory, Demography, and Effective Control." *Public Culture* 30 (2): 199–220.

Comaroff, John. 1997. "Images of Empire, Contests of Conscience: Models of Colonial John L. Domination on South Africa." In *Tensions of Empire: Colonial Cultures in a Bourgeois World*, edited by Ann Laura Stoler, and Frederick Cooper, 137–163. Berkeley: University of California Press.

Crane, Sheila. 2011. *Mediterranean Crossroads: Marseille and Modern Architecture*. Minneapolis: University of Minnesota Press.

Crinson, Mark. 1996. *Empire Building: Orientalism and Victorian Architecture*. London: Routledge.

Dovey, Kim. 1999. *Framing Places - Mediating Power in Built Form*. London & New York: Routledge.

Dovey, Kim. 2009. *Becoming Places:Urbanism/Architecture/Identity/Power*. London: Routledge.

Escobar, Arturo. 1995. *Encountering Development: The Making and Unmaking of the Third World*. Princeton: Princeton University Press.

Ferguson, James. 1990. *The Anti-Politics Machine, "Development," Depoliticization, and Bureaucratic Power in Lesotho*. Cambridge: Cambridge University Press.

Fuller, Mia. 2006. *Modern Abroad: Architectures, Cities, and Italian Imperialism in the Mediterranean and East Africa*. London & New York: Routledge.

Goldhagen, Sarah, and Réjean Legault, eds. 2000. *Anxious Modernism, Experimentation in Postwar Architectural Culture*. Montreal: Canadian Centre for Architecture.

Gordon, Neve. 2008. *Israel's Occupation*. Berkeley: University of California Press.

Gorenberg, Gershom. 2007. *Occupied Territories: The Untold Story of Israeli's Settelments Accidental Empire*. New York: I.B. Tauris.

Heinze-Greenberg, Ita. 2010. "Erich Mendelsohn's Mediterranean Longings." In *Modern Architecture and the Mediterranean: Vernacular Dialogue, Contested Identities*, edited by Jean Francois Lejeune, and Michelangelo Sabationa, 175–191. Oxon: Routledge.

Herzfeld, Michael. 2005. "Practical Mediterraneanism: Excuses for Everything, from Epistemology to Eating". In *Rethinking the Mediterranean*, edited by William V. Harris, 45–63. Oxford: Oxford University Press.

Jabary Salamanca, Omar. 2016. "Assembling the Fabric of Life: When Settler Colonialism Becomes Development." *Journal of Palestine Studies* 45 (4): 64–80.

Jones, Paul. 2011. *The Sociology of Architecture. Constructing Identities*. Liverpool: Liverpool University Press.

Jones, Paul. 2015. "Modelling Urban Futures." *City* 19 (4): 463–479.

King, Anthony. 2004. *Spaces of Global Cultures: Architecture Urbanism Identity.* New York: Routledge.

Legg, Stephan, and Colin McFarlane. 2008. "Ordinary Urban Spaces: Between Postcolonialism and Development." *Environment and Planning A: Economy and Space* 40 (1): 6–14.

Lejeune, Jean Francois, and Michelangelo Sabatino, eds. 2010. *Modern Architecture and the Mediterranean: Vernacular Dialogue, Contested Identities.* Oxon: Routledge.

Levin, Ayala. 2016. "Haile Selassie's Imperial Modernity: Expatriate Architects and the Shaping of Addis Ababa." *Journal of the Society of Architectural Historians* 75 (4): 447–468.

Levin, Ayala. 2019. "South African 'Know-How' and Israeli 'Facts of Life': The Planning of Afridar, Ashkelon, 1949-1956." *Planning Perspectives* 34 (2): 285–309.

Lustick, Ian S. 1993. *Unsettled States, Disputed Land: Britain and Ireland, France and Algeria, Israel and the West Bank–Gaza.* Ithaca, NY: Cornell University Press.

Markus, Thomas, A. 1993. *Buildings and Power: Freedom & Control in the Origin of Modern Building Types.* London & New York: Routledge.

McLaren, Brian L. 2006. *Architecture and Tourism in Italian Colonial Libya: An Ambivalent Modernism.* Seattle: University of Washington Press.

Ministry of Labor, Department of Public Works (DPW) [Israel]. 1973. "Building Refugee Housing Projects in the Strip: Interim Report". Jerusalem: Ministry of Labor, Department of Public Works. Israeli Architecture Archive (IAA).

Nitzan-Shiftan, Alona. 2017. *Seizing Jerusalem: The Architectures of Unilateral Unification.* Minneapolis: University of Minnesota Press.

Porter, Libby, and Oren Yiftachel. 2019. "Urbanizing Settler–Colonial Studies". *Settler Colonial Studies* 9 (2): 177–186.

Prakash, Vikramaditya. 2002. *Chandigarh's Le Corbusier: The Struggle for Modernity in Postcolonial India.* Seattle, WA: The University of Washington Press.

Pullan, Wendy. 2011. "Frontier Urbanism: The Periphery at the Centre of Contested Cities." *The Journal of Architecture* 16 (1): 15–35.

Robinson, Jennifer. 2006. *Ordinary Cities: Between Modernity and Development.* London: Routledge.

Rouhana, Nadim N., and Sabbagh-Khoury Areej. 2014. "Settler-colonial Citizenship: Conceptualizing the Relationship Between Israel and its Palestinian Citizens." *Settler Colonial Studies.* doi:10.1080/2201473X.2014.947671.

Roy, Sarah. 1995. *The Gaza Strip: The Political Economy of De-Development.* Washington, DC: Institute of Palestinian Studies.

Sachs, Wolfgang. 1992. *The Development Dictionary: A Guide to Knowledge as Power.* London: Zed Books.

Said, Edward. 1978. *Orientalism.* London: Penguin Books.

Scott, James C. 1998. *Seeing Like a State: How Certain Schemes to Improve the Human Condition Have Failed.* New Haven and London: Yale University Press.

Sharon, Smadar. 2017. *And Thus a Homeland is Conquered: Planning and Settlement in 1950s Lakish Region.* Haifa: Pardes Publishing. [in Hebrew].

Shoked, Noam. 2020. "Design and Contestation in the Jewish Settlement of Hebron, 1967–87." *Journal of the Society of Architectural Historians* 79 (1): 82–102.

Shoshani, Mordechai. 1973. "I am Disappointed by the Profession, Many Architects are Willing to be Sell-Swords." *AA – The Architects' Monthly Publication – The Architects' and Engineers' Society in Israel* 2 (September): 8–11. [in Hebrew]

Sorek, Tamir. 2003. "Arab Football in Israel as an 'Integrative Enclave'." *Ethnic and Racial Studies* 26 (3): 422–450.

Tatour, Lana. 2019. "Citizenship as Domination: Settled Colonialism and the Making of Palestinian Citizenship in Israel." *Arab Studies Journal* XXVII (2): 8–39.

Vale, Lawrence. 1992. *Architecture, Power and National Identity*. New Haven, CT: Yale University Press.

Van der Heuvel, Dirk. 2015. "The Open Society and its Experiments: The Case of the Netherlands and Piet Blom." In *Architecture and the Welfare State*, edited by Mark Swenarton, Tom Avermaete, and Dirk Van der Heuvel, 133–152. Oxon: Routledge.

Veracini, Lorenzo. 2006. *Israel and Settler Society*. London, U.K: Pluto Press.

Weizman, Eyal. 2007. *Hollow Land: Israel's Architecture of Occupation*. London: Verso Books.

Wolfe, Patrick. 2006. "Settler Colonialism and the Elimination of the Native." *Journal of Genocide Research* 8 (4): 387–409.

Wright, Gwendolyn. 1991. *The Politics of Design in French Colonial Urbanism*. Chicago: Chicago University Press.

Yacobi, Haim. 2003. "Everyday Life in Lod: on Power, Identity and Spatial Protest." *Jamaa* 10: 69–109. (Hebrew).

Yacobi, Haim. 2015. *Israel and Africa: A Genealogy of Moral Geography*. Abington: Routledge.

Yaneva, Albena. 2017. *Five Ways to Make Architecture Political: An Introduction to the Politics of Design Practice*. London: Bloomsbury.

Yiftachel, Oren. 1994. "The Dark Side of Modernism: Planning as Control of an Ethnic Minority." In *Postmodern Cities and Spaces*, edited by Sophie Watson, and Katherine Gibson, 216–239. Oxford: Basil Blackwell.

Yiftachel, Oren. 2006. *Ethnocracy: Land, and the Politics of Identity Israel/Palestine*. Philadelphia, PA: University of Pennsylvania Press.

Yiftachel, Oren. 2010. "From Sharon to Sharon: Spatial Planning and Separation Regime in Israel/Palestine." *HAGAR Studies un Culture, Polity and Identities* 10 (1): 73–106.

Yiftachel, Oren, and Haim Yacobi. 2003. "Urban Ethnocracy: Ethnicization and the Production of Space in an Israeli Mixed City." *Environment and Planning D: Society and Space* 21 (6): 673–693.

Songs of subordinate integration: music education and the Palestinian Arab citizens of Israel during the Mapai era

Oded Erez ⓘ and Arnon Yehuda Degani

ABSTRACT

This article traces the role of music in Arab public schools during Israel's early decades, as a unique window into the dynamics of inclusion and exclusion that underline the encounter between the state and its Palestinian citizens. We interpret the case of music education in Arab schools through the lenses of a larger historical process of the "subordinate integration" of Palestinians into the Israeli polity. In addition to reviewing the emergence of formal music education for the separate Arab school system, we analyze state-sponsored songbooks produced in the 1960s, discussing editorial motivation and the musical practices reflected and inscribed therein. We then focus on the role of a well-known Independence Day song, exploring both its emergence and early reception, and its persistent function as a *lieu de mémoire*, representing the larger trauma of forced spectacle of loyalty for an entire generation of Palestinian citizens of Israel schooled during those years.

In his 2009 film *The Time That Remains*, director Elia Suleiman (b. 1960) tells the story of his Nazarene family from the time of its Israeli occupation in 1948 to the present. One of the film's most striking tableaus depicts a choir of girls singing an Israeli march—*Mahar* ("tomorrow")—expressing a yearning for a better, peaceful future. It is delivered in Hebrew with a thick Arabic accent. When the song concludes, a Jewish official from the Ministry of Education rises to address those present in Hebrew:

> I am proud and happy to award the school's wonderful choir the first prize in the Hebrew song competition. This award, given to a school of the minorities, is another sign of our desire to instil in our students the principles of democracy and equality.

Figure 1. Nabila Abu-Shkara (née Azzam) conducts the *Natsaret Bet* school's girls choir during an Arab choir convention celebrating Israel's 20th anniversary. Frank Sinatra Hall, Nazareth, 1968 (Photo: *ha-Hinukh ha-Muziqali* 14–15, p. 25). This event was likely the main inspiration for the scene depicted in Suleiman's 2009 film.

Following the award ceremony, the choir performs a second song, this time in Arabic: "ʿId istiqlal israʾil" ("Israel's holiday of independence") (Figure 1).

This deeply ironic scene serves in Suleiman's film as a potent musical metaphor for the double charade of equality and loyalty that was the staple of Arab public schooling in the young State of Israel.[1] It marks Independence Day songs as a key symbol for the lived experience of this charade, in the memories of Palestinian citizens of Israel schooled during those years. Inspired by Suleiman's striking use of music in this scene, the purpose of our article is to offer a genealogy of the realities behind such memories, highlighting the place of music in the Arab school during Israel's early decades. Following a summary discussion of how music entered Arab public schools through formal channels, we focus on the story of a single Independence Day song, which serves as the point of articulation between the domain of the performance of citizenship, and that of music in school life. By analyzing policy documents and songbooks that provide insight into the construction and implementation of a music curriculum, and coupling them with the memories of teachers and students, collected through interviews and from written sources, we aim to shed light on an understudied aspect of the dynamic between Jewish and Palestinian Arab agents of music education. We further seek to trace the cultural and political vision for Arab citizenship reflected in material for the music classroom, and elucidate ways in which music fits into broader attempts to promote Arab pupils' identification with the state, while keeping them culturally and politically separate from the Jewish Israeli majority group (Nassar 2017, 60).

Background[2]

This study considers Zionism comparable to other settler-colonial national movements, and Israel as comparable to other settler-colonial states. As has been established by Patrick Wolfe (1999) and Lorenzo Veracini (2010), settler-colonial movements have a propensity to violently dislocate indigenous communities, yet they also have a complementary tendency to absorb the remaining indigenous population into the settler body politic. Indeed, all cases of settler-colonial consolidation feature some form of indigenous elimination through violence (genocide, ethnic cleansing, mass expulsion, etc.) and through assimilation into settler political order. The touchstone policy of settler-colonial assimilation is the extension of citizenship, which formally endows indigenous people with the same individual rights as settlers. It thus extinguishes claims for collective rights based on indigeneity, i.e. on "being there first."

In Israel, too, indigenous assimilation included the granting of citizenship to those Palestinians who remained within its borders after the mass exodus that took place during the 1948 War (referred to in Arabic as al-Nakba, "the catastrophe"). At the same time, the state immediately subjected these citizens to a multi-layered system of surveillance, segregation, disenfranchisement, material deprivation, political repression, and, for the better part of the first two decades, a form of martial law known as the Military Government (Zureik 1979; Bauml 2007; Degani 2014). In 1966, after having gradually alleviated its most burdensome restrictions, the state abolished the Military Government altogether. However, Palestinian citizens remained structurally marginalized in Israeli society and politics.

Degani (2018) refers to the processes of assimilation that Palestinian Arabs in Israel underwent as "subordinate integration." This term encapsulates both the "incompleteness" of Arab integration into Israeli society, and its liminality: integration that is weak but just robust enough to elicit from the Palestinians conformity to the political structure of Israeli society and confines their political opposition to the state to mostly non-violent and rights-based forms of resistance. The term also connotes that this assimilation is qualitatively different from other cases such as the United States, Canada, Australia, and New Zealand, where the indigenous communities no longer pose any major threat, real or perceived, to the settler-state, and the settler-state recognizes aspects of indigenous culture to be part of its national heritage. Nevertheless, the net effect of subordinate integration was that, by the

1980s, most of the Palestinian citizens of Israel willingly assumed the category of "Arab Israelis" (Smooha 1999; Bishara 1999). Even today, after a long period of heightened ethnic tensions in Israel/Palestine and virulent anti-Palestinian discourse coming from the ascending Israeli right, around 10% of the Palestinian Arabs in Israel continue to claim that they primarily identify as Israeli, and close to 65% claim that they are "rather proud" or "very proud" of their "Israeliness" (Hermann et al. 2019).

While the settler-colonial perspective effectively accounts for this dynamic, understanding how the new state negotiated the place of the Arabic language, Arab music, and other manifestations of Arab cultures necessitates taking into account unique local factors, such as the related integration of incoming Jews from Arab and Muslim lands (Arab Jews, or *Mizrahim*), and the divergent educational goals set by the state for these populations (Levy 2005). While in a cultural sense, the latter often had much in common with the local Palestinian Arab population, the state, applying an ethno-religious criterion, designated almost opposite routes of integration for these two populations. Palestinian Arabs were generally expected to renounce any political aspirations grounded in Arab nationalism, but were encouraged to maintain their cultural difference. Arabic-speaking Jews, on the other hand, were expected (like other Jewish immigrants) to fulfil their *Jewish ethnicity* as *Israeli nationality* by stripping of their diasporic culture in favour of a Modern Hebrew one, the course for which was plotted largely by Jews of European descent (Shohat 1999; Shenhav 2006). The fact that the Israeli settling core largely avoided the cultural assimilation of the Palestinian Arabs, and indeed cultivated a cultural Jewish-Arab divide, reflects the unique constellation of religious, ethnic, and inclusion/exclusion dynamics that endow the case of Israel with its specificity vis-à-vis other settler states (Wolfe 2012).

Music education as an ideological state apparatus

Unsurprisingly, education was a central arena for enacting these divergent visions of integration. Modern social theory has often stressed the central role of education as a site for social reproduction and for the mediation of material power structures into the realm of culture. In the writings of Antonio Gramsci, education and educators are seen as essential to the attainment, maintenance, or subversion of hegemony by a ruling or aspiring-to-rule social group (Landy 1986). Later Marxist theorists of ideology, such as Louis Althusser, elaborated on the rôle of schools as a central ideological state apparatus, where state power is consolidated and exerted not by means of violence but by means of ideology (Althusser 1971).

This basic ideological function of education is arguably nowhere more patent than in the emergence of modern nation-states and the making of "peoples." The idea that music in particular is an essential component of national identity and should be cultivated through education is as old as nationalism itself, going back to the foundational writings of Johann Gottfried Herder (1744–1803).[3] After Herder, the interlaced operations of the study of folk music and its mobilization in the service of the national idea through composition, performance, and instruction, has been a mainstay of every national movement in its formative stages (Taruskin 2001). As such, music education has been increasingly recognized as a political domain (Hebert and Kertz-Welzel 2012; Schmidt and Colwell 2017).

As was the case with other forms of cultural expression, minorities and their music often presented a challenge for musical nationalisms (Stokes 1994), exposing the latter's contingent and invented nature, and intensifying what Ochoa-Gautier (2006) has termed "epistemologies of sonic purification." Here, too, settler societies in particular often exhibited policies of elimination via integration. For example, in the United States, the Federal Office of Indian Affairs (OIA) operated, from the 1880s to the 1930s, many boarding schools where Native American children were introduced to Euro-American ways of life. In these schools, music education was of great importance in the task of uprooting tribalism, indigenous languages, and indigenous music and dance, while inculcating a repertoire shared with White schoolchildren (Troutman 2009, Ch. 3). At the same time, these schools also instructed students on "proper" ways of performing their "Indianness," using music authorized and adapted by state-sponsored music anthropologists (ibid., Ch. 4).

As we will show, the paths taken in Israeli music education for Arab schools varied markedly from this model. Rather than set as its goal the assimilation of Palestinian pupils into the national culture of the Jewish majority (perhaps while maintaining some indigenous elements as a source of communal pride), music education was de facto designed to promote a distinct "Arab-Israeli" identity, grounded not only in the Arabic language but also in the transnational Arab musical system of maqam,[4] yet detached from Arab nationalist songs, including songs about Palestine and the Nakba that were popular in the region in the heyday of Nasserism (McDonald 2013, 75–105). In emphasizing Arab music as a transnational cultural idiom—a cultural element all but banned from the curriculum in Jewish schools, including those attended primarily by Jewish immigrants from Arab lands—music education contributed to the isolation and marginalization of Palestinian citizens in the Jewish state as much as it was part of the attempt to inscribe Israel as their sole national framework.

Israeli education and the Palestinian citizens Israel

The separate Arab education system in Israel suffered from deep disparities in relation to the Jewish one, disparities that still exist today. Al-Haj (1995, 165) considers the Israeli education system as largely pursuing the British Mandate government's "policy of producing ignorance" (*siyasat al-tajhil*). Nonetheless, Arab education in Israel was different from the British system by virtue of its mass scale, placing an unprecedented percentage of Palestinian Arab children in classrooms.

Yet in other ways the political goals of the Arab public school system during the Military Government years resembled those a colonial administrations in that it was highly preoccupied with monitoring and suppressing dissent, real or perceived. The discourse on Arab dissent, as expressed in memoranda, meeting protocols, and press reports, constantly referred to the term "loyalty" (*ne'emanut*) which meant, depending on the context, anything between a pragmatic willingness to abide by Israeli law to a true appreciation of the good fortune in being Israeli citizens. State officials constantly pondered if the Arabs were genuinely loyal to the state, if loyalty can be instilled, and how. These concerns were not pure paranoia; the popular culture of the Arab world, including music, was rife with anti-Zionist and anti-Israel themes. Within the Israeli establishment's discourse on "loyalty", constant references were made to the notion, based on reality, that many Arabs listened to radio stations broadcasting anti-Israeli content from Arab capitals (Degani 2018, 178–181; Massad 2003). The Israeli anxiety about Arab loyalty formed the backdrop for Israeli educators' (Both Jewish and Arab) constant demands for displays of loyalty from Palestinian citizens. Palestinian educators were well aware of the fact that they were being watched and knew exactly what the state and its representatives expected them to do or not to do (Al-Haj 1995, 162–168).

Despite its salience, the security-oriented approach to "Arab loyalty" was not the only one. Contributing to the "integration" aspect of "subordinate integration" in Israeli education were civic-minded officials such as Yehuda Leib Benor (Blum), the first Head of the Department of Arab Education and Culture, who was disinclined to force "loyal behaviour" upon Arab citizens. However, it is likely that the Palestinian Arab principals' and teachers' decisions were shaped more by the repressive measures of the Military Government than by the liberal attitudes of civilian education officials. Moreover, the particular intersections of religion, nationalism, and ethnicity in Israeli society hampered, to say the least, the development of a widespread and deep sentiment of Palestinian Arab identification with the state. In 1957, Benor (now Deputy Director of the Ministry of Education) admitted that there was a basic problem in developing an Israeli civic ethos that would be relatable to Arabs: "On the one hand, we should not replicate, of course, the culture of Jewish-Israeli nationalism in Arab schools, yet, on the other hand, we have yet to work out [even amongst us Jews] a general Israeli civic culture," he wrote (quoted in Tsameret 2003, 66). By 1973,

Benor's successor as head of the Department for Arab Education concluded that

> we cannot, and we do not wish, to instil in the heart of the Arab pupil "the common fate and destiny of the Jewish people," [specified in the 1953 "General Education Law" as one of the goals of general education] .... [A]s the main goal of Arab education, we should set the values of Arab culture. (Kopelovitch 1973, 325)

A study of music education yields illuminating examples of how such ideas permeated the practice of Jewish and Palestinian educators. As we will show, by excluding Western music theory from the curriculum of Arab teacher's training, or by purging elements of Western tonality (the basic "grammar" of Western music) in new melodies composed for Arab school songbooks (both examples are discussed later in this article), music educators were de facto giving such abstract principles a concrete musical interpretation.

Music education in the Arab schools

The foundations of music education in Israel were laid within the framework of Jewish settlement during the pre-state era. The guiding principle of its pioneers—mostly European Jews—was in line with the larger cultural agenda of the Zionist mainstream, which sought to cultivate a unique sense of nationhood through music (Hirschberg 1996). This meant that in addition to the strong European foundations of their musical outlook, ideologues and theorists of music education such as Leo Kestenberg (1882–1962) believed that they had to devise a vision premised on the synthesis of Western music with local or traditional-Oriental elements (Hirschberg 1996; Tauber 2017, 51–52; Cohen 2009).

In the field of music education, the main figure charged with addressing these and other challenges was Emanuel Amiran-Pougatchov (1909–1993), a Warsaw-born composer who in 1945 co-founded, with Kestenberg, the first seminar for music teachers in Tel Aviv. In 1949, Amiran was appointed Inspector General for Music in the Ministry of Education, a position he held until 1975. During this long tenure, Amiran, together with a core group of music pedagogues (many of them his students), laid the foundations for formal music education in Israel in terms of its organization, its pedagogical practices, and its cultural content. A key effort in this operation was the production of educational materials—mainly songbooks—to provide common ground for the different schools.

This organized and vibrant operation is the backdrop against which we should evaluate music education in Arab schools.[5] Once pieced together, the general picture painted by historical evidence concerning formal music education in the separate Arab school system is one of neglect. To put it concisely, the Arab education system was a low priority for the state, and music education was a low priority for the Arab education system. It is clear, however, that music education officials believed that Arab schools fell within their realm of responsibility (Amiran-Pogachov 1955, 275). Despite what Amiran reported as "great efforts" (ibid.), it was more than a decade before any significant progress was made in music classes for the separate Arab school system. The seeds of change were planted when, in the mid-1950s, Amiran finally had a certified Palestinian Arab music teacher, Suheil Radwan (b. 1931, Bisan, Palestine). Raised in Nazareth, Radwan first worked there after the war teaching math, and later music. He received his early musical training in Western music theory and piano from Jewish and Armenian teachers, and also sang in the choir of the Communist Party of Israel's youth movement, *al-Taliʿa* (Radwan, interview, 2019). In 1952, all teachers affiliated with the Communist Party were fired—Radwan among them—leading him to leave the Party.

That same year, Amiran visited his school and asked Radwan to join the first class of a music teacher training programme in a kibbutz near Haifa. Although the curriculum focused on Western music, it was in part the frequent requests from European-Jewish students and teachers at the seminary that Radwan introduce them to Arab music which eventually pushed him to pursue this music as a musician and teacher (ibid.). In 1959, Radwan moved to Haifa, taking up teaching in the adjacent towns and villages. It was around this time that he was also recruited to co-edit the first Arab songbook produced by the State of Israel, as we discuss below. Between 1966 and 1988, Radwan served as acting superintendent of music for the Arab sector. In 1962, he founded and directed a two-year training programme for Arab music teachers at the Rubin Conservatory in Haifa. As he noted in a report from 1965, "in the study of solfege, theory, form, and other subjects, we concentrate on the foundations of Arab music, and primarily on the *maqamat*. Harmony and counterpoint are not taught in this department" (Radwan 1965). This stood in sharp contrast to the curriculum of the central teacher training programme in Tel Aviv, designed mainly for Jewish teachers (Tauber 2017, 62–66, 110). By 1972 Radwan's programme produced close to 60 graduates, comprising the first cadre of certified music teachers in Arab schools.

In many ways, Radwan's personal story exemplifies the dynamics that characterize the enterprise of Arab music education in which he played a leading role. It was most likely his early training in Western music that made him an appealing candidate for Amiran. Yet once selected, he was expected to act as an ambassador of "Arab music" and was thus channelled into this musical realm. Moreover, without the repressive measures which pushed him to renounce his affiliation with the Communist Party (the almost exclusive political platform for Palestinian national sentiment inside

Israel at the time), he would probably never have met Amiran and developed a career in music pedagogy.

Songbooks of the 1960s

Starting in the late 1950s, Radwan was responsible for the production of at least five songbooks that he edited together with Jewish music educators under Amiran's supervision. Of these, we discuss two that bookend the formative period of the 1960s and provide the best (however partial) glimpse into both the intentions of music educators and into the repertoire used in the classroom.

The 1961 songbook *Baqa al-Alhan: Anashid ʿArabi* ("A Garland of Melodies: Arab Hymns"), was a tri-lingual publication sponsored by the Central Office of Information (a propaganda branch of the Prime Minister's Office that targeted mostly immigrant and minority populations) and funded by the America-Israel Cultural Foundation. The editors credited with the booklet's compilation are Issachar Miron (famed author of the song *"Tzena tzena,"* popularized by the Weavers), Radwan, and the Armenian-Palestinian Michel Dermalkonian, Radwan's mentor and friend. Amiran's name is the first in a long list of editorial board members that includes most of the songwriters and composers who contributed to the collection.

Despite the fact that it is not the product of curricular planning, the booklet betrays a clear intention that music education for the Arab school be grounded in Arab music, specifically in the system of modes and practices known as *maqam*. While it was not used as a classroom textbook, it represents what the various contributors, and those teachers trained by them, taught in their respective classrooms (Radwan, interview, 2019; Abu-Shkara, interview, 2019). The thirty songs included are mainly new compositions, with melodies created or adapted by musicians such as Sudqi Shukri, Hikmat Shaheen, and Radwan himself. Eight songs draw on Palestinian folk melodies (such as the *dalʿuna*) and on well-known Arab melodies of the urban tradition (e.g. the tune of the famous *muwashah "Lamma Bada Yatathanna"*). The song lyrics were by various poets and teachers, among them Palestinian Arabs such as Jamal Qaʿwar and George Najib Khalil, and the Jewish Iraqi authors Salim Shʿashuaʿ and Zakai Aharon (under the pen name "Zaki Binyamin"). Most of these lyricists were associated with the League of Arabic Poets (*Rabitat al-Shuʿaraʾ al-ʿArabiyya*)—a literary association founded in 1955 by Michel Haddad and Shaʿshuʿ (Nassar 2017, 211n138)—and published their writings in the state-funded daily newspaper *al-Yawm,* as well as in Michel Haddad's monthly literary journal *Mujtamaʿ* (Nassar 2017, 70–73; Nashif 2017; Kabaha 2006).

In 1966, Radwan, Amiran, and Ovadia Tuvia (1920–2006), the latter a Jewish-Yemeni musician and educator who was the director of the National

Seminary for Music Teachers in Tel Aviv, set out to compile a series of songbooks for grades Three through Eight, modelled after the books for the Hebrew school. These were to comprise the core of the Arab schools' music curriculum, ensuring its wide implementation and creating a common body of songs for a new generation of students. The first edition was released in 1969 as *al-Anashid al-Madrasiyya* (*The School Songbook*), published by the Arab Department of the Histadrut, Israel's largest trade union and an important Zionist institution. Across its three volumes, the series encompassed well over one hundred songs (although several songs appear in more than one of the volumes), some new and others reprints of songs from earlier publications. Close to fifty songs were in Hebrew, seven of them by Amiran. Ten songs used tunes taken from international music literature, including Mozart and Beethoven (based on the model of songbooks for the Jewish sector). Referring to the editorial process, Radwan recalled that Amiran and Tuvia "did not understand and did not care about the lyrics, so that was my domain" (Radwan, interview, 2019). When it came to the music, however, Radwan mentioned that they would make him change the melodies he proposed for the Arabic songs if there was a hint of Western tonality in them—that is, if they did not sound "Arab" enough (ibid.).

Songs in *al-Anaashid al-Madrasiyya* can be divided thematically into three categories: (1) general didactic topics ("mother," "my school," "my book"); (2) nature and rural life (agriculture, the changing of seasons); and (3) holidays (see also Ben-Zeev 2006, 30–42). These topics generally overlap with those of the Hebrew songbooks, with a number of notable differences. First, the Hebrew books feature a hefty portion of Jewish religion-themed songs that contain biblical texts, or draw on Jewish tradition. In the Arabic songbooks, as in the Arab school's general curriculum, there was almost no religious material, due to the diverse religious background of pupils and teachers (Muslims, Christians, and Druze). As a result, the few holiday songs refer either to a general, ambiguous "holiday joy," or to the secular, national Independence Day (redubbed in Arabic "ʿid-ul-istiklal [sic]"—the "Holiday of Independence"). The only other holiday featured in the booklet is the Jewish *tu bishvat*, redressed in Arabic as "ʿid ash-shajar [sic]," meaning "Holiday of the Tree." A second difference has to do with the meaning of agricultural themes. Despite the agricultural ethos of Zionist settlement, the vast majority of the Jewish population lived in urban and suburban settlements. As such, the large portion of agricultural songs and songs about the land in the Hebrew songbooks were heteronomous to corresponding Zionist ideals. They evoked biblical images, or highlighted the cultivation of land as a historic return of the Jew to his homeland, and to the lifestyle of a sedentary autochthonous nation. For the largely rural Arab population, however, these same themes took on a different meaning, as we discuss below.

Al-Anashid al-Madrasiyya booklets were in circulation for many years, and in 1989 Radwan's successor, Munir Abu-Shkara, published an almost identical re-issue. Nevertheless, many music teachers expressed dissatisfaction with the booklets, or are said to have never used them. In two invaluable sets of interviews with Arab music educators conducted in the late 1990s (Shay 2001) and early 2000s (Ben-Zeev 2006), the most common points of criticism raised by teachers were that Palestinian folk music was not represented in its authentic form, that the melodies are artificial, and that the themes are detached from and irrelevant to the world of the Arab pupils.

"On my country's holiday": Independence Day celebrated in song

Throughout the 1950s and 1960s, but particularly during the early years, the Ministry of Education banned textbooks, re-wrote chapters, constantly monitored the curriculum in the Arab schools to make sure it contained no content that conveys Arab national sentiment (Shemesh 2009, 225), and generally steered clear of cultivating a civic national ethos of any kind. However, one context in which Palestinian Arabs were actively encouraged to recognize their Israeli citizenship was the annual celebration of Israel's Independence Day. In scenes bearing many similarities to the one depicted in Suleiman's film, educational authorities coerced Palestinian Arabs to celebrate the state in an environment saturated with Zionist symbols and laudatory texts.

Testimonies and contemporary reports of Independence Day celebrations in Arab schools reveal elements that were common countrywide. In preparation for the day, Arab municipalities and schools would ubiquitously hang Israeli flags and images of the state's Menorah emblem and even construct victory arches. Schools and local councils staged elaborate ceremonies, which included sports competitions, traditional Palestinian dancing, poetry contests, and speeches by Jewish and Arab officials (Degani 2018, 190). The school headmasters and teachers forced the children under their care to play a leading role in what Shira Robinson (2013) aptly defined as "spectacles of sovereignty." The symbolic vocabulary offered by the state, however, was hardly adequate for its non-Jewish citizens. During the years of the Military Government, schoolchildren (and occasionally also teachers) revolted by vandalizing some of those symbols, defiling photographs of Israeli presidents and Zionist leaders, and the blue and white flag. A strong point of contention was the state's national anthem, "*ha-Tikva*," with its expression of a "*nefesh yehudi homiya*" ("yearning Jewish soul"). For instance, the late educator and Israeli parliamentarian Walid Sadeq recalled that during his days as a pupil, his Egyptian-Jewish teacher tried to teach the anthem to the class. As soon as the pupils heard the melody, Sadeq writes, they "mutinied," some of them pulling small firecrackers from their pockets and throwing them on the floor to create a cacophony of explosions and laughter. The teacher then lost his temper, screamed, and threatened to bring in the military governor (Sadeq 2012, 55–56). Ahmed Yunes (b.1947), a music teacher from the village of 'Ara, had similar recollections:

> I had a beautiful singing voice. When I was in the Fifth grade, our music teacher from Nazareth ... selected me to be a soloist for songs in Arabic and Hebrew, including the national anthem, which he taught us to sing. We had [in our village] educated people, who said to the principal: "as Arabs we shouldn't have to sing the anthem." I didn't understand what an anthem was or what the lyrics meant ... They warned [the principal] against an uprising and trouble with the Military Government and the police, but still we had to sing it, in the presence of the military governor. (Yunes, interview, 2019)

The problem with Arabs singing "*ha-Tikva*" was not entirely lost on Jewish educators. Emanuel Amiran, Radwan recalled, strongly objected to this practice, and so Radwan relied on the former's authority when opposing Raif Zo'abi—a supervisor of Arab schools in the 1960s who strictly enforced grandiose Independence Day celebrations and the singing of the national anthem (Radwan, interview, 2019). It is clear, however, that such performative norms varied widely from school to school, with some schools singing the anthem well into the 1970s (Abu-Shkara, interview, 2019). In light of Amiran's objection to the idea that Arabs should sing "*ha-Tikva*," it is possible that one reason for the emergence of Independence Day songs written specifically to be used in Arab schools was to provide an Arabic alternative that would facilitate the display of loyalty while avoiding the absurdity of non-Jews singing about the yearning of the Jewish soul.

We find Independence Day songs in both the 1961 and 1969 songbooks. The 1961 booklet features two such songs. The first, plainly titled "'*Idul 'istiklal* [*sic*]" ("Independence Holiday"), is curiously labelled a "folk song." While it is possible that the melody alone was of folkloric origins, it is just as likely that the true author of this song was reluctant to claim it as their own. The other song is titled "'*Id istiqlal isra'il*" ("Israel's independence holiday") and is credited to the Acre-based musician Sudqi Shukri (1922–2018).[6] A prominent performer and teacher of Arab music in Mandate Palestine, Shukri, who attended the Cairo Conservatory in 1946, was one of just a few formally trained Palestinian Arab musicians to remain within the borders of Israel after the 1948 War (Radwan 1997). And it was his song—the one featured in Suleiman's film—that became enshrined in practice. The song, identified in everyday parlance by its first two lines, "*bi-'id istiqlal biladi / ghard al-tayr al-shadi*" (On my country's independence holiday / the songbird chirped), was by far the most widely performed, achieving notoriety as a symbol of the humiliation and coercion of Independence Day spectacles. The song's lyrics (see below) proclaim the joy of the holiday, but above all describe (in practice, prescribe) the way it should be celebrated: the hanging of flags and light decorations, the singing of songs, and the recitation of poems. The melody is notated in *maqam kurd*, yet in practice the song was probably performed in *maqam bayat*, which is ubiquitous in Palestinian folk music. This would accentuate the already folkloric character of the melody. As such, the melody lent itself to popular taste and implied a sense of locality, rather than mobilize fully the celebratory and military undertone of musical genres such as the march, often used in both Arab-nationalist and Zionist national songs.

Israel's Holiday of Independence	عيد استقلال إسرائيل
On my country's Holiday of Independence / The songbird chirped	بعيد استقلال بلادي / غرّد الطير الشادي
Happiness spread through the lands / Reaching the plain and the valley	عمّت الفرحة البلدان / حتى السهل والوادي
On my country's holiday	بعيد بلادي
Above the houses / In all places	فوق المساكن / بكل الأماكن
Ornaments are hanging / And everyone is happy	ارتفعت الزينات / وتمت الفرحات
On my country's holiday	في عيد بلادي
We fly the flags / we sing the chants	رفت الاعلام / صدحت الأنغام
The homes are decorated / With joy and light	ازدانت الدور / بالبهجة والنور
On my country's holiday	في عيد بلادي
The people sing / happily rejoicing	الشعب يغني / فرحان متهني
The song of their liking / On Israel's holiday	يحلا له الترتيل / بعيد إسرائيل
Long live my country	دمتِ يا بلادي

The impoverished state of music instruction in many schools, combined with the disproportionate role of Independence Day celebrations in school life, sometimes led to the complete conflation of these two activities. For example, Thabet Abu-Ras (b.1955) from Qalansawe, stated simply that in his recollections "music class was a class in Israeli patriotism." Like many others, Abu-Ras recalled singing "*'Id istiqlal isra'il*" at school, citing the first two lines from memory. He believed, however, that the song was written by his own teachers (Abu-Ras, interview, 2019). This "localization" of the song's provenance is another salient feature in the recollections of students from various places (e.g. al-Naqib, interview, 2019). By the end of the 1960s, the song had become so prevalent that on occasion even those who went to private church schools, where it was not performed, picked it up from their friends who attended public schools (Barbara, interview, 2019).

While the memories of pupils often highlight the coercive nature of singing this Independence Day song, the composer, Shukri, had publicly expressed a nuanced outlook on the cultural and political status of Palestinian Arabs in Israel. Like Radwan, he acknowledged the discrimination against Palestinian Arabs, and at the same time adopted the rhetoric of integration as a route for advancing the indigenous Arab citizens and their art. In a 1968 interview detailing his compositional and educational endeavours, printed in the Hebrew daily ʿAl ha-Mishmar, the interviewer noted that Shukri "wishes to make no claims against the establishment for not helping him along" (Dor 1968). After some persuasion, however, Shukri let on that "whatever he accomplished, he accomplished alone [i.e. with no help from the Jewish authorities]." He then goes on to protest that the radio will devote no more than five minutes of airtime to his orchestra. The reason, he explained, is that there is not a single "Israeli Arab" working in the Arab Department of Kol Yisrael: "they are all Iraqi Jews."

> They broadcast Lebanese and Egyptian Songs but no [Arab] Israeli songs, and when they do [play locally composed Arab songs] these are in the Iraqi style. Some ask me, "where is the Arab-Israeli melody?" What should I reply? Abroad they pay me 50 Israeli Lira per tune, and here I'll give it away for free. I'm not after the money, just the opportunity to propagate Arab-Israeli tunes. (ibid.)

These comments reveal a discursive strategy by which Shukri conforms to the rhetoric of "Arab Israeli" identity, while holding on to his indigenous privilege: it is *his* music (and, by extension, that of Palestinians at large) that deserves recognition as the representative Arab music of Israel, as opposed to the music of recently arrived Iraqi Jews, framed here as a foreign style.[7] This is a position that accepts the civic framework of Israeli citizenship while challenging the legitimacy of Jewish ethnocracy through cultural means.

Regardless of whether Shukri lent his musical talent to the creation of "ʿId istiqlal israʾil" in the spirit expressed in the above comment (to which we are privy only through the ideological filters of the Socialist-Zionist organ in which they were printed), or did so to protect and promote his standing with the authorities, he was surely neither the author nor the chief propagator of the ways in which it was put to use under duress. In any case, despite or perhaps *because* of its growing notoriety, "ʿId istiqlal israʾil" was omitted from the 1969 booklets. It was replaced, however, by two other Independence Day songs that were included in the booklet for the Seventh and Eighth grades. Interviewees who were familiar with the 1969 booklets from their school days could not recall ever singing these Independence Day songs. Coinciding with the gradual easing of restrictions and surveillance that followed the dismantling of the Military Government in 1966, it almost seems like the Independence Day songs we find in the 1969 booklet were included there—in lieu of Shukri's composition—so as *not* to be used, which was, in practice, their fate.

"Am I not allowed to love the olive tree?" on the Ambiguity of "Homeland" and the Afterlife of "ʿId istiqlal israʾil"

In the years following the abolition of the Military Government, and especially after the appointment of Yigal Alon as Minister of Education in 1970, the

Israeli establishment was compelled to reconsider the organization and goals of Arab education. A key administrative element in this process was the dismantling of the Division of Arab Education so as to integrate the administration of Arab schools into the same bodies within the Ministry of Education that managed Jewish schools (Al-Haj 1995, 66–67). While this process only began to take effect in 1978 and was not completed until 1987, the 1970s saw a series of committees entrusted with determining new goals for Arab education. The last of these was the Peled committee, headed by the former general, peace activist, and professor of Modern Arabic, Mati Peled (1923–1995).

In the course of deliberations, Palestinian members of the Peled committee suggested adding "love of the *shared* Homeland", rather than just "love of the Homeland," as an educational goal for the Arab school. At a meeting of the committee held in December 1974, Dr. Sami Mar'i mentioned, in support of this addition, that a "non-extremist" national song was disqualified (censored) because it declared love of the homeland. "One asks," Mar'i ventured, "am I not allowed to love the olive tree? the land? my village?" Another member of the committee, Rasmi Biadsi, suggested adding the words "shared by Arabs and Jews." In this way, he said, "when we speak in textbooks or songs about 'the homeland' it will be obvious that we are talking about the State of Israel, and we will have avoided the problem or question of 'which homeland we are talking about'" (State Archive file GL-11/1770).

These comments by Mar'i and Biadsi provide another backdrop for an evaluation of civic and national topics in school songbooks. Mar'i's account of banning songs or poems with the word "homeland" (*wattan*) is in line with several others, especially going back to the 1950s (Robinson 2013, 140). Yet the 1961 songbook 'Anashid 'arabi features a song called "Hadha wattani" ("This is my homeland"), set to music by Sudqi Shukri. It is an ode to the beauty of nature in Galilee and the Carmel mountain range, expressed from the mouths of anthropomorphized birds, flowers, and trees. In the culmination of this song, it is the birds who exclaim: "*hadha wattani!*" The license to write such a text was afforded, not surprisingly, to an Iraqi Jew: the poet Zakai Aharon (b. 1929).

More importantly, the emphasis that Mar'i places on the meaning of the relationship between the Palestinian Arabs and the natural landscape allows us to rethink the content of the 1961 and 1969 songbooks, rife with such amorous descriptions of the land. Arguments that this rural emphasis was an effect of Zionist pastoral romanticism and an attempt to deprive Palestinians of their modernity notwithstanding (Ben-Zeev 2006, 39–42), with the loss of the urban elites in 1948 (and while taking into account the fact that attending a private Christian school was an available option in cities such as Nazareth, Haifa, Acre, and Jaffa), the songbooks considered in this article were indeed catering to a largely rural population. While

Radwan distanced himself from *"'Id istiqlal isra'il,"* his comments on editorial goals in compiling the 1969 songbooks seem to echo Mar'i's words:

> As for me, I tried to include songs that talked about nature, the village, taking pride in the landscape, seasons, things like that .... I wanted the child to be able to express himself with reference to things that are close-at-hand: he sees a mountain, a tree, a pomegranate, olives ... he can go with his teacher and see it with his own eyes; to link the songs to his environment and his life is very important .... That is his *"wattan"*: his village, the Galilee .... (Radwan, Interview, 2019)

Despite the recognition that songbooks for the Arab classroom did include such ambivalent occasions for the expression of a Palestinian connection to land, in retrospect, none of the educational experiences facilitated by these landscape songs (to the extent that they were used at all) gave rise to a resilient narrative to rival the trauma of *"'Id istiqlal isra'il."* Independence Day scenes like the one recreated in Suleiman's film are ubiquitous in various testimonies, memoirs, and texts produced by Palestinian Arabs who were schooled in the 1950s, 60s and 70s. These texts often use the Independence Day celebration as a *lieu de memoire*, an experience that epitomizes the entire period of the Military Government, with *"'Id 'istiqlal 'isra'il"* as a recurring element. As poet and journalist Salman Masalha (b. 1953) noted: "Everyone my age remembers the lyrics and the tune to this day. Sometimes they even hum it at social gatherings, in a sort of sarcastic nostalgia" (Masalha 2017).

In a manner similar to other symbols cultivated through acts of commemoration (Sorek 2015), *"'Id istiqlal isra'il"* today represents a site of collective trauma that both encapsulates feelings of animosity toward the state *and* serves to cement a distinct sense of community among Palestinians in Israel, apart from those living in Gaza, the West Bank, or the diaspora. In a 2014 online article, Suliman Jubran, Professor Emeritus of Arabic at Tel Aviv University and former President of the Israeli Academy of Arabic, almost laments the fact that the "young generation doesn't know of this song." Jubran writes that "this naturally leaves them with a large cultural gap, and I shall now transfer to them what remains in my memory from the many times I have heard it and was disgusted by it ... " (Jubran 2014).

Conclusion

The story of music and its role in Arab public schooling during Israel's first decades is difficult to recount. It does not conform easily to previous narratives highlighting Palestinian music as a site of resistance (McDonald 2013), co-existence (Brinner 2009), or Orientalism (Beckles-Wilson 2013). In part, it is the story of the generation that experienced the *Nakba*, trying to rebuild their lives and make a living in a new repressive and restrictive political environment. It is the story of a handful of musicians—Radwan, Shukri, Shaheen, and others—who were leading an effort to sustain, modernize, and pass along a local sense of musicality in their communities, under conditions of extreme adversity. It is also the story of Jewish music educators such as Amiran and Tuvia, whose sustained investment in questions of East and West in music education was largely subsidiary to the cultural dimension of a Jewish national revival. Amiran's early writings demonstrated a "one-size-fits-all" approach wherein the synthetic Oriental-style compositions produced by Zionist composers like himself should be the blueprint for *all* Israeli students. Looking at the songbooks produced under his supervision, however, makes clear that in practice, rather than serve as a "bridge of understanding" (Amiran-Pogachov 1955), the teaching materials his department produced for the Arab classroom contributed to the solidifying of cultural borders between Jews and Arabs.

This article demonstrated how these Jewish and Palestinian educators negotiated the Arab music curriculum. While the former did so from a much more powerful position, the latter were not entirely devoid of agency and also benefited from the freehand afforded by the neglect of Israeli officials, who focused their efforts of censorship on other subjects, such history and literature. The Israeli education authorities used music to disseminate cultural identification with a general, cultural "Arabness" that was stripped, to the extent possible, of any explicit nationalist content. Combined with modernist ideals held by both Jewish and Palestinian music educators, this led to a school repertoire that was largely divorced from local traditions, which in turn became a recurrent point of criticism on the part of Palestinian students and teachers.

However, these conflicting demands inevitably fostered certain ambiguities: from musical elements resistant to the forced separation from the rest of the Arab world, to textual elements that cultivated a sense of propriety over the homeland's landscapes, entangled with a flattering outlook of the State. Regardless of the motivations and intentions of song authors, coercing educators and pupils into singing a song of praise for the state such as "ʿId istiqlal israʾil" had, unsurprisingly, the effect of searing into the collective memory of an entire generation feelings of humiliation and resentment. The song became a symbol of oppression in ways that at once hindered a sense of civic inclusion and, paradoxically, contributed to the solidifying of a distinct Arab-Israeli identity. The editors of the 1969 Songbook were not blind to this effect and expunged the song from the curriculum of the 1970s. From the late 1970s on, the Ministry of Education ceased to demand extravagant Independence Day celebrations. Nevertheless, as the internal debates of the Peled committee show, Palestinian educational leaders still hoped that the state would sponsor some sort of civic nationalism, perhaps one that recognized two nations living in Israel. The government's answer came in the subsequent mission statements on the goals of Arab education that include no recognition of (not to mention support for) any national expression in Israel other than the Jewish one.

Finally, the case of Arab music education in Israel produces some valuable theoretical insights. The extant literature on music and politics often recognizes the role of music in the making of modern nations, both in its pre-state stages (by fuelling the consciousness of a national uprising) or in the making of a nation-state (through the creation of a shared, embodied ethos for populations that have thus far been divergent in one or several ways: cultural, linguistic, religious, etc.). Our case study highlights another function of music, namely, as a vehicle for the subordinate integration of indigenous populations and a site of negotiation between the settler elites and indigenous educators. Importantly, the peculiarity of the Israeli case illuminates aspects that diverge from other settler-colonial models, where state education sought to "Kill the Indian to save the man." While this logic of political integration via oppressive acculturation was applied to incoming Jewish populations, and particularly to Arabic-speaking Jews, we have demonstrated how the indigenous Palestinian population was encouraged to cultivate its own repertoire of state rituals. As such, the study of music education reveals the dynamics through which in Israel— in the absence of distinct racial boundaries—indigenous populations were integrated into the settler state while also maintaining a structural cultural alterity, bolstering an ethnic division that acts as a self-evident justification for marginality.

As HaCohen (Pinczower) and Ezrahi (2017) recently argued, the conditions that enable music to facilitate the making and maintaining of a political community are the creation of a "shared semiotic reservoir" (202). Measured against this condition, it becomes evident that music education in Israeli Arab schools could only integrate Palestinian citizens as a group-apart, relating to the authority of the state using a separate musical semiotic reservoir. If we now revisit the two songs performed in Suleiman's cinematic reconstruction and evaluate them in the context of the curricular vision of their time (the late 1960s), it becomes apparent how they are performances of collective subordination rather than civic inclusion: for the children singing, the first (Hebrew) song was not fully theirs, while the second was not fully Israeli. This perspective thus exposes the need to theorize the political function of music beyond paradigms of consolidation/co-option and resistance, as a field of negotiation (however unequal the parties may be) that can yield ambivalent political collectivities, and express more complex political arrangements.

Notes

1. When referring to state institutions and policies pertaining to the Palestinians who became citizens of Israel, we retain the word "Arab," as it reflects both

the term used by Israeli bureaucracy, and the latter's outlook according to which this population should not develop an independent territorial nationality. When otherwise referring to this population, its member, or its culture, we use the terms "Palestinian" or "Palestinian Arab."

2. This segment draws from research conducted as part of Arnon Degani's PhD thesis submitted to the University of California at Los Angeles and supervised by David N. Myers and Gershon Shafir.

3. For a recent evaluation of Herder's ideas on music and nationalism, see Herder and Bohlman 2017.

4. *Maqam* is the elaborate system of modes and melodic practices which characterizes the traditional urban styles of the Arab world, as well as much of its modern popular music.

5. The topic of music education in Arab schools in Israel was previously addressed in an extensive and well-researched MA thesis in Hebrew by Noam Ben-Zeev (2006). Further information is found in a survey by Radwan (1997) and a more recent article by Essica Marks (2014)

6. While Shukri is indeed the composer of this tune, he is not the author of the lyrics. Through our conversations with Palestinians on this topic, we learned that the identity of the lyricist is an open secret: it is known to many, but no one wishes to discuss it, as it is considered a shameful legacy. We have concluded that it is not our place to make the identity of the lyricist public.

7. On the music of Arab Jews in Israel, see Perlson 2006.

Disclosure statement

No potential conflict of interest was reported by the author(s).

ORCID

Oded Erez ⓘ http://orcid.org/0000-0002-7137-4304

References

Al-Haj, Majid. 1995. *Education, Empowerment, and Control: The Case of the Arabs in Israel*. Albany: State University of New York Press.

Althusser, Louis, ed. 1971. "Ideology and Ideological State Apparatuses." In *Lenin and Philosophy and Other Essays*, 127–193. New York: Monthly Review Press.

Amiran-Pogachov, Emanuel. 1955. "Music Education." In *The Teachers Association Jubilee Book, 1902–1952*, edited by Dov Kimhi, 272–278. Tel Aviv: Histadrut ha-Morim. (Hebrew).

Bauml, Yair. 2007. *A Blue and White Shadow: The Israeli Establishment's Policy and Actions among Its Arab Citizens: the Formative Years: 1958–1968*. Haifa: Pardes. (Hebrew).

Beckles-Wilson, Rachel. 2013. *Orientalism and Musical Mission: Palestine and the West*. Cambridge: Cambridge University Press.

Ben-Zeev, Noam. 2006. "Music Instruction in Schools of the Arab-Palestinian Population in Israel." MA Thesis, Tel Aviv University (Hebrew).

Bishara, Azmi. 1999. "The Israeli Arab: Studies in a Split Political Discourse." In *Between "I" and "We": The Construction of Identities and Israeli Identity*, edited by Azmi Bishara, 169–191. Jerusalem: Van Leer Institute and ha-Kibbutz ha-Me'uhad. (Hebrew).

Brinner, Benjamin. 2009. *Playing Across a Divide: Israeli-Palestinian Musical Encounters*. Oxford: Oxford University Press.

Cohen, Judith. 2009. "Leo Kestenberg and the Vision of Music Education in Israel." *Min-Ad: Israel Studies in Musicology Online* 7 (1). https://www.biu.ac.il/hu/mu/min-ad/8-9/Kestenberg-JC.pdf (Hebrew).

Degani, Arnon. 2014. "The Decline and Fall of the Israeli Military Government, 1948–1966: A Case of Settler-Colonial Consolidation?" *Settler Colonial Studies* 5 (1): 84–99.

Degani, Arnon. 2018. "Both Arab and Israeli: The Subordinate Integration of the Palestinian Arabs into Israeli Society, 1948–1967." PhD diss., UCLA.

Dor, Dvora. 1968. "Is 'Ya Mustapha' an Arab or a French song?" *'Al ha-Mishmar*, May 24th, 1968 (Hebrew).

HaCohen (Pinczower), Ruth, and Yaron Ezrahi. 2017. *Composing Power, Singing Freedom: Overt and Covert Links Between Music and Politics in the West*. Jerusalem: Van Leer and ha-Kibbutz ha-Me'uhad. (Hebrew).

Hebert, David G., and Alexandra Kertz-Welzel, eds. 2012. *Patriotism and Nationalism in Music Education*. London: Ashgate.

Herder, Johan Gottfried, and Philip V. Bohlman. 2017. *Song Loves the Masses: Herder on Music and Nationalism*. Berkeley: University of California Press.

Hermann, Tamar, Or Anabi, William Cubbison, Ella Heller, and Fadi Omar. 2019. *A Conditional Partnership: Jews and Arabs, Israel 2019*. Jerusalem: Israel Democracy Institute.

Hirschberg, Jehoash. 1996. *Music in the Jewish Community of Palestine 1880–1948: A Social History*. Oxford: Oxford University Press.

Jubran, Suliman. 2014. "'bi-'Id Istiqlal Biladi!'" *al-Madar*, June 3, 2014. http://www.almadar.co.il/news-13,N-47285.html.

Kabaha, Mustafa. 2006. "Mizrahi Jews in the Arab Press in Israel, 1948–1967." *Iyunim* 16: 445–461. https://in.bgu.ac.il/bgi/iyunim/16/mustafa.pdf (Hebrew).

Kopelovitch, Emanuel. 1973. "Arab Education: Facts and Issues." In *Education in Israel*, edited by Haim Ormian, 323–334. Jerusalem: Ministry of Education (Hebrew).

Landy, Marcia. 1986. "Culture and Politics in the Work of Antonio Gramsci." *boundary 2* 14 (3): 49–70. The Legacy of Antonio Gramsci (Spring).

Levy, Gal. 2005. "From Subjects to Citizens: On Educational Reforms and the Demarcation of the 'Israeli-Arabs'." *Citizenship Studies* 9 (3): 271–291.

Marks, Essica. 2014. "Culture and Education: Musical and Cultural Aspects in the Teaching Methods of Two Arab Music Teachers in Israel." In *Music and Minorities from Around the World: Research, Documentation and Interdisciplinary Study*, edited by Ursula Hemetek, Essica Marks, and Adelaida Reyes, 25–46. Newcastle: Cambridge Scholars.

Masalha, Salman. 2017. "'Id Istiqlal Biladi." *Ha'aretz* Online, April 30, 2017. https://www.haaretz.co.il/opinions/.premium-1.4060876.

Massad, Joseph. 2003. "Liberating Songs: Palestine put to Music." *Journal of Palestine Studies* 32 (3): 21–38.

McDonald, David A. 2013. *My Voice Is My Weapon: Music, Nationalism, and the Poetics of Palestinian Resistance*. Durham, NC: Duke University Press.

Nashif, Isma'il. 2017. *'Arabic': The Story of Colonial Masque*. Jerusalem: Van Leer and ha-Kibbutz ha-Me'uhad. (Hebrew).

Nassar, Maha. 2017. *Brothers Apart: Palestinian Citizens of Israel and the Arab World*. Stanford, CA: Stanford University Press.

Ochoa-Gautier, Ana María. 2006. "Sonic Transculturation, Epistemologies of Purification and the Aural Public Sphere in Latin America." *Social Identities* 12 (6): 803–825.

Perlson, Inbal. 2006. *Great Joy Tonight: Judeo-Arab Musicians and Mizrahi Identity in Israel*. Tel Aviv: Resling. (Hebrew).

Radwan, Suheil. 1965. "An Arab Department at the Rubin Conservatory in Haifa." *Music Education [ha-Hinukh ha-Muzikali]* 8: 34. (Hebrew).

Radwan, Suheil. 1997. "The Performance of Arab Music in Israel." In *The Performance of Jewish and Arab Music in Israel Today: A Special Issue of the Journal Musical Performance*, edited by Amnon Shiloah, 35–50. Amsterdam: Harwood Academic Publishers.

Robinson, Shira. 2013. *Citizen Strangers: Palestinians and the Birth of Israel's Liberal Settler State*. Stanford, CA: Stanford University Press.

Sadeq, Walid. 2012. *Exile in His Own Land: From Taibeh to the Knesset*. Petah Tikva: Sifrut Akhshav. (Hebrew).

Schmidt, Patrick K., and Richard Colwell, eds. 2017. *Policy and the Political Life of Music Education*. New York: Oxford University Press.

Shay, Tsiona. 2001. "The Goals of Music Education in the Arab Sector According to the Views of Arab Musicians." MA Thesis, Bar-Ilan University (Hebrew).

Shemesh, Hanna. 2009. "Shaping the Past in History Textbooks in Arab Schools in Israel (1948–2008)." PhD diss., Hebrew University of Jerusalem (Hebrew).

Shenhav, Yehuda. 2006. *The Arab Jews: A Postcolonial Reading of Nationalism, Religion, and Ethnicity*. Stanford, CA: Stanford University Press.

Shohat, Ella. 1999. "The Invention of the Mizrahim." *Journal of Palestine Studies* 29 (1): 5–20.

Smooha, S. 1999. "The Advances and Limits of the Israelization of Israel's Palestinian Citizens." In *Israeli and Palestinian Identities in History and Literature*, edited by Kamal Abdel-Malek, and David C. Jacobson, 9–33. New York: St. Martin's Press.

Sorek, Tamir. 2015. *Palestinian Commemoration in Israel: Calendars, Monuments, and Martyrs*. Stanford, CA: Stanford University Press.

Stokes, Martin. 1994. "Introduction: Ethnicity, Identity and Music." In *Ethnicity, Identity, and Music: The Musical Construction of Place*, edited by Martin Stokes, 1–28. Oxford: Berg Publishers.

Taruskin, Richard. 2001. "Nationalism." *Grove Music Online*. https://doi.org/10.1093/gmo/9781561592630.article.50846.

Tauber, Sarit. 2017. "Fifty Years of Teacher Training in Israel: The Seminary for Music Teachers, Tel Aviv (1945–1996)." PhD diss., Tel Aviv University (Hebrew).

Troutman, John W. 2009. *Indian Blues: American Indians and the Politics of Music, 1879–1934*. Norman: University of Oklahoma Press.

Tsameret, Tsvi. 2003. The Development of the Education System (Israel during the first decade), Unit 7. Ramat Aviv: Open University (Hebrew).

Veracini, Lorenzo. 2010. *Settler Colonialism: A Theoretical Overview*. New York: Palgrave Macmillan.

Wolfe, Patrick. 1999. *Settler Colonialism and the Transformation of Anthropology: The Politics and Poetics of an Ethnographic Event*. London and New York: Cassell.

Wolfe, Patrick. 2012. "Purchase by Other Means: The Palestine Nakba and Zionism's Conquest of Economics." *Settler Colonial Studies* 2 (1): 133–171.

Zureik, Elia. 1979. *The Palestinians in Israel: A Study in Internal Colonialism*. London: Routledge.

Interviews

Abu-Ras, Thabet. December 18, 2019
Abu-Shkara, Nabila. December 9, 2019
Al-Naqib, Maha. February 13, 2019
Barbara, Adel. December 19, 2019
Radwan, Suheil. February 4, 2019; September 23, 2019
Yunes, Ahmed. December 9, 2019

State Archive Files

GL-11/1770
GL-145/1292

Self-categorization, intersectionality and creative freedom in the cultural industries: Palestinian women filmmakers in Israel

Amal Jamal ⓘ and Noa Lavie

ABSTRACT

The cultural industries are major fields of producing, distributing and reflecting national icons and norms. They form major sites of contestation and conflictual self-categorization, especially in conflict zones. Our article explores the intersection between nationality and gender in cultural production in such contexts. It examines the engagement of Palestinian women filmmakers within the Israeli cultural industry, seeking to facilitate a better understanding of national minorities in the field of cultural production in conflict zones. Palestinian women filmmakers in Israel have introduced new themes that do not only address national issues that stand in tension between the Palestinian experience of oppression and the hegemony of the Zionist narrative in the Israeli cultural industries, but also challenge the prevalent patriarchal social values in Palestinian society. Exploring their experience allow us to better explicate the intersection of professional, gender and national factors in conditioning the cultural production of creative labour in conflict zones.

Introduction

Palestinian cultural production in Israel has been undergoing tremendous transformations in recent years. These transformations are expressed in the quantity and quality of cultural products, especially in the field of music (Broeske-Danielsen 2013), cinema (Dabashi 2006) and theatre (Al-Saber 2018). Given that this production takes place under the shadow of the Israeli-Palestinian conflict, the experiences of Palestinian cultural creators in Israel presents an interesting avenue of study which could expand Bourdieu's political treatment of cultural production (Bourdieu 1993). In more concrete terms, examining Palestinian cultural production in Israel, especially women filmmaking, enables us to examine the relevance of Bourdieu's theory in an active colonial context, where the collective narratives of the colonizers and the colonized are prevalently perceived as antagonistic. Furthermore, such a venture allows us to explore how the lack of political legitimacy resulting from the national conflict between Israelis and Palestinians determine not only the freedom spaces allowed to the latter to produce art, but also influences its type and value. It also allows us to explore the impact of the location of creative agents on cultural production and thereby contribute to the literature on cultural industries in colonial contexts.

Notwithstanding the rising attention given to ethnic, racial and gender minority creative workers in the cultural industries (Lee 2017; Alacovska and Gill 2019; Saha 2018), little attention has been devoted to women filmmakers in conflict zones. Given that conflicts, especially ethnic and national conflicts, have material and symbolic dimensions, cultural production could become a battlefield on which images, representations, identities and justifications are contested and promoted (Swartz 2013). Therefore, exploring these complexities from the standpoint of Palestinian women filmmakers could enhance our understanding of the intersection between national, commercial and gender factors in determining the creative freedom they have in the cultural industries in colonial contexts. Such a venture could also assist in identifying the challenges women filmmakers from ethnic minorities face as a result of being located between their professional aspirations, funding conditions and national affiliation, and the ramifications of this location on the topics they decide to tackle.

Choosing to explore the experiences of Palestinian women filmmakers in television and cinema in Israel is based not only on the fact that their number has been rising, but also since women filmmakers allow us to better observe and explicate the intersection of professional, gender and national factors in conditioning the cultural production of creative labour in conflict zones. Palestinian women filmmakers in Israel have not only addressed national issues that tackle the tension between the Palestinian experience of oppression and the hegemony of the Zionist narrative in Israeli cultural industries (Nathanson, Gazala, and Pisam 2016), but also have challenged the prevalent patriarchal social values in Palestinian society (Abu-Rabia-Queder and Weiner-Levy 2013). Furthermore, since television and cinematic production are major fields of producing, distributing and reflecting social icons and norms (Olesen 2018) and therefore, are major sites of contestation and conflictual self-categorization, the examination of the experience of Palestinian women filmmakers in Israel enables us to pinpoint the challenges they face as being dependent on Israeli funding, on the one hand, and addressing the Israeli-Palestinian conflict from a Palestinian viewpoint, on the other. Exploring the experience of Palestinian women filmmakers vis-à-vis funding necessities and working in a patriarchal industry and society could explicate the centrality of the "female gaze" (Taylor 2014) in their works. It could also demonstrate their double bind, as manifested in the unresolvable expectations they face as women filmmakers on the one hand and as Palestinians acting in the Israeli context on the other (Jenkins 2014; Conor, Gill, and Taylor 2015). Tackling the unique gendered patterns of disadvantage, discrimination and exploitation they experience could deepen our understanding of the complexities of cultural production in conflict zones through a gender based angle.

This study relies on interviews conducted with Palestinian women TV and film creators involved in the Israeli cultural industry. The article is divided into five main parts. First, we review the available literature on minority creative workers in conflict settings, focusing on the intersection of national and gender factors. Second, we provide an overview of the creative industries in Israel. The third part presents the methodology adopted to explore this complex topic. Only then do we present our analysis of the interviews and we conclude with a short discussion of the data and provide a few general insights of broad theoretical importance.

Minorities and gender in cultural production in national conflict zones

The study of cultural production has aroused interest not only as a primary means of producing symbolic goods and texts in capitalist societies (Bourdieu 1993; Hesmondhalgh 2007), but also as a major field of identity formation and construction of collective consciousness in nation states (Lee 2017; Castello 2015; Schlesinger 1991). The media and its poetics have been conceived not only as crucial in the process of nation building and the construction of national consciousness (Schlesinger 1991; Cormack 1993; Watson 2002), but also as a central mechanism in promoting cultural hegemony through the production of meaning and building consent for existing social relations (Coban 2018; Jamal 2009). Tamar Ashuri, focusing on television productions, states that "television programmes are crucial in the formation, maintenance and reflection of national identity" (Ashuri 2005, 423). Castello (2015) also argues that "television dramas are ideological and cultural products that project a point of view about our society and our nation through their narrative ideology" (51).

Bourdieu (1993) has demonstrated that cultural production is distinguished from other fields of production by the unique interpenetration of material and symbolic dimensions, translated into not only the production of material objects, but also producing their value and thereby the recognition of artistic legitimacy. This argument of Bourdieu, which is made in the context of a free market of ideas, where artists struggle either to gain recognition for their product as "real art" or to make a profit, could take a different course in conflictual colonial contexts. In such contexts, not only that the structure of power determines the legitimacy of the narratives manifested in cultural production, but also that the ability of colonized artists to produce and the cultural value of their art are determined by political legitimacy granted by the colonizer. As a result, "different social groups enjoy not only different levels of access to different forms of artistic and cultural engagement, but also different access to the power to bestow value and legitimize aesthetic and cultural practices" (Belfiore 2018, 2). These differences make the self-categorization (Turner and Reynolds 2012) of colonized artists more challenging, for being located in the struggle between their national identity, their gendered social identity and the identity of the ethno-national state in which they create.

Since cultural production, especially filmmaking, is deeply related to economic considerations (Lee 2017), any effort to better understand the behaviour and experiences of filmmakers must pay attention to the economic dimensions of their work. The precariousness of cultural production is manifested in institutional, contractual and wage relationships that imply risk, insecurity and even exclusion (Lee 2017; McGuigan 2010). This reality is even harsher for racial and ethnic minority groups and especially harsh for women creative workers from these minority groups, affecting them emotionally, psychologically and economically (Belfiore 2018; Banks 2017). As Conor, Gill, and Taylor (2015) demonstrate, gendered patterns of disadvantage and exclusion in the creative industries are complicated by divisions of class, race and ethnicity. The intersectionality of disadvantage and exclusion becomes even more complex in conflict zones, in which there is a deep affinity between creative labour, personal autonomy, national identity and gender (Hesmondhalgh and Baker 2015; Bielby 2009). In such contexts, the ethnic, national or gender identity of creative workers shape the extent to which they feel autonomous (Hesmondhalgh and Baker 2015; Hillman, Cannella, and Harris 2002). Although some minority creative workers, including women, manage to integrate and succeed in carving out fertile spaces in the fields of cultural production (Saha 2016, 2017; Mayer 2017), their unique position in such a harsh reality invites greater attention than given in the literature.

As Gill (2002) has demonstrated, despite the fact that the creative industries seem to look "cool, creative and egalitarian", they facilitate "new forms of gender inequality" (Gill 2002, 71; cited in Lee 2017, 9) that are deeply related to identity. The glass ceiling that women and minorities encounter in the field, forcing them to be more qualified in order to be able to compete (Òbrien 2014; Hillman, Cannella, and Harris 2002), seems to be thicker and lower for women from minority backgrounds. The harsh reality that women face explains why they opt out of media work (Òbrien 2014). Their working conditions are deeply related to the societal culture in which they act. These are more complicated and challenging in traditional societies, as the cases of women in the cultural industries of Iran and Turkey demonstrate (Şerban and Grigoriu 2014; Uğur Tanrıöver 2016).

The working conditions of Palestinian filmmakers are determined by the intersection between the political, cultural and economic conditions set by their Israeli environment, which are partially enabling, but are also deeply discriminatory against them as Arab-Palestinians on the one hand, and being women in a predominantly traditional society in which patriarchal customs and norms remain deeply persistent on the other (Abu-Rabia-Queder and Weiner-Levy 2013). Furthermore, Palestinian women filmmakers are discriminated against in their society and by the state in which they are citizens. In such a reality, filmmaking, which is inherently related to meaning making and identity becomes a very challenging task, especially for women, who have to struggle not only against Israeli discriminatory policies, but also against their traditional roles in their own patriarchal society.

Tackling the intersection between these two interrelated forces becomes a unique challenge, especially since addressing national issues may lead to less financial support from the state and addressing gender issues in their own society invites harsh critique and accusations of betrayal. This means that the intersection between professional, national, and gender factors magnify the labour constraints they face beyond the aggregate of either of them alone. This unique location between gender hierarchies, national conflict and the precariousness of the market invites unique attention that may help us facilitate a deeper understanding of the challenges and dilemmas facing women filmmakers in conflict zones. Such an attention in a colonial context enables us to go beyond Bourdieu's insights not only regarding the relationship between the material and symbolic dimensions of art, but also regarding the interaction between political legitimacy and art making in colonial contexts.

Israeli cultural industries, funding policies and national narratives

The creative industries in Israel have been developing rapidly in the last few decades (Nathanson, Gazala, and Pisam 2016). As in many other nation states, there is a deep link between commitment to national narratives and the production of symbolic goods (Feder and Katz-Gerro 2012, 2015; Katz and Sella 1999, 363). This is of special importance since Israel is a nation state in conflict, partially with a large community of its own indigenous citizens (Jamal 2011). One of the avenues that reveals the convergence of financial and cultural factors in cultural production is state funding policies. Feder and Katz-Gerro (2012) present three main characteristics of the funding policies of the Israeli government in the field of culture. First, the great majority of funding goes to art created by Jewish artists and toward the preservation of the heritage associated with Jewish culture and history, and in "cultural domains" such as "literature [and] theater", "there is preference for the funding of works in the Hebrew language" (2012, 363). Second, "most types of art that are supported by the government are of Western origin or influenced by European and North American artistic traditions" (2012, 363). Third, financial support to the arts is mostly provided directly to individual artists or arts organizations (2012, 363). Although some funding is indirectly allotted through semi-independent organizations, the main policies indicated above haven't considerably changed. As a result, the Ministry of Culture "reproduces the existing social-cultural order and contributes to the maintenance of the ethnic and national hierarchies that characterize Israeli society" (Keshet et al. 2011, 3; cited in Feder and Katz-Gerro 2015, 78–79). It also "restricts the freedom of artists" and promotes art "desired by the state" (Feder 2018, 17). Therefore, art which does not achieve the desired effect will not be supported, but rather, defunded or even censored (Ibid: 17; Schejter 2009).

Notwithstanding these firm conclusions, funding policies have always been complicated and have been strongly politicized in the last several years (Ronen 2018). The provocative moves made by former Minister of Culture Miri Regev have revealed the growing efforts to establish a conditional relationship between funding and cultural production. Regev's treatment of major cinema foundations, through which most of state funding is channeled[1] and her efforts to bring major theatres to change their policies of not holding productions in the Jewish settlements in the occupied Palestinian territories[2] mirror the changes taking place in the relationship between the state and cultural institutions. Although this relationship is not one-dimensional, and different ministers have introduced slightly different policies, the aggressive interventions made by Regev revealed the sensitivities of the relationship between politics and creative work, especially when it comes to the Israeli-Palestinian conflict and to ethnic relations in Israeli society. It also revealed that, given the dependency of major creative fields, such as cinema, television and theatre, on state funding, the contents produced are not only dependent on rational market-oriented calculations of audience making, but also on their reception by the state and the extent to which they serve its image and socio-cultural policies.

These complications and sensitivities of funding are even more apparent when funding Arab cultural production in Israel. The ministry has traditionally singled out all productions viewed as radically politicized, namely, those critical of the state of Israel and its policies towards its Arab citizens and the Palestinian people.[3] Most funding, whether directly extended by the Ministry of Culture, via semi-independent foundations, such as in the field of cinema, or through television channels, has encouraged works that tackle local social issues (Ronen 2018). Although some political works have been funded, they have mostly addressed the complicated relationship between Arabs and Jews inside Israel. Daring films, such as "Beyond the Walls"[4] and creative series such as "Arab Labor"[5] provide good examples of the delicate balance maintained between critiquing the oppressive hand of the Jewish majority and the existential need of the minority to accept its role as a submissive minority that seeks sophisticated ways to meet the expectations of the hegemonic majority and thereby survive the tense relationship resulting from the Israeli-Palestinian conflict.

There is tangible evidence that the allocation of financial resources for Palestinian-Israeli artistic institutions has slightly increased in the last few years.[6] Notwithstanding, the rise is very small and increasingly differentiates between "acceptable" and "unacceptable" art. In recent years, new regulations have been introduced that deepen the conditional relationship between funding and the cultural contents produced by Palestinian-Israeli artists[7] and have had a chilling effect on all cultural fields, including cinema, art, music and television. Although these new policy outlines have slightly changed as a result of the change in the identity of the minister of culture, they have longstanding effects that deserve special attention. One way to do that is through the experience of Palestinian women filmmakers in Israel and the extent to which they conceive of them as disciplinary measures which narrow their spaces of creative freedom and establish conditional dependency.

Methodology

This research is based on in-depth interviews with seven Palestinian women TV and film directors in Israel, who agreed to be named in the study. Obtaining the interviews was very challenging for many reasons. First, the number of Palestinian women filmmakers in Israel is 16, some of whom have either produced one film only or have opted out of the field. Second, some showed inherent suspicion towards being interviewed about the funding complexities in a reality in which the spaces of critique are constantly shrinking (Jamal 2020). However, given that all seven interviewees are major and active cultural creators in the audio-visual fields in Israel, they provide us with a broad picture of the interplay between national identity, social structure and state funding in the cultural industries in conflict zones.

Most of the women were interviewed in public cafes. One chose to be interviewed in her working environment and another was interviewed in the office of the first author. Each interview lasted for around two hours. The interviewees were asked about the structural conditions in which they operate, especially their relationships with, first, state funding policies and second, social norms in their own society, and their creative freedom. Most interviews were conducted in Arabic, the native language of both the first author and the interviewees. One of the interviews was conducted in Hebrew by the second author. All interviews were recorded, transcribed, translated into English and then thematically analyzed. The interpretative analysis of the interviews was conducted on three levels. First, we looked at the individual story, ascertaining the central themes that emerged (Braun and Clarke 2006; Boyatzis 1998). Second, we connected the themes to the different spheres of life that were mentioned in the interviews: occupation, working conditions, financial support, social context and national identity. Finally, we analyzed the impact of these multiple contexts on their work. In our thematic analysis, we followed the steps proposed by Braun and Clarke (2006), namely, we familiarized ourselves with the data, generated initial codes, searched for themes, reviewed them and then defined and named them. We avoided fitting our coding of the data into a preexisting coding frame or into any analytic preconceptions that we came with in advance (Chamaz and Belgrave 2018). In the last stage we interpreted the data and formulated the main insights that emerged. In the following we present the three main interrelated themes that emerged from the interviews.

Data analysis: overcoming economic and cultural factors

Funding and the challenges of self-categorization

Film director Suha Arraf introduced us to the harsh circumstances that minority women filmmakers face when their national group is in direct conflict with the state in which they are citizens. She illustrated this point when speaking about the scandal around the funding of her film "Villa Touma".[8] Facing major difficulties to independently raise money for her film, she ended up largely relying on state funds. After the film was completed, she participated in a film festival in Venice and there the film was defined as Palestinian. She explained that she had done so as she herself was Palestinian and that the film addressed an upper-class Palestinian family. That decision led to a major crisis with the Israeli Ministry of Culture.

Arraf's venture raised a very interesting question of self-categorization. She, as an Israeli citizen entitled to taxpayers' rights, justified her decision to fund her film from state sources. When asked about private funds, she explained that "there are no available funds for such ventures in my society". When asked about sources from other countries, she explained that

it is almost impossible to raise funds in Europe, for Europeans want us to focus on their common stereotypes about Palestinian women ... They expect us to deal with the relationship between Arabs and Jews, or deal with the separation wall, the conflict between Fatah and Hamas, or draw attention to the backwardness and folklore in our own society. One of the examples is women being killed for what is called 'family honor'.

Arraf, it seems, refuses to be pushed into the corner of a stereotypical female film maker who produces films for an orientalist-chauvinist gaze.

Arraf's decision to define the film as Palestinian led the Ministry of Culture to demand that she return the funds.[9] The scandal, she admits, led to "the Israeli Cinema Funds ... [being] asked to add new clause to the contracts with directors" in order to be sure that this type of incident would not recur. According to her, the new clause demand that "if you want to take money from Israeli funds, you must submit your film as an Israeli film, period."[10] She criticizes this step, reflecting the dilemmas that Palestinian creative workers face in Israel. She says it "identifies you as Israeli" and thereby enables the "Israeli cultural industry to use you ... to show Israeli democracy". In her view, "[i]f you make different films and show dissimilar perspectives, you end up being outside".

Maysaloun Hammoud was not hesitant about defining her film "In Between"[11] as "a Palestinian-Israeli film, reflecting a Palestinian reality". She claimed against Palestinian critics, "I am not ashamed of taking Israeli funding. I prefer to be realistic and make something influential out of it", denying the argument that it damages the essence of the film. Hammoud argued that most Palestinian filmmakers in Israel must rely on state funds at the beginning of their careers. She argues that, being taxpayers entitles Palestinian citizens to state funds.

Aware of the critique voiced by some in Palestinian society regarding dependence on Israeli funds which, in the view of critics, influences the narrative she promotes and the issues she tackles, Hammoud argues:

> Many condemn us for taking Israeli money but don't offer a realistic alternative ... I prefer Arab funding which makes things easier and helps me get rid of the conflict and of questioning the film's nationality. Moreover, it opens possibilities like screening it in Dubai for instance.

Hammoud's dilemma concerning the relationship between funding and self-categorization is echoed in the name of her film, "In Between". She argues that she manages to disconnect between the source of funding and her ability to subvert and criticize. By asserting "I want to take money and spit in the face of colonialism", Hammoud shows self-certainty that she can bypass state surveillance and carve her autonomous space that allows her to translate her creativity into her work. This standpoint, taken by many artists in the cultural industries, reflects Hammoud's effort to categorize herself first and foremost as an artist, who is able to establish a balance between the opposing forces that exert great pressure on her.

This position is challenged by Aida Kaadan, who directed the film "Farawla".[12] Kaadan states that she has avoided official state funding since "money equals influence". She wonders, "How could I challenge them if I take money from them. I am not interested in letting them have any impact on my creative work". When asked about filmmakers who receive funds from the ministry, she clarifies, "It is not possible to demolish the house of the master with his own tools ... If you get involved in receiving Israeli funds, you can hardly get away from it ... It is something bad". In her view, taking state money means letting the state "intervene in the creative process", since a "film's identity is not determined solely by the identity of the director". Kaadan acknowledges that distancing herself from the Israeli cultural industry and its funds means having to reconcile herself to producing modest films or leaving the country and working abroad. The dichotomous options posed by Kaadan mirror the challenges and dilemmas that many Palestinian filmmakers face in Israel and therefore we find that several of them have chosen what Albert Hirschman (1970) coined as the "exit" strategy and have left to work either in Europe or the US.[13] Most of those who have chosen the exit rather than the voice strategy are men for, as Ibtisam Mara'ana, a veteran filmmaker maintained, "culturally and socially it is much more difficult for women and they have less courage to leave their families and work abroad".

Mara'ana, a veteran filmmaker, confirms the relationship between funds and content. But unlike Kaadan, she tries to balance between wanting to maintain creative autonomy while being dependent on state funding, and simultaneously expressing some frustration about lacking alternatives. Her dilemma echoes what Hammoud has admitted. She is very cautious, when reflecting on her position. She shows much self-consciousness by lowering the expectations from Palestinian filmmakers and admits that

> this is the field of Israeli cultural production. Give me an alternative and I shall work differently ... They [the Israelis] are much more sophisticated than us [the Palestinians] ... As long as this is the case, we have to work from within the rules of the field.

However, Mara'ana argues that the Israeli cultural industry "gives us space". But she admits that "they make us speak the way they want us to". Aware of the lack of alternative funding, she avoids a dichotomous perception of the relationship between being an artist and a Palestinian operating in the Israeli context. Her self-categorization, like other creators interviewed, is more professional than national. She and Hamoud might also be exhibiting a strategy used by many women in the TV and film industry – that is, the willingness to work under different conditions than men, because it is more difficult for women to enter this industry (Lavie and Jamal 2019).

Mira Awad, a well-known singer, actor and TV creator tackles the issue of funding with caution and establishes a clear distance between her own experience and the broader picture. When asked about her own place in this situation, she stated, "If I want to succeed in my country ... if I want to reach the national level and be in theater, on TV, I have to leave my society and work in Israeli society". She admits that doing so, "I am being exploited by the Israeli authorities, as a fig leaf". The price for her is to be rejected by her own society as "'Judaized', 'Israelized', 'a collaborator'". She complains that "when we make art, we also make politics". Being aware of the hardships endured by Palestinian cultural creators in Israel, Awad remains reluctant to engage in dichotomous self-categorization. Like Hammoud and Mara'ana, she seeks to cautiously navigate her way in a highly complicated field of cultural production.

A similar line of thought is presented by Rana Abu Fraihah, a much younger Palestinian filmmaker who has directed a film about her family "In Her Footsteps".[14] She says, "When what we create depends on the government, there is censorship ... the most dangerous sort, self-censorship ... Fear exists". Abu Fraihah argues that when she deals with issues of minorities or occupation, internal censorship starts working. In her view, "there is always a price ... and silencing".

It is very interesting to note that in talking about working and being funded by the state of Israel, the female creators interviewed for this study seemed to put their national identity – as Palestinians – before their gender identity – as females. This may be because, when facing the state of Israel directly, they are more inclined to connect to the national part of their identity than with their gender.

Filmmaking, national narratives and White-Washing

As demonstrated, the difficulties that Palestinian women filmmakers increasingly face when applying for state funds are clearly related to the national contents that their films seek to tackle. Scripts that normalize the Palestinian narrative or those dealing with the Israeli occupation of the Palestinian territories are viewed as illegitimate by the Ministry of Culture. Mara'ana affirms that the policies of ministry funding, especially during Culture Minister Miri Regev's term, are based on loyalty. Mara'ana clarifies that state intervention in funding creative work in Israel is not new. As an example, she speaks of her experience with her first film, *Paradise Lost*. The script slightly related to her father's job, digging collective graves in Tantura village where the Israeli army conducted a massacre in 1948. She shares that the head of the Rabinovich Foundation, supporting the films at the time, said that mentioning collective graves "cannot pass". According to him, the Palestinian narrative of the massacre is doubtful, and the entire story had to be cast in doubt. Therefore, she shares, "the entire voiceover of the film had to be changed". Mara'ana clarifies that "this is the Israeli cinema" and that Israeli cinema foundations "100 percent" have an impact on the contents of films whose production they support.

Kaadan is more straightforward about the relationship between funding and the propagating of the Zionist narrative. She argues that Israeli cinema foundations are engaged in "whitewashing" the state. "The master", she argues, "uses his tools vis-à-vis the slave in order to whitewash his image before the world". In her view there is a direct contradiction between wanting to produce films with Palestinian content and state funding. She indicates the hegemony of the Israeli narrative about the region and adds that Palestinian filmmakers relying on state funds "have to speak in Israeli terms, since Israelis give them a stage". She provides the example of the Israeli series Fauda to argue that "it is impossible to separate the Israeli cultural production from the colonial mind. The Israelis have their own views and they will not give them up".[15]

This direct position concerning the relationship between funding and the dispute over national narratives is also expressed by Rana Abu Fraihah, who shares that during the production of her film "a lot of pressure was exerted by the public relations people of the New Israel Fund … not to engage with the 1948 war". She admits that these people, members of a liberal and private foundation that receives no money from the state and is heavily criticized by the nationalist government of Benjamin Netanyahu,[16] wanted her to avoid saying that Palestinians "were deported or escaped". They "wanted me not to mention the entire issue", thereby censoring topics that may cause unease in the Israeli public sphere. In her view "there was an issue with every sentence that subverted the common knowledge". She clarifies that although the New Israel Fund is a liberal foundation, when addressing issues related to the conflict and presenting the Palestinian narrative, "they behave exactly like Miri Regev".

Mara'ana's realism about the price that Palestinian filmmakers must pay is translated into frustration and dissatisfaction in Kaadan's and Abu Fraihah's words. They mirror the impossible position of most Palestinian filmmakers in Israel. Being aware of the way the Israeli hegemony rules over their narratives, Palestinian women filmmakers are on the losing side, no matter what option they choose. On the one hand, giving up state funds may mean risking not being able to remain in the field, and as Palestinian-women they are doubly marginalized in the TV and film industry, which probably makes relying on state funds even more important On the other hand, relying on state funds means risking the loss of their creative autonomy and submitting to state demands of self-censorship. Their aspiration to translate their national identity and narrative into their films must be censored, something that not only violates their creative autonomy, but also feeds the whitewashing efforts of the Israeli government in their eyes. This puts them in a very conflicted position.

Between creativity and the patriarchal social structure

Palestinian women TV and cinema creators not only have to deal with dilemmas of funding and their implications on their art, but also with challenges that arise from being women who belong to a largely traditional society. Although Palestinian society is not monolithic and is structurally, religiously and culturally pluralistic, its social structure is mostly traditional, organized around family affiliation and patriarchalism, in which men remain dominant, as manifested in public institutions and the public sphere (Abu-Rabia-Queder and Weiner-Levy 2013; Sa'ar 2016). Despite tremendous changes taking place in Arab towns in Israel, especially when relating to women's education and integration into the job market, dominant customs and norms remain traditional (Ibid.). Their critique by the new generation of men and women must face the growing influence of the Islamic Movement, which seeks to facilitate religious values and oppose liberalization related to the traditional social structure (Ghanem and Mustafa 2018).

The dominant role of traditional social forces, manifested in all Arab towns, sets a challenge for women in general and those working in the cultural industries, women filmmakers, in particular. Unlike men, women must not only face the discriminatory policies of the Israeli state and cultural industries, but also the sensitivities of addressing the oppression of women in their own society. Gender mainstreaming of creative work and the highlighting of social pathologies related to the killing, battering, exploitation and rape of women becomes an internal challenge that women filmmakers must face alone. Challenging the dominant social customs and norms related to women demands a lot of courage and risk taking. This effort is even more complicated when done with Israeli state funding. It not only clashes with the prevalent social structure but is also conceived by many people in Palestinian society as part and parcel of Israeli cultural colonization of Palestinian society. The subordinate status of women in Arab society and the violation of their rights by their environment is not addressed by male filmmakers (Farah 2016) and is also conceived of as betraying national and social norms, especially when done with the support of Israeli funds. As Mira Awad summed it up, addressing women oppression is not tolerated since it is viewed by the male dominated society as "hanging out the family laundry", something that clashes with basic norms in society.[17]

Hammoud's experience in this regard is very interesting. Her film, which tackles the most sensitive issues in Arab society, such as sexual relations before marriage, rape within the family, sexual harassment, and battered women, has led to a tremendous outcry in the Arab public, especially among religious sectors.[18] They viewed the film as heretical and a violation of the most sacred values in Muslim society.

Hammoud admits that "[t]he attacks were essentially from a standpoint that the movie was critical". She mentions how the mayor of Umm al-Fahm stood at the centre of the mosque and stated: "I didn't see it, but the movie 'In Between' is forbidden (haram)". This call led many men to protest against the movie. In her view this was amazing because "they are precisely reflecting the way they are shown in the film; a patriarchal community". When Hammoud was asked about how she dealt with the critique, she states, "I want to believe that my community is strong enough to face these subjects, which show how ugly we are. When I made the film, I was not criticizing the Bahamas, I was criticizing myself". Only after asserting her firm position that her depiction is accurate, does she establish a surprising connection between liberating women and liberating Palestine from Israeli occupation; "Without liberating our minds, we can't liberate one centimeter of our land". This statement seems to legitimize her effort to mobilize change in her society by challenging its negative habits and negative norms, especially relating to women and their autonomy. Even if this effort comes with state money, she seems to assert her patriotism to her society since, according to her, what matters is the intention behind the work. In other words, she seems to enlist the Palestinian cause in order to justify her critical gaze on what she believes is Arab patriarchal society.

Mara'ana perceives of herself differently, but still raises the difficulties she has faced in her career as a woman. She views her cinematic experience as an opportunity to enter the world of men. She shares that when she was working on her movie *Paradise Lost*, she entered cafes in her village that were open to men only. She admits, "My female identity was crystalized during this period". But when asked about challenging the patriarchal structure of her society, she expresses contradictory messages. On the one hand, she confesses: "I was at war with everybody, my family and the entire society ... I sought to break down all social structures". On the other, she states that "now it is different", as if she is afraid to continue criticizing her own heritage. Mara'ana reveals that becoming a mother made her more cautious and aware that change must be created gradually and that pushing too far may lead to a backlash that women do not need. She reveals that she has "no intention of taking revenge against the patriarchy". In her view, Arab society is not monolithic. There are people who understand her work and welcome her art. Notwithstanding, she admits that in order to have room for her own creativity and feel free to practice her work as an autonomous filmmaker, she had to leave her village. Although she comes to visit, she ended up living and marrying in Tel Aviv. Summing up, it seems that she is torn between her obligation to her Arab heritage and her own feminist views.

Although Awad defines herself differently, she still admits that she feels trapped between wanting to free herself from the patriarchy in Arab society and the stereotypes about it in Jewish society. She argues,

> I have to show great caution and understanding ... although my parents are very liberal. But they have people around them ... it is a narrow collar around one's neck ... We are talking about a woman in Arab society in a Jewish state ... It means that you are on the lowest rung of the ladder.

When asked about her series "Muna", which tells a side story of a battered woman, she states that "you don't know much about woman being battered in society ... You cannot imagine how many times I have seen women being battered". That is why the women in her series are strong and manage to face their challenges in their own way. In her view, she seeks to open a window for other women and make them think that they can do something about their lives. She adds, "I have done things that not everybody agrees with ... and women do not have to follow my lead, but they need at least to think that there are available options to choose from". In her view, women have a price to pay, but have the option to choose what price to pay. It seems that this is the choice she has made by working in the Israeli TV industry. She has chosen to have the space to address social issues in her society, even at the expense of contributing to whitewashing the Israeli cultural industry. Here it seems that she has put her gender before her national identity.

Abeer Haddad admits that while preparing for her film "The Women of Freedom",[19] about sexual harassment in Arab society, everyone she spoke to about it told her, "It is going to be impossible to find women to speak up about this topic". When asked how the film was received in Arab society, she stated reluctantly,

> It is more difficult for women ... If you count the number of women in the field, there are very few ... If you ask me whether the difficulties have to do with being an Arab, being Palestinian, being a woman, being a mother ... yes ... the difficulties are related to all of these factors ... but I have always tried to overcome them.

Haddad's statement mirrors the intersectional challenges that Palestinian women filmmakers in Israel face. Nevertheless, all interviewed filmmakers insist that they must pave the way for future women creators, who will continue challenging both Zionist hegemony and Arab patriarchy.

Discussion and conclusion

This paper has delved into the complexities that Palestinian women filmmakers experience in Israel and their ramifications on their self-categorization. All interviewed filmmakers show that filmmaking entails a constant inner battle that goes beyond what men in their society face and what women filmmakers in other societies experience. Palestinian women filmmakers in Israel have to constantly face the inherent tension between their sources of funding in the Israeli culture industry, their national identity and the patriarchal social values and norms in their society. The intensity of the intersection between professional, political, national and gender factors determine the path they take, the topics they address in their films and the way they face the critique against them in their own society. Hammoud's, Awad's and Mara'ana's experience reflect their triple bind, manifested in the fact that their creative production deals with social values, identities and narratives in an already precarious field in which the rigidity of the intersection of national, ethnic and gender factors strictly condition their work. They have asserted their conviction for challenging common cultural values, norms and customs in their society against all odds, but have also raised the fear of being blamed as playing into the hands of the Israeli authorities in stigmatizing their own society and thereby serving Israeli delegitimizing policies. As Arraf and Abu Fraiha have demonstrated, Palestinian filmmakers, especially women are expected to be loyal to their society, including the customs and norms that oppress them. Most interviewees have admitted that they are asked in the name of national loyalty to practice censorship on gender issues and thereby ignore the tragic implications of the patriarchal social structure for women. The interviews show how the creators walk the thin line between sometimes highlighting their gender and sometimes their nationality; a strategy that male filmmakers usually do not have to face.

The experience of Palestinian women television and cinematic filmmakers allows us to shed light on the complex interconnection between cultural production and national conflicts. Our analysis of the interviews at hand shows that this field is marked by contestation and struggle on various levels; political, social, economic and moral. As such it goes beyond the mere illustration of Bourdieu's argument that cultural production does not only produce the materiality of its object, but also its value and the recognition of its artistic legitimacy (Bourdieu 1993). Bourdieu wrote his theory in relation to a context where there is a relatively free market of ideas. Addressing the colonial conditions under which Palestinian women filmmakers produce their art and their need not only for Israeli funding, but also for recognition of their narratives, which are mostly antagonistic to the hegemonic Israeli narratives, demonstrates the dialectical relationship between artistic legitimacy and political recognition. Notwithstanding Bourdieu's important insights that social formation is structured by way of a hierarchically organized series of fields and that each field is relatively autonomous but structurally homologous with the others. Exploring the experience of Palestinian women filmmakers demonstrates that the structure of the field of cultural production is determined by the relations between the positions agents occupy in the field. In colonial contexts, such as the one addressed here, cultural production and cultural value (Belfiore 2018) are fully dependent on women filmmakers gaining political legitimacy from their colonizer, thereby submitting filmmaking to political considerations antagonistic not only with their creative freedom, but also with the sensitive intersection between their national and gender identity.

The dynamics of the bifurcated sphere of cultural production in colonial contexts is further complicated by the gender dimension. Gender roles and patriarchy, as debated in the Arabic public sphere, remain dominated by traditional social and moral values. As a result, cinematic production made by women and addressing gender relations in society is deeply influenced by the intersection between the internal patriarchal social structure and being located in the midst of a national conflict. The lack of political legitimacy in the Israeli public sphere and the existential anxiety, resulting from the national conflict, impose political and national considerations on the treatment of gender issues. Put differently, the examination of Palestinian women filmmaking demonstrates the tension embedded in the loyalty to various value systems – personal, professional, national and genderial – and the ramifications they have on creative agency and self-categorization in the cultural industries in colonial contexts.

Examining the narratives of Palestinian women TV and film creators in a patriarchal society in the context of a national conflict enable us to mirror the female gaze in tackling social, cultural and genderial topics that are not addressed by men filmmakers. As we demonstrate, the experience of Palestinian women TV and cinema creators in Israel, as a case study for other women creators of minority groups in conflict zones, demonstrate that they must tread a thin line with hardly any safety net to secure their fall. Therefore, it is understandable that any funding of such creative workers necessitates great sensitivity that enables them to have some freedom and autonomy to be creative.

Notes

1. Olivier, Einat, "Miri Regev Introduces a Reform in Cinema: Limiting the Power of the Foundations that Support Films." *Maariv*, 9.7.2018. https://www.maariv.co.il/culture/movies/Article-650500
2. Anderman, Nirit, "Ministry of Culture: No Cultural Institution was Punished for Refusing to Perform in the Occupied Territories". *Haaretz*, 19.6.2019. https://www.haaretz.co.il/gallery/theater/1.7394906
3. Staff, Toy. "Regev demands defunding of Haifa film festival for screening 'subversive' movies", The Times of Israeli, 18.9.2018. https://www.timesofisrael.com/regev-demands-defunding-of-haifa-film-festival-for-screening-subversive-movies/ (last retrieved 24.12.2019).
4. An Israeli film from 1984 directed by Uri Barbash and dealing with Jewish and Palestinian prisoners in an Israeli jail. It was nominated for an Academy Award for the Best Foreign Language Film. https://www.imdb.com/title/tt0087699/
5. Israeli sitcom television series created by Sayed Kashua and premiering on Channel 2 between 2007 and 2012. https://www.imdb.com/title/tt0904447/
6. Based on a calculation made by the first author on a database of the Israeli Ministry of Culture, the average funding for Arab cultural activities is between 3.6% and 6.4% of the ministry's budget in the years 2007–2018.

7. See note 3 above.
8. Villa Touma is a film about three Palestinian Christian sisters who lose their land during the 1967 war with Israel. For more details: https://ica.art/films/villa-touma (last retrieved 24.12.2019).
9. Sagi Ben-Nin, "The Ministry of Culture and The Pais Company Are Examining Demanding Back 1.5 million ILS from Suha Arraf after Defining her Film as Palestinian", *Walla*, 30.7.2014. https://e.walla.co.il/item/2770273 (Last retrieved 17.12.2019).
10. Rutha Kopfer, "Following the Scandal with Suha Arraf the Ministry of Culture Changed Criteria of Supporting Films", *Haaretz*, 5.4.2015. https://www.haaretz.co.il/gallery/cinema/1.2607989 (last retrieved 17.12.2019).
11. "In Between" talks about three Palestinian women, citizens of Israel, living in Tel Aviv and caught between their hometown conservative lifestyle and big city's lifestyle. For more details: http://intl.filmfund.org.il/films/?nom=002769&film=In%20Between (last retrieved 24.12.2019).
12. The film Farawla deals with "the stolen small pleasures of day-to-day life of the Palestinian citizens living under occupation". For more details: http://www.institut-icfp.org/page.php?id=569a3y354723Y569a3&p=1 (last retrieved 24.12.2019).
13. Two major examples are Elie Sleiman, who works from Paris, and Hanni Abu Asa'ad, who works from the US.
14. The film documents an entire family torn between fulfilling the [Muslim] mother's last wish [to get buried in the Jewish town Omer] and social codes that cannot be ignored. For more details: https://nfct.org.il/en/movies/in-her-footsteps-وَراءك%D9%90/ (last retrieved 24.12.2019).
15. Relating to Fauda as an example of whitewashing is especially interesting since media and the professional literature have already indicated that the second season of the series is based on a dichotomous narrative between the Israeli good guys and the Palestinian villains (Gertz and Yosef 2017).
16. On the critique of Prime Minister Netanyahu of the New Israel Fund see: Judy Maltz, "Israel's public enemy no. 1 or the poster boy for Zionism?" *Haaretz*, 23.8.2018. https://www.haaretz.com/israel-news/.premium.MAGAZINE-mickey-gitzin-new-israel-fund-branded-by-netanyahu-israel-s-public-enemy-1.6408542
17. Hlehel, Alaa. "With Beauty Only?", Hlehel Blogspot, 1.8.2008. http://hlehel.me/ بالجمال-وحده؟ / (last retrieved 24.12.2019); Hammash, May. "Palestinian Citizens of Israel and "Muna" T.V Series", *Alhadath*, 25.9.2015. https://www.alhadath.ps/article/106116/منذ-مسلسل-و-الداخل-فلسطينيو (last retrieved 24.12.2019).
18. Athamleh, Riham Y. "After the Attack Against Her: Fear of Attempts to Assault Maysaloun Hammoud", *Bokra*, 8.1.2017. https://bokra.net/Article-1358668 (last retrieved 24.12.2019).
19. The film tells the stories of women who were killed in the name of "honor killing", others who survived murder attempts and women who are under death threat. For more details: https://nfct.org.il/en/movies/women-of-freedom/ (last retrieved 24.12.2019).

Disclosure statement

No potential conflict of interest was reported by the author(s).

Funding

This work was supported by Israel Science Foundation [grant number 845/17].

ORCID

Amal Jamal ⓘ http://orcid.org/0000-0002-8516-1473

References

Abu-Rabia-Queder, Sarab, and Naomi Weiner-Levy. 2013. "Between Local and Foreign Structures: Exploring Agency of Palestinian Women in Israel." *Social Politics: International Studies in Gender, State & Society* 20 (1): 88–108.

Al-Saber, Samer. 2018. "Jerusalem's Roses and Jasmine: A Resistant Ventriloquism Against a Racialized Orientalism." *Theatre Research International* 43 (1): 6–24. doi:10.1017/S0307883318000032.

Alacovska, Ana, and Rosalinda Gill. 2019. "De-Westernizing Creative Labour Studies: The Informality of Creative Work from an Ex-Centric Perspective." *International Journal of Cultural Studies* 22 (2): 195–212. doi:10.1177/1367877918821231.

Ashuri, Tamar. 2005. "The Nation Remembers: National Identity and Shared Memory in Television Documentaries." *Nations and Nationalism* 11 (3): 423–442. doi:10.1111/j.1354-5078.2005.00212.x.

Banks, Mark. 2017. *Creative Justice: Cultural Industries Work and Inequality.* London: Rowman and Littlefield.

Belfiore, Eleonora. 2018. "Whose Cultural Value? Representation, Power and Creative Industries." *International Journal of Cultural Policy* 26 (3): 1–15. doi:10.1080/10286632.2018.1495713.

Bielby, Denise. 2009. "Gender Inequality in Culture Industries: Women and Men Writers in Film and Television." *Sociologie du Travail* 51 (2): 237–252.

Bourdieu, P. 1993. *The Field of Cultural Production.* New York: Columbia University Press.

Boyatzis, Richard. 1998. *Transforming Qualitative Information: Thematic Analysis and Code Development.* Thousand Oaks: Sage Publications, Inc.

Braun, Virginia, and Victoria Clarke. 2006. "Using Thematic Analysis in Psychology." *Qualitative Research in Psychology* 3 (2): 77–101. doi:10.1191/1478088706qp063oa.

Broeske-Danielsen, Brit Aagot. 2013. "Community Music Activity in a Refugee Camp – Student Music Teachers' Practicum Experiences." *Music Education Research* 15 (3): 304–316. doi:10.1080/14613808.2013.781145.

Castello, Enric. 2015. "The Production of Television Fiction and Nation Building: The Catalan Case." *European Journal of Communication* 22 (1): 49–68. doi:10.1177/0267323107073747.

Chamaz, Kathy, and Linda Liska Belgrave. 2018. "Thinking About Data with Grounded Theory." *Qualitative Inquiry* 25 (8): 743–753. doi:10.1177/1077800418809455.

Coban, Sava, ed. 2018. *Media Ideology and Hegemony.* Leiden: Brill.

Conor, Bridget, Rosalind Gill, and Stephanie Taylor. 2015. "Gender and Creative Labour." *The Sociological Review* 63 (S1): 1–22. doi:10.1111/1467-954X.12237.

Cormack, Mike. 1993. "Problems of Minority Language Broadcasting: Gaelic in Scotland." *European Journal of Communication* 8 (1): 101–117.

Dabashi, Hamid. 2006. *Dreams of a Nation: On Palestinian Cinema.* London: Verso.

Farah, Maria. 2016. "Palestinian Female Directors in Israel: Between a Rock of a National-Masculine Discourse and a Hard Place of a Struggle for Change and Gender Empowerment." Unpublished MA Thesis. Haifa University.

Feder, Tal. 2018. "Normative Justification for Public Arts Funding: What Can we Learn from Linking Arts Consumption and Arts Policy in Israel?" *Socio-Economic Review* 18 (1): 193–213. doi:10.1093/ser/mwy001.

Feder, Tal, and Tally Katz-Gerro. 2012. "Who Benefits from Public Funding of the Performing Arts? Comparing the Art Provision and the Hegemony–Distinction Approaches." *Poetics* 40: 359–381. doi:10.1016/j.poetic.2012.05.004.

Feder, Tal, and Tally Katz-Gerro. 2015. "The Cultural Hierarchy in Funding: Government Funding of the Performing Arts Based on Ethnic and Geographic Distinctions." *Poetics* 49: 76–95. doi:10.1016/j.poetic.2015.02.004.

Gertz, Nurit, and Raz Yosef. 2017. "Trauma, Time and the 'Singular Plural': The Israeli Television Series Fauda." *Israel Studies Review* 32 (2): 1–20. doi:10.3167/isr.2017. 320202.

Ghanem, As'ad, and Mohanad Mustafa. 2018. *Palestinians in Israel: The Politics of Faith After Oslo*. Cambridge: Cambridge University Press.

Gill, Rosalind. 2002. "Cool, Creative and Egalitarian? Exploring Gender in Project-Based New Media Work in Europe." *Information, Communication & Society* 5 (1): 70–89. doi:10.1080/13691180110117668.

Hesmondhalgh, David. 2007. *The Cultural Industries*. London: Sage.

Hesmondhalgh, David, and Sarah Baker. 2015. "Sex, Gender and Work Segregation in the Cultural Industries." *The Sociological Review* 63 (1): 23–36. doi:10.1111/1467-954X.12238.

Hillman, Amy, Albert Cannella Jr., and Ira Harris. 2002. "Women and Racial Minorities in the Boardroom: How Do Directors Differ?" *Critical Sociology* 28 (6): 747–763.

Hirschman, Albert. 1970. *Exit, Voice and Loyalty: Responses to Decline in Firms, Organizations and States*. Cambridge, MA: Harvard University Press.

Jamal, Amal. 2009. *The Arab Public Sphere in Israel: Media Politics and Cultural Resistance*. Bloomington: Indiana University Press.

Jamal, Amal. 2011. *Arab Minority Nationalism in Israel: The Politics of Indigeneity*. London: Routledge.

Jamal, Amal. 2020. *Reconstructing the Civic: Palestinian Civil Activism in Israel*. New York: State University of New York Press.

Jenkins, Catherine. 2014. "'That's Not Philosophy': Feminism, Academia and the Double Bind." *Journal of Gender Studies* 23 (3): 262–274.

Katz, Elihu, and Hed Sella. 1999. *The Beracha Report: Culture Policy in Israel*. Jerusalem: Van Leer Jerusalem Institute and Beracha Foundation.

Keshet, Shulah, Dorit Abramovitch, Ortal Ben-Dayan, Rafe Aharon, and Clarisse Harbon, eds. 2011. *The Bureaucracy of Inequality: Discrimination in the Allocation of Cultural Resources in Israel, the Case of the Mizrachi Culture in 2009*. Heart at East: The Coalition for Equal Distribution of Cultural Funds in Israel, Tel Aviv (in Hebrew).

Lavie, Noa, and Amal Jamal. 2019. "Constructing Ethno-National Differentiation on the Set of the TV Series, Fauda." *Ethnicities* 19 (6): 1038–1061.

Lee, Hye-Kyung. 2017. "The Political Economy of 'Creative Industries'." *Media, Culture & Society* 39 (7): 1078–1088. doi:10.1177/0163443717692739.

Mayer, Vicky. 2017. *Almost Hollywood, Nearly New Orleans: The Lure of the Local Film Economy*. Los Angles: California University Press.

McGuigan, Jim. 2010. "Creative Labour, Cultural Work and Individualization." *International Journal of Cultural Policy* 16 (3): 323–335.

Nathanson, Roby, Itamar Gazala, and Dathna Pisam. 2016. *Creative Industries in Israel.* Tel Aviv: The Center for Political Economics.

Olesen, Thomas. 2018. "Adaptation and Self-Celebration: The Formation of Injustice Icons in a North-South Perspective." *International Journal of Politics Culture and Society* 31: 313–328.

Òbrien, Anne. 2014. "Producing Television and Reproducing Gender." *Television & New Media* 16 (3): 259–274. doi:10.1177/1527476414557952.

Ronen, Diti. 2018. *Art as a Driver for Social Change in Israel.* New York: Jewish Funders Network.

Sa'ar, Amalia. 2016. "The Gender Contract Under Neoliberalism: Palestinian-Israeli Women's Labor Force Participation." *Feminist Economics* 23 (1): 54–76.

Saha, Anamik. 2016. "The Rationalizing/Racializing Logic of Capital in Cultural Production." *Media Industries Journal* 3 (1): 1–16. doi:10.3998/mij.15031809.0003. 101.

Saha, Anamik. 2017. "The Politics of Race in Cultural Distribution: Addressing Inequalities in British Asian Theatre." *Cultural Sociology* 11 (3): 302–317. doi:10. 1177/1749975517708899.

Saha, Anamik. 2018. *Race and the Cultural Industries.* Cambridge: Polity press.

Schejter, Amit. 2009. *Muting Israeli Democracy: How Media and Cultural Policy Undermine Freedom of Expression.* Urbana: University of Illinois Press.

Schlesinger, Phillip. 1991. "Media the Political Order and National Identity." *Media Culture and Society* 13: 297–308.

Şerban, Silviu, and Anita Grigoriu. 2014. "Feminism in Post-Revolutionary Iranian Cinema." *Journal of Research in Gender Studies* 4 (2): 967–978.

Swartz, David. 2013. *Symbolic Power, Politics and Intellectuals.* Chicago: University of Chicago Press.

Taylor, Jessica. 2014. "Romance and the Female Gaze Obscuring Gendered Violence in *The Twilight Saga.*" *Feminist Media Studies* 14 (3): 388–402. doi:10.1080/14680777. 2012.740493.

Turner, John, and Katherine Reynolds. 2012. "Theory of Self-Categorization." In *Handbook of Theories of Social Psychology*, edited by Paul A.M. Van Lange, Arie W. Kruglanski, and E. Tory Higgins, 399–417. London: Sage Publications.

Uğur Tanrıöver, Hulya. 2016. "Women as Film Directors in Turkish Cinema." *European Journal of Women's Studies* 24 (4): 321–335. doi:10.1177/1350506816649985.

Watson, Iarfhlaith. 2002. "Irish-Language Broadcasting: History, Ideology and Identity." *Media, Culture and Society* 24 (7): 39–57. doi:10.1177/016344370202400601.

Religious symbolism and politics: hijab and resistance in Palestine

Samira Alayan and Lana Shehadeh ⓘ

ABSTRACT

The covering of Muslim women has become a topic of contention on a global level. Relying on in-depth interviews in the Palestinian territories, our study illustrates the motivation to wear hijab under a colonial context and compares the justifications women give for wearing the hijab under two different types of political subjugation. Palestinian Muslim women in both the West Bank and East Jerusalem, frequently provided political justification for wearing the hijab. In the West Bank, where interactions with the occupier are limited to tense encounters with soldiers, they use the hijab as a defiant symbol against the Israeli occupation. In East Jerusalem, Palestinian women use the hijab as a visible representation of their identity and resilience, but at the same time they are more cautious and consider the way the hijab might be viewed by Jewish-Israeli civilians, whom they encounter on a daily basis.

Introduction

The covering of a Muslim woman's body has become a controversial and heavily contested issue (Rosenberger and Sauer 2012; Scott 2007). Although hijab is perceived as a religiously mandated garb covering a woman's head, hair, neck and ears while leaving only the face showing (Williams and Vashi 2007); it has become a controversial and politically scrutinized symbol providing a source of identity for women who choose to wear it (Heath 2008). Fanon (1959) famously analysed the veiling of Muslim women as a political statement and act of anti-colonial resistance. In his work on hijab, Fanon's insight remains unique, mainly because of the scarcity of contemporary active colonial projects. Similarly, a comparable context to the colonial era described in Fanon's work, can be seen within the occupation of the Palestinian territories. The case of Muslim Palestinian women under Israeli occupation provides for ample opportunity to reexamine, update, and refine this body of literature as it relates to a woman's dress code within a colonial context.

In understanding this context and its relation to a woman's donning of the hijab, we specifically asked what motivates Muslim women in the highly politicized region of the Palestinian territories, the West Bank and East Jerusalem, to cover and the effect of political occupation on that decision. Through in-depth interviews conducted with Muslim Palestinian women in East Jerusalem and the West Bank, this paper demonstrates how donning the hijab symbolizes a complex assortment of visibility, identity and empowerment within the context of Palestinian resistance as opposed to the predominant understanding of hijab as a strictly religious act.

Building on Scott (1985), Vinthagen and Johansson (2013) suggested that "everyday resistance" is contingent due to changing contexts and situations. At the same time, it needs to be understood as intersectional as the powers it engages (not engaging with one single power relation). Our analysis examines both of these dimensions: (1) We examine the justifications women give to donning the hijab in two different contexts of colonial domination. (2) We examine the meaning of donning the hijab vis-à-vis the occupation, as well as vis-à-vis patriarchy.

We argue that the Israeli occupation and the political oppression it provides has a direct impact on the way women justify wearing the hijab. Based on our interviews, we find that women see the hijab not only as a religious symbol but a symbolic political act of resilience and resistance to reality in the territories. We also find a difference in the perception of oppression and occupation between women in East Jerusalem and the West Bank. Women in East Jerusalem, although they encounter Israelis as occupiers, they also encounter Israelis as neighbours, colleagues, and supervisors, among other titles. We on the other hand, Palestinians in the West Bank, who encounter overt occupation and repression, see Israelis only as occupiers at checkpoints and in Israeli settlements. This difference has implications on the justification women in each location provide for wearing the hijab. At the intersection of patriarchy and occupation, we argue that women find themselves entangled in multiple systems of power, thus strengthening one form of power over themselves – patriarchy – while attempting to resist another – occupation.

Hijab as a religious symbol and political tool

Although both scholars and the general public disagree whether the hijab is religiously mandated (*fardh*) (Smith 1999; Asad 1980), there is little doubt that it is popularly considered a religious symbol and has certain grounds within Islamic theology. Advocates of the hijab interpret donning the hijab as a divinely ordained solution to the sexual appetites of men and women (Siraj 2011), with the Quran as a central point of reference. The *hijab* (حِجَاب), coming from the word *"hajib"*(حَاجِب) refers to a "barrier". It is understood that a form of barrier, whether it be a piece of cloth or other forms of covering, must remain between the opposite sexes.

Religious symbolism, though, has been used as a form of political representation in many contexts and can serve as a form of unity between peoples or a significant flag of differentiation and rejection of a current reality. It can be used to strengthen division and support the building of barriers between one's self, one's community and the so-called other (Guven 2010). In most cases, when religious symbolism is entreated within the context of political conflicts, the line between secularism and religiosity is blurred. In such instances, religiosity becomes "de-privatised" and seeks a larger and more active role within the public sphere and political arena (Mancini and Rosenfeld 2010). Hijab, more precisely, has been clearly effective in disrupting the social reality within most non-Muslim contexts. In France, the banning of hijab came from the mentality that its mere presence within the public sphere would "disrupt the tranquility of [...] life" (Mancini 2008). Within the context of pre-AKP Turkey,[1] secularism was actively practiced and maintained within the public sphere. The practice of wearing the hijab in a public space became a distinct challenge to the authority and government in place. Hence, within that context, the physical practice of donning the hijab became a highly political act of protest to the enforced secular public space present (Göle 2002).

Perhaps the most extreme form of politicization of the Hijab has been taking place among Muslim communities within colonial contexts. Communities under colonial rule and occupation are usually forced to rise up furiously in any way they can. In many instances they are able to do so with whatever resources they have against the colonial power. Fanon shed light on the role of women in the face of colonialism. In the view of a colonizer, a veiled woman symbolizes a challenge against the western notion of civilization, as the custom of wearing the veil is considered primitive and abiding by traditional rules of dress code. According to Fanon, Western men see the veil as a challenge to the system. Thus, successfully colonizing the land goes hand in hand with liberating and removing the veil from the customary dress code of the colonized woman (Fanon 1959).

Hijab in Palestine

Israeli colonialism, though, has its own particular characteristics that shape the way the colonized react it. Historically, following the war of 1948 and the expulsion of 750,000 Palestinians, Israel declared its independence in May of 1948 (Bardi 2016). After the war of 1967, Israel expanded its occupation to the West Bank, among other territories; yet it strategically avoided official annexation to ensure a Jewish majority in the state. Although Israeli law was extended to East Jerusalem with a possible, yet significantly complicated path to Israeli citizenship, it practically barred the majority of East Jerusalemites from receiving Israeli citizenship, leaving them with permanent residency status. As part of the 1994 Oslo Peace Process, other West Bank cities became part of the Palestinian Authority.[2] Thus, West Bank cities, with the exception of East Jerusalem, were under Palestinian control creating two very different political and social contexts between West Bank cities and East Jerusalem (Alayan 2019; Israeli 2014; Jefferis 2012; Klein 2001; Khalidi 1992).

Hijab has not always been such a distinct political symbol within Palestinian dress code. Before the start of the first Intifada (1987–1993), the hijab was actually considered part of the dress code of older Palestinian women, a symbol of modesty and respectability and an end to material pursuits and fashion (Dakkak and Mikulka 2012). Shortly after the start of the second Intifada (2000–2004), it became a head piece worn by young women in the Palestinian territories. Unenforced by their parents, girls from as early as the age of seven were seen wearing the hijab diversified with many various levels and styles (Dakkak and Mikulka 2012). The hijab in these territories, according to some, has become part of a growing form of fundamentalism. In many cases, the hijab is worn as a reaction to the frustration built up by the Israeli occupation of the Palestinian lands, the lack of a prospect for peace and the lost hope of promised improvement of quality life for Palestinian (Dakkak and Mikulka 2012). It can be claimed that wearing the hijab conveys a message of defiance to the presence of the Israeli soldiers and Israeli settlers in the Occupied Palestinian Territories, and at the same time a visual message stating their presence in their (occupied) homeland. According to Wolfe (2006), the mere essence of settler colonialism depicts the elimination of the indigenous presence as a means of consolidating state claims to indigenous territory (Wolfe 2006). The keen sense of identity for Palestinian women is illustrated when donning the hijab. For many Palestinian women, the hijab symbolized a visible and physical representation of their own defiance against the reality created by their enemy. In a way, Palestinian Muslim women use their hijab to showcase themselves as the "other" opposing the occupier, be it the soldiers or the settlers.

However, the difference in the political status of Palestinians in the West Bank and East Jerusalem is reflected also in the justification they provide for using the hijab. In the West Bank, women deal with a very overt Israeli occupation encountered at checkpoints, during home invasions and near Israeli settlements in the territories. Palestinians in East Jerusalem have a very different experience with the Israeli occupation. Although Israeli policy in this territory could not be characterized as a direct Israelization of the Palestinians, it is a strong instrumental process in accessing state resources for Palestinians in the city (Shlomo 2017).

In East Jerusalem, Palestinians live under complete Israeli rule. This means civil and security branches are controlled by the Israeli government, and both Israeli and Palestinian societies live in very close proximity. Although Palestinians in East Jerusalem face numerous human rights violations within their everyday lives (Shalhoub-Kevorkian 2010, 2014a), they have relatively frequent encounters with Jewish-Israeli civilians, an experience which has become unfamiliar to most West Bank residents. Therefore, women in East Jerusalem are able to see Israelis both as occupiers and as civilians, given that the two populations–Palestinian and Israeli–come into contact more often (Shalhoub-Kevorkian 1999). Hence, Palestinian women's agency in Israel is not only dictated by Arab cultural boundaries but also by the cultural realities put forth by Israel (Abu-Rabia-Queder and Weiner-Levy 2013). West Bankers, although under political occupation, do not have the ability to perceive these dimensions of Israeli society, except through soldiers they interact with at checkpoints.

Research methods

To conduct our study, we contacted 143 Palestinian female participants through extended networks followed by searches conducted at local universities in the West Bank and East Jerusalem. Wearing a hijab was a condition for the women taking part in the study. The participants were given the option of participating in a survey with open ended questions or an in-depth sit-down interview. Of those contacted, 110 (76 from East Jerusalem and 34 from the West Bank) agreed to answer survey questions while 33 (15 from East Jerusalem and 18 from the West Bank) sat down for in-depth interviews between June and November of 2019. The self-report surveys and in-depth interviews took place during the same period of research, however each interview and survey was conducted separately at a different time. Participants ranged in age between nineteen years of age and forty-nine years and were interviewed by two female Palestinians living in Israel who do not wear the hijab. It was important to ensure that women of Arab descent conducted the interviews in order to give participants a sense of comfort and ease throughout the conversation. All of the interviews were transcribed to standardize the analysis process more effectively. All participants were given identifications that represent their age and where they originate from, instead of their actual names, in order to protect their identities and ensure confidentiality. Participants were informed that no personally identifiable aspects of their interviews would be shared, nor were given names exchanged or recorded during the interviews. The questionnaires also included a consent form without any identification of their names or identities.

As two Palestinian women living in very different realities, we have found that our own understanding of our communities and the driving forces behind our actions are strikingly different. One of us is a Palestinian American from the West Bank who dons the hijab. Since she is located in the West Bank her experience with Israelis is limited to the interaction experienced at checkpoints with Israeli soldiers as occupiers. While the Palestinian author who resides in Jerusalem interacts with Israelis very differently as she works at an Israeli university with Israeli colleagues and friends, meeting and interacting with Israelis not just as occupiers. The differences in our experiences with the occupation strengthen the differences we found in the data collected for our study.

Due to our backgrounds, we were able to connect with our research subjects and understand their contexts and communities. Since travel during our fieldwork period proved to be difficult for both parties, we utilized Zoom as a resource to ensure at least one researcher was present during the interview proceedings.

Findings

Each of the following sections will explain the justifications participants illustrated as contributing to their choice to don the hijab. It is important to note that although most participants chose politics as the primary reason behind wearing the hijab, some participants, at times, mentioned more than one reason as their motivation.

Political motivation

The interviews consistently revealed that the political conditions that participants live under contribute to their motivation in wearing the hijab. The most common justification was the strengthening of one's identity in the context of the occupation. We labelled this justification as "political" since the elaboration given by participants illustrated their feeling of resistance through a visible representation of what they believe their oppressor does not want to see. The hijab as a mode of resistance is not as pronounced as more commonly understood methods of resistance such as riots and revolutions. However, in the contexts of the Palestinian territories, it is a form of what is known as "everyday resistance" (Scott 1985). Everyday resistance ultimately has the potential to undermine power in a non-dramatic way, engages with intersectional powers, and is enacted by individuals in various ways without formal leadership (Vinthagen and Johansson 2013). For approximately 64 per cent of the participants (75 per cent of West Bankers and 57 per cent of East Jerusalemites), the political conditions in the Palestinian territories contributed to the motivation behind their decision to wear hijab.

This quantitative gap between the West Bank and East Jerusalem might relate to the harsher mode of occupation in the former, which in turn enhances the tendency of our interviewees to politicize their donning of the hijab. The content of their justification indicates to a similar pattern. West Bankers revealed that the degrading treatment they receive from Israeli soldiers at security checkpoints invigorated their urge to strengthen their political identity through donning the hijab. Many women tie their own feelings toward the occupation to their ability to use the hijab as a visible representation of their rejection of the occupation and the reality they live in. Respondent WB-23-B[3] asserts her understanding of head covering as a form of resistance: "A woman wearing hijab is a political power against the Zionist enemy."

Of the respondents, twenty-six West Bankers said that they began wearing the hijab after the Second Intifada and the construction of the separation wall.[4] A time in which hopelessness increased among Palestinians following much destruction and loss of life in the West Bank translated into Palestinian women using their bodies, and the donning of the hijab, as a symbol of fighting back against the oppression they felt. WB-23-B continued:

> The Zionists want to kick us out of our land and become the majority in Palestine. They erected the Wall to impose a separation between in order to stop seeing us. My hijab is a tool for me to show them that we exist and will forever stay on this land.

Another respondent, WB-BZ,[5] spoke of the humiliation that she experienced at checkpoints during her frequent visits to family in the West Bank:

> We receive humiliating treatment from the disgusting female soldiers they put at the checkpoints, they always leave us in the scorching heat or the cold for a long time when we want to go from one place to another. They ask us a lot of questions even though I am only visiting my parents and not entering Jerusalem. Even in our country they demonstrate their power and so the way to fight them is for them to see me wearing the hijab, it infuriates the female soldiers and scares them ...

There is a predominant sense of humiliation among respondents when they pass checkpoints at large. Their use of hijab as a political tool is effective, according to them, in illustrating a sense of existence and resistance to whatever force they see. One respondent, WB-20[6], deems the hijab not only as a symbol of religiosity, but also as a symbol of political resistance to the status quo brought about by the occupation. Her sense is that she can physically illustrate an objection to the norm in a way that may seem threatening to her perceived "enemy". For her, wearing the hijab became a form of protest. From our own experience, members of the Palestinian community, specifically in the West Bank, consistently describe religion as the most visible rejection of the occupation and so called "westernization" of the Palestinian existence. Respondent WB-20 also added, "When female soldiers at the checkpoints see a woman with a hijab it scares them."

For women under occupation, covert and overt acts of violence transform gender relations in complex, contradictory, and diverse ways. Civilian women in the context of occupation realize the existence of and learn about survivors' counter-discourse. In response, they produce new modes of resistance in order to make their lives richer, stronger, and more meaningful under the conditions (Shalhoub-Kevorkian 2008). As respondent WB-B[7] explained:

> I wanted to identify with my husband's sense of humiliation that the soldiers always try to cause him at checkpoints and take him to a small side room for a physical check, this way the female soldiers can take me and I will go through the same feeling.

Respondent WB-32 explained that the occupation will not frighten her nor will it prevent her from bringing her Muslim identity to the forefront: "Yes, I am a Muslim Palestinian and this is my identity, the occupation will not scare us."

For women in East Jerusalem, the realities are a bit different. They live in an area that is completely controlled by Israel without possessing the benefits of citizenship. Many East Jerusalem Palestinian residents are not given Israeli citizenship, rather they possess Jerusalem ID cards allotting them residency status in the city. This status in and of itself precludes them from any voting rights in the general election and in many cases, they can lose their status depending on the will of the Israeli authorities (Shalhoub-Kevorkian 2014b). Interestingly, the findings from 57 per cent of East Jerusalem interviewees (fifty-two of ninety-one respondents) reveal that hijab is mostly used as a tool for political representation and identity. For respondents, it serves as a flag of survival and resilience among Jewish-Israelis. A thirty-two-year-old respondent from East Jerusalem stated (EJ-32):

> Look what's going on in East Jerusalem in recent years. Jews are trying to build everywhere and take over everything, they are trying to erase everything that shows there Palestinian have the right so I with my hijab show them we are resilient (*samidun*) and are staying here.

This respondent used the term *samidun* in Arabic, which means the plural of steadfast, or resilient, a term which testifies to the deep embeddedness of her discourse in the Palestinian narrative of national resistance, and therefore is a stark illustration for the politicization of wearing the hijab. For anyone who has spent time within the Palestinian community, in the West Bank or in East Jerusalem, would understand the significance of the word *samidun*. This concept of resilience stands strong within the existence of the Palestinian identity and agency.

Women like EJ-32 see themselves as a group that has lost their agency amid the conditions they live under. They often mention incidents of home demolitions, seizure of land and the Israeli monopoly over the education system. A main difference between the realities in East Jerusalem, for

Palestinians, and that of the West Bank is the fact that East Jerusalem's education system is completely controlled by the Israeli Ministry of Education. Although Palestinian schools in East Jerusalem are given Palestinian curricula, even the textbooks are censored and controlled by Israeli authorities (Rempel 1997, Alayan 2019). Interestingly, many Palestinian women lose their sense of agency within East Jerusalem and Israel proper. This is because the society, being Israeli, rejects their identity as Palestinian. In fact, among the interviewees, Palestinians in the West Bank consistently referred to Israel or the state of Israel as the occupier, while Palestinians in East Jerusalem referred to the Israeli state and the Israeli authority as opposed to just the occupier.

According to EJ-22-DYC, "Jews do not want to see Arabs in Jerusalem. They want us to disappear and instead we are here, and we show our presence by wearing the hijab." This respondent's answer resembles the answer of another respondent, WB-23-B, differing only in the fact that EJ-22-DYC's motivation stems from the existence as a minority group in East Jerusalem. For Palestinians in East Jerusalem, the hijab has a stronger notion of existence more specifically in East Jerusalem where Palestinians are not only part of a Palestinian community that they belong to but are also subjected to the guidelines and framework of the Jewish–Israeli culture. The Palestinians of East Jerusalem, thus, find themselves in a similar context to Palestinians within Israel proper (Abu-Rabia-Queder and Weiner-Levy 2013).

Another respondent, EJ-HU says:

> Every evening I hear shouting that the soldiers are destroying houses in our village and arresting our boys while at school. We are obliged to teach what they want and how they want, they leave us with nothing. The way I dress is my choice to demonstrate that we are surviving here and no one will force us out of our village.

Respondent EJ-24, who lives in Issawiya, a village in the Jerusalem district and constantly experiences clashes between the inhabitants of the village and the Israeli army, explains: " … They […] see us wearing hijab everywhere, working in every shop, speaking different languages. They aim their weapons at us […] we [women] are strong with the hijab." The respondents and their experiences illustrate the extent to which Palestinian women are willing to go to resist what they see as an injustice; hence their hijab becomes a political act in the face of the occupation. It becomes a force of resistance.

Religious motivation

Although politics has been a significant justification for wearing the hijab among women in the Palestinian territories, it is ultimately considered a religiously mandated decree (see section Political motivation).[8] Among West Bank participants, 48 per cent (twenty-five of fifty-two Participants) of the participants stated that they chose to wear the hijab for religious purposes, while

30 per cent (twenty-seven of ninety-one Participants) of the Jerusalem-based participants chose religion as the motivation. While a gap in level of religiosity between Jerusalem and the rest of the West Bank could partially explain the difference, it is important to remind in this context the significant difference in the realities Palestinian communities live in the West Bank as opposed to the reality in East Jerusalem. In East Jerusalem, Palestinians are much more exposed to the tendencies of Israeli society with relative western leniency as opposed to the West Bank which is classified as a conservative Muslim society. Those who did state that religion was their motivation chose to wear it at a young age. Some stated that they wore it as early as six or seven years old.[9] Others wore it at puberty and stated that they were raised in homes in which it was a religious norm to wear hijab at puberty. Respondent WB-28-BZ, a mother of two explained:

> I wore the hijab at the age of 14, all of the women in my family wear a hijab. This is what Muslim women are supposed to wear, and this is what our Quran mentioned. I am a religious woman and follow our religion and tradition.

This illustrates that coming from a conservative family does not leave women much choice. Thus, women are, due to familial pressures, expected to cover and abide by the expectations of the family due to the patriarchal nature of the Palestinian community. In traditional Palestinian societies, women are often expected to weigh collective interests more heavily than their personal needs, and many are expected to censure their own individual interests (Rapoport 1989). Such women do not have the freedom to choose what to wear but rather follow the collective norm.

In some cases, it is evident that even religious motivation to wear the hijab has a background in the political circumstances. Some respondents' fear of the unknown under the constant change in the political conditions in the Palestinian territories have invoked their own religious motivation to wear the hijab. For respondent WB-20-B, her fear of the Israeli soldiers that broke into her home late at night prompted her own fear of God and her abiding by what she believes is a religious ordinance in Islam. She explains:

> On the day the soldiers broke into our house and took my father in front of my eyes, a moment I will never forget [...] humiliation, violence and screams, there were feelings of fear that only God can help us break through this violent force [...] At that same moment, I decided that I have to pray and wear the hijab [...] the hijab gave me a feeling of power and that God is with us, and this is enough.

Respondent WB-20-B illustrates her fear from soldiers as she experienced them entering her home during the late hours of the night and took her father in as a political prisoner. Interestingly, however, her fear translates into a religious motivation to wear the hijab. This fear renders her own fear of God and her belief in the need to fulfil her own religious obligation.

Hence, religiosity and political motivation collide in a Palestinian woman's purpose behind wearing the hijab.

Social pressure

Other than political and religious motivations to wear the hijab, Palestinian women interviewed expressed other factors that played a part in motivating them to wear the hijab. Among them is the societal pressure on women through their clothing which has become a spatial practice that reflects power-relations, hierarchies and agency. Thus, women's bodies become both a socio and political instrument within a community increasing their oppression within a patriarchal society, regardless of the political realities (Alfasi and Fenster 2009). The findings illustrate the societal pressures on women to abide by a certain dress code. The pressure on women to wear the hijab is part of the structure of a patriarchal society that has pressure on women to be conservative and follow the norms and customs of the society in which they belong. This structure is one reinforced by the occupation and the structures at play (Hamamra 2020).

Among the respondents, 17 per cent (nine from fifty-two) of West Bankers and 21 per cent (nineteen from ninety-one) of Jerusalemites stated that societal pressure is among the many reasons in which they have decided to don the hijab. In recent years because of the social and political realities of Palestinian society, many women feel that hijab has given them a degree of honour within their respective societies. Due to the patriarchal nature of the Palestinian society, women tend to feel the need to dress modestly specifically in the presence of men. This translates into a version of honour code where the Palestinian woman's honour emanates into the honour of the family. EJ-26-DYC explains:

> All of my aunts including my mother decided to wear the hijab early on. And that's where my mother's pressure began. For months, my two aunts and their daughters began irritating me with their pressure in trying to convince me to wear a hijab. The pressure was too strong, and I succumbed to it. I covered my hair. As a result, my mom threw a big party and invited all the aunts.

Another respondent, EJ-HU, says:

> I teach in a conservative neighborhood in East Jerusalem, over the last few years many teachers including the principal started coming to school with hijab; myself and very few teachers remained without it. The social pressure that was directed towards us was overwhelming. Over time I decided that I cannot continue like this and wore the hijab.

Being a devout Muslim woman wearing a hijab, with all the commitments and social responsibilities the hijab grants you, makes the decision to remove it almost impossible. The findings illustrate that 12 per cent of respondents from both East Jerusalem and the West Bank mentioned their inability to remove it in the event that they did not feel connected to it any longer, making it an irrevocable choice. Women stated that wearing the hijab in front of the community, as a whole, makes it almost impossible to take it off if one regrets wearing it. EJ-33 explains:

> When I wore the hijab a few years ago I didn't do it for a religious reason, it was my mother and sister's pressure on me and I did it to please them, and today I think I made a big mistake. Unfortunately, I do not have the courage to take it off. The whole society saw me wearing the head cover so how do I take it off?

The hijab, paradoxically, served as a liberating factor in many of the lives of the respondents. Of these respondents, many of the women (23 per cent of the overall sample and 19 per cent of West Bankers versus 25 per cent of East Jerusalemites) stated that without the hijab they would not be able to leave their homes to attend college, university or even work outside of the house. Respondents from both East Jerusalem and the West Bank explained that for many of their conservative Muslim Arab families leaving the house without a hijab was a serious deviation from their traditional customs and social norms. Hence, to ensure their ability to leave for work or pursue higher education, many choose to wear the hijab. For them, the hijab provides a sense of liberation from the restrictions of their society allowing them to pursue their everyday lives. However, this was a factor more prevalent in East Jerusalem due to the daily contact with Jews in the city preventing families from feeling as though their daughters are safe. For them, safety seemed to be more readily available in the event that a young woman chose to wear the hijab. Respondent EJ-23 said:

> My brother constantly bothered me about going to school with jeans and tight shirts, claiming they don't comply with the social codes. He has always been giving me trouble and said if I don't cover my head he would keep me from studying. In the end and in order to be able to go out and continue to study I had to cover my head.

On the other hand, for some women living in East Jerusalem, wearing the hijab posed an obstacle instead. Some women in East Jerusalem expressed their concern that the hijab has decreased progress in their workplace and their advancement within the Israeli-Jewish society. Many of these women have stated that their employers prefer that they do not wear the hijab. Respondent EJ-23-DYC said:

> As a student from East Jerusalem, I am looking for a job that fits my school hours. Anytime I go for an interview and see other Arab girls without hijab, I know they will get the job. Jews do not like a Muslim girl with a headcover, they prefer Christian or Muslim Arabs without it.

Regardless of how hijab should be worn or how it was ordained to be worn, it is obvious that many of our respondents have chosen their own way of wearing the hijab and have interpreted it the way that not only suits them, but also suits their society and culture.

Conclusion

In understanding hijab as a social and political phenomenon within Palestinian communities, this study examined the motivation behind wearing the hijab for women living under occupation and political oppression in the West Bank and East Jerusalem. Similar to Fanon (1959), we illustrate that resilience plays a significant role in the political justification for wearing the hijab, resilience in the face of occupation – whether it be overt occupation as displayed in the West Bank or an indirect control over authority and everyday life as in East Jerusalem. We find, though some differences between the two contexts. In the West Bank a larger share of the interviewees used political reasoning for explaining their choice to do the hijab, although those who did use political justification use similar themes and vocabulary in both contexts. We interpret this gap as a reflection of the higher exposure of West Bankers to the direct violence of the occupation, which leads to more frequent politicization of mundane practices.

West Bank women were also more likely to provide explicit religious justifications for wearing the hijab. However, in the West Bank interviewers sometimes connected the religious justification to their exposure to violence and experience of humiliation by the occupation forces. If we accept Vinthagen and Johansson's assertion that everyday resistance is first and foremost a practice, which may or may not be politically conscious, we could see how even if the reasoning is explicitly religious, wearing the hijab could still be considered a form of resistance. In the West Bank the daily events might bring the political dimension more frequently to the surface, as in the case of our interviewer who recalled being helpless during a military raid of her home, an experience which pushed her toward religiosity and wearing the hijab.

While social pressure to wear the hijab was found to be similar on the two regions, in East Jerusalem we found also some counterpressure. While in the West Bank the encounters with Israeli soldiers encourage some women to wear the hijab as a defiant in act, in East Jerusalem, where Palestinian women frequently encounter Jewish Israelis, we found that respondents were cognizant of their visibility or lack thereof within their own reality, For Palestinian Jerusalemites, displaying one's visibility through hijab may be a minor yet powerful projection of their resistance to the status quo, but at the same time, it might reduce their chances in the job market. The potential of the hijab to be seen as threatening for Israeli Jews might deter some women from wearing it. . In other words, the set of considerations for wearing the hijab depends on the particular type of colonial domination.

While the essence of wearing the hijab as practice of everyday resistance to the occupation is clear, it is less so in the way it relates to patriarchy. Respondents in both the West Bank and East Jerusalem described family pressures to wear the hijab and lack of freedom in making a future decision about wearing it or not. While scholars found that in contexts where Muslims are a minority, some women experience donning the hijab as a symbol of female Muslim identity and therefore a source of empowerment (for example, Siraj 2011) our interviewees experienced the empowerment only in their interaction with the occupier. Vis-à-vis their own family they describe donning the hijab as abiding by the rules. We do agree with Scott (1985) that everyday resistance should be intentional, and therefore we identity an inter-sectional discrepancy across contexts. When Palestinian women face the occupier, they display conscious and explicit resistance to the occupation, and more subtle resistance to patriarchal power by taking upon themselves a resisting role. Despite the sense of fear and injustice that Palestinian women face, we can see that these women are able to act in unconventional ways, transforming their identity – political and religious – into a more expressive and active one against the occupation. Facing their own family, though, we did not identify a similar tendency toward resistance.

Notes

1. The Justice and Development Party, also known as the AKP, is the party founded by the current Turkish president Recep Tayyip Erdoğan in possession of the majority of seats in the Turkish parliament. It is considered an Islamic religious political party in Turkey (Kumar 2014).
2. The Palestinian National Authority, also known as the PA or PNA, is known as the interim self-government body established by the Palestinian people in 1994 following the Gaza–Jericho Agreement to govern the Gaza Strip and Areas A and B of the West Bank. This split took place as a result of the 1993 Oslo Accords. The lands of the West Bank were split into Area A (civil and security control by the PA), Area B (civil control by the PA and security by Israel), and Area C (civil and security control by Israel).
3. Identification for respondents are done based on location (West Bank: WB; East Jerusalem: EJ), Age, University Name if applicable (Birzeit: BZ; Al-Quds: AQ; Bethlehem: B; David Yellin College: DYC; Hebrew University: HU).
4. Israel began construction on the Separation Wall in 2000 shortly after the beginning of the Second Intifada. Israel considers it a security barrier against terrorism, while Palestinians call it a racial segregation or apartheid wall (Stewart 2013; Hanauer 2011).
5. No age given.
6. No University affiliation.
7. No age given.
8. Previous studies have found similar motivations among Muslim women in other parts of the world; see Ali (2005), Mohammadi (2016), Dakkak and Mikulka (2012), El Guindi (1999), Gole (2002), Franks (2000) and Wagner et al. (2012).

9. According to many scholars who explain that hijab is religiously mandated, they agree that its mandate is designated for young women who reach puberty (Rita 2017; Ali 2005; Ahmed 1992).

Disclosure statement

No potential conflict of interest was reported by the author(s).

ORCID

Lana Shehadeh ⓘ http://orcid.org/0000-0001-6891-0447

References

Abu-Rabia-Queder, S., and N. Weiner-Levy. 2013. "Between Local and Foreign Structures: Exploring the Agency of Palestinian Women in Israel." *Social Politics* 20 (1): 88–108.

Ahmed, L. 1992. *Women and Gender in Islam: Historical Roots of a Modern Debate*. New Haven: Yale University Press.

Alayan, S. 2019. *Education in East Jerusalem: Occupation, Political Power and Struggle*. London: Routledge.

Alfasi, N., and T. Fenster. 2009. "Between the 'Global' and the 'Local': On Global Locality and Local Globality." *Urban Geography* 30: 543–566.

Ali, S. 2005. "Why Here, Why Now? Young Muslim Women Wearing Hijab." *The Muslim World* 95: 515–530.

Asad, T. 1980. "Ideology, Class and the Origin of the Islamic State." *Economy and Society* 9 (4): 450–473.

Bardi, A. S. 2016. "The 'Architectural Cleansing' of Palestine." *American Anthropologist* 118 (1): 165–171.

Dakkak, H., and J. T. Mikulka. 2012. "Palestinian Girls and the Multiple Meanings of Hijab." *International Journal of Applied Psychoanalytic Studies* 9: 266–272.

El Guindi, F. 1999. *Veil: Modesty, Privacy, and Resistance*. Oxford: Culture.

Fanon, F. 1959. *A Dying Colonialism*. New York: Grove/Atlantic, Inc.

Franks, M. 2000. "Crossing the Borders of Whiteness? White Muslim Women Who Wear the Hijab in Britain Today." *Ethnic and Racial Studies* 23: 917–929.

Gole, N. 2002. "Islam in Public: New Visibilities and new Imaginaries." *Public Culture* 14: 173–190.

Guven, I. 2010. "Globalisation, Political Islam and the Headscarf in Education, with Special Reference to the Turkish Educational System." *Comparative Education* 46 (3): 377–390.

Hamamra, B. T. 2020. "The Misogynist Representation of Women in Palestinian Oral Tradition: A Socio-Political Study." *Journal of Gender Studies* 29: 214–226.

Hanauer, D. I. 2011. "The Discursive Construction of the Separation Wall at Abu Dis: Graffiti as Political Discourse." *Journal of Language and Politics* 10: 301–321.

Heath, J. 2008. *The Veil: Women Writers on Its History, Lore, and Politics*. Berkeley: University of California Press.

Israeli, R. 2014. *Jerusalem Divided: the Armistice Regime, 1947–1967*. London: Routledge.

Jefferis, D. C. 2012. "Institutionalizing Statelessness: The Revocation of Residency Rights of Palestinians in East Jerusalem." *International Journal of Refugee Law* 24 (2): 202–230.

Khalidi, R. 1992. "The Future of Arab Jerusalem." *British Journal of Middle Eastern Studies* 19 (2): 133–143.

Klein, M. 2001. *Jerusalem: The Contested City.* New York: NYU Press.

Kumar, S. M. L. K. 2014. "Examining AKP's Impact on Turkey's Domestic and Foreign Policy." *Contemporary Review of the Middle East* 1 (2): 207–230.

Mancini, S. 2008. "The Power of Symbols and Symbols as Power: Secularism and Religion as Guarantors of Cultural Convergence." *Cardozo Law Review* 30: 2629.

Mancini, S., and M. Rosenfeld. 2010. "Unveiling the Limits of Tolerance: Comparing the Treatment of Majority and Minority Religious Symbols in the Public Sphere." Cardozo Legal Studies Research Paper 309.

Mohammadi, O. 2016. "The Personal, the Political, and the Public: Performing Hijab in Iran." *Liminalities*: 1.

Rapoport, T. E.-F. 1989. "Female Subordination in the Arab-Israeli Community: The Adolescent Perspective of 'Social Veil'." *Sex Roles* 20: 255–269.

Rempel, T. 1997. "The Significance of Israel's Partial Annexation of East Jerusalem." *The Middle East Journal* 51 (4): 520–534.

Rita, A. A. 2017. "Assertion of Wearing Hijab in the Community: an Analysis." *American Scientific Research Journal for Engineering, Technology, and Sciences* 29 (1): 340–347.

Rosenberger, S., and B. Sauer. 2012. "Framing and Regulating the Veil: Introduction." In *Politics, Religion and Gender: Framing and Regulating the Veil*, edited by S. Rosenberger and B. Sauer, 74–94. New York: Routledge.

Scott, J. C. 1985. *Weapons of the Weak.* New Haven: Yale University Press.

Scott, J. W. 2007. *The Politics of the Veil.* Princeton: Princeton University Press.

Shalhoub-Kevorkian, N. 2008. "The Gendered Nature of Education under Siege: A Palestinian Feminist Perspective." *International Journal of Lifelong Education* 27: 179–200.

Shalhoub-Kevorkian, N. 2010. "Palestinian Women and the Politics of Invisibility: Towards a Feminist Methodology." *Peace Prints: South Asian Journal of Peacebuilding* 3 (1): 1–21.

Shalhoub-Kevorkian, N. 2014a. "Criminality in Spaces of Death: The Palestinian Case Study." *British Journal of Criminology* 54: 38–52.

Shalhoub-Kevorkian, N. 2014b. "Palestinian Children as Tools for 'Legalized'state Violence." *Borderlands* 13 (1): 1–24.

Shalhoub-Kevorkian, N. 1999. "Towards a Cultural Definition of Rape: Dilemmas in Dealing with Rape Victims in Palestinian Society." *Women's Studies International Forum* 22 (2): 157–173.

Shlomo, O. 2017. "The Governmentalities of Infastructure and Services Amid Urban Conflict: East Jerusalem in the Post Oslo era." *Political Geography* 61: 224–236.

Siraj, A. 2011. "Meanings of Modesty and the Hijab Amongst Muslim Women in Glasgow, Scotland." *Gender, Place & Culture* 18: 716–731.

Smith, J. 1999. *Islam in America.* New York: Columbia University Press.

Stewart, D. J. 2013. *The Middle East Today: Political, Geographical and Cultural Perspectives.* London: Routledge.

Vinthagen, S., and A. Johansson. 2013. "'Everyday Resistance': Exploration of a Concept and Its Theories." *Resistance Studies Magazine* 00 (1): 00–00.

Wagner, W., R. Sen, R. Permanadeli, and C. S. Howarth. 2012. "The Veil and Muslim Women's Identity: Cultural Pressures and Resistance to Stereotyping." *Culture & Psychology* 18: 521–541.

Williams, R. H., and G. Vashi. 2007. "Hijab and American Muslim Women: Creating the Space for Autonomous Selves." *Sociology of Religion* 68 (3): 269–287.

Wolfe, P. 2006. "Settler Colonialism and the Elimination of the Native." *Journal of Genocide Research* 8: 387–409.

Anniversaries of 'first' settlement and the politics of Zionist commemoration

Liora R. Halperin ⓘ

ABSTRACT
This article centres on stylized commemorative events staged in Israel in 1962 and 1982 to mark, respectively, 80 and 100 years since the consensual beginning of the "First Aliyah," the first wave of Jewish rural settlement in Palestine. Focusing on protocols of 1962 and 1982 Knesset sessions, commemorative medals, military parades, summer camps, and local commemorations, it shows that multiple completing Zionist parties used the rhetoric of "firstness" to negotiate and redefine primacy in light of the political present. Drawing from scholarship on settler memory in other settings, it also positions the settlement event as not a onetime historical occurrence but a sacralized referent used to frame and justify ongoing settlement and participate in historical erasures.

On 4 December 1962, the Israeli parliament (Knesset) held a special session to celebrate the "Year of the First Ones" (Shenat Rishonim), a year of country-wide festivities to mark the eightieth anniversary of the nationally-recognized beginning of the first wave (First Aliyah) of European Jewish rural settlement in Palestine (Ben-Artzi 1997; Eliav 1981). Nearly twenty years later, on 8 February 1982, it convened again to mark the 100th anniversary of that date. The settler colonial project, Patrick Wolfe has notably written, is "a structure, not an event" (Wolfe 2006, 388). Indeed, in both 1962 and 1982, Israel was continuing the pre-1948 Zionist project of land settlement on behalf of the Jewish people, in the former case within the boundaries established by the 1949 ceasefire, and in the latter case also in territories Israel had conquered during the 1967 war, including the West Bank, Gaza, the Golan, and East Jerusalem. But emphasis on settler structures and ongoing practices, though useful in clarifying certain logics of ongoing Israeli state formation (Robinson 2013; Degani 2015), can cause us to forget the significance of the settlement "event," not only as a discrete moment or period of encounter in the late nineteenth century that must be evaluated in the context of its own time and place (Shafir 1996; Ben-Bassat 2009; Ben-Bassat 2013), but also as a sacralized form suitable for integration into subsequent commemorative discourses, which themselves generate and reinforce structures (Trouillot 1995; Bruyneel 2016).

Indeed, celebrations of the past never simply narrate the past: the past is structured by acts of memory themselves (Matsuda 1996; Ross 2002). Scholarship on Zionist collective memory (Zerubavel 1995; Gertz 2000) has ably reflected the function of mythic and mythicized past events in navigating the politics of the present, but has evaded the centrality of modern settlement events per se. Instead, they and other more recent work has emphasized the way modern Zionist commemorative rhetoric centres ancient myth, specifically myths of Jewish heroic death or defeat, in contexts of contemporary loss or casualties (Bitan 1997; Guesnet 2004; Helman 2006; Brog 2010). This historical and discursive ancient past, no doubt, is one of several distinctive feature of the Zionist project. The 1962 and 1982 Knesset events, however, were explicit commemorations of modern settler "firsts." Zionist members of Knesset delivered reflections for the occasion that narrated the beginning of settlement, and its associated places, processes, and figures, as sites of memory that embodied their own parties' political stances. As Jill Lepore argues regarding the collective memory of the American Revolutionary War, founding pasts exist outside the political dynamics of the present and are easily consolidated into sites of collective trans-political values that can be coopted by multiple groups (Lepore 2010, 7).

The year 1882 in fact had predated—by 15 years—the Zionist movement that would later claim it as its settlement starting date. It was not in fact the first effort at Jewish rural land settlement in this era, which had been attempted several years prior by urban Jews from Jerusalem and Safed (Bartal 2010). Moreover, the agricultural colonies founded with private capital in the last decades of the nineteenth century, in search of economic productivization and enhanced spiritual connection to the land, didn't seem entirely "Zionist" to all observers even in retrospect. Unlike the secularized, Socialist Zionists who became the hegemonic leadership of Jewish Palestine come the 1920s under the banner of "Hebrew [Jewish-only] Labor," the "First Aliyah" farmers, in communities known initially as *kolonyot* and later as moshavot, (a Hebrew translation of "colonies") were notable for their religiosity, capitalistic orientation, reliance on foreign Jewish philanthropic support, and tendency to hire Arab rather than Jewish Labor well into the twentieth century. Erstwhile workers in the established colonies, Socialist (Labor) Zionist elites in fact labelled their predecessors "First" and themselves "Second" after World War I—in speeches, opinion pieces, and historical scholarship—in order to mark the former as retrograde, reactionary, and exploitative. The presumption that the "Second Aliyah" superseded the first pervades scholarship about Zionism across political divides (Penslar 1991; Shafir 1996; Shafir 2007; Piterberg 2008, 65; Dowty 2012, 36; Shapira 2012, 46). Yet the First Aliyah, as a retrospective commemorative framework, also allowed the private colonists themselves, part of the Jewish economic—though not political or cultural—elite during the mandate period (Lissak 1981; Ben-Porat 1999; Karlinsky 2005), to articulate their own support for private enterprise within the very framework of "firstness" meant to sideline them (Halperin 2021). With the rising hegemony of Labor, moreover, several other Zionist constituencies on the political centre and right also looked to the nineteenth century colonies and their narrative of the past in search of an alternative settler narrative, one rooted in values that they accused the Labor governments of the Yishuv and Israel of neglecting: religiosity military force, and economic pragmatism, which they had earlier cited in justifying their use of native Palestinian labour. Articulations of these "firsts," both by those who denigrated them and those who praised them and their economic model, participated in an internal process of commemorating and constituting a useable Zionist past.

In rescuing or elevating "firsts," these acts of memory-making simultaneously participated in erasing and forgetting other competing pasts. Jean M. O'Brien, in her study of the nineteenth century New England colonies, calls this process "firsting." Firsting, which consists of repeated and exhaustive litanies of "first" people and things—roads, schools, births, harvests, and most of all, settlements—identifies instances of land settlement as moments of historical rupture. In the American case, they constitute "a straightforward scripting choice that subtly argues for the sole legitimacy of New English ways" (O'Brien 2010, 6). In 1948, just months after Israeli statehood, the Petah Tikva colony (est. 1878; re-est. 1883) northeast of Tel Aviv and Jaffa, published an anniversary book complete with historical narratives, photographs, and a 10-page section enumerating firsts including "first manufacturing," "first houses," "first roads," "first granary," "first borders," "first budget," "first taxes" and "first casualties" (Trofe 1948, 36–45). Firsting, as we will see, displaces native claims (including, in some cases, native Jewish claims), in part by evading the existence of other populations and emphasizing (or resolving) disputes about primacy within an internal settler discourse. As Massachusetts and Connecticut towns feared declining influence relative to larger manufacturing centres down the Atlantic coast, they turned with enthusiasm to commemorative activities (O'Brien, xix). Firsting, O'Brien argues, enabled colonists to articulate settler history as the sole legitimate history, erase indigenous rights to place, and claim their own primacy within an American society in which they had ceased to dominate politically. Similarly, attention to memory in the mid-twentieth century by the towns and cities that had emerged out of the "First Aliyah" colonies occurred not despite being overshadowed within Zionist narrative, but because of that occlusion. However, the very discourse about "firstness" between First and Second Aliyah spokespeople not only took the supersession of Palestine's Palestinians and Palestine-ness as their agreed upon goal, but produced and reproduced that supersession via these retrospective discourses. To adapt Wolfe's insight about the frontier, the discourse of "firstness" is not simply "misleading"; it is a "performative representation" that helps displacement to occur (Wolfe 1999, 165). In this article, I follow the construction Zionist of "firstness" by examining commemorative sites including protocols of the 1962 and 1982 Knesset sessions, medals, military parades, summer camps, and local commemorations.

The 1962 "Year of the First Ones"

Though private agriculturalist interests initiated both the 1962 and the 1982 commemorative events, in practice these celebrations of the past became opportunities for multiple parties to claim "firstness." On July 22, 1962, Yitzhak Ziv-Av, head of the Israeli Farmers' Federation, wrote to Prime Minister David Ben Gurion with a suggestion: declare the upcoming Hebrew year, 1962–1963, "The Year of Farmers" (*Shenat ikarim*). He thanked Ben Gurion for his opening greetings at a commemorative event held a few days earlier, where the leader of the Labor Zionist ruling Mapai Party commented that the First Aliyah "brought about a historical turning point in the vision of the national revival [*hazon ha-tekumah*]." Ziv-Av imagined that a commemorative year would be marked in schools, youth groups, and immigrant absorption centres. Eighty years before, he said, the year 1882 had been "the year of a change of values [*shinui 'arakhin*] in the national revival" and this moment deserved to be commemorated.[1] Ben Gurion agreed, saying that such a recognition would "give glory to the state." The Knesset ultimately approved a planned year of events and publications, many in the former colonies (moshavot) themselves, but decided on the broader term "Year of the First Ones (*rishonim*)."[2]

In placing the First Aliyah on the symbolic national agenda, Ziv-Av hoped for the revision of a historical narrative that he believed had systematically excluded the achievements of the farmers he believed mattered: those who cultivated land under private ownership. In an interview with Yosef (Tommy) Lapid in *Maariv* in December 1962, Ziv-Av called moshavot the exemplar of transhistorical Jewish Palestine settlement: "the moshavot are the red thread in Jewish history since ancient times ... and to today." Unfortunately, Ziv-Av thought, the mainstream Israeli narration of settlement history focused on socialist-oriented immigrants rather than those who had preceded them in the late nineteenth century: "The First Ones, long may they live, would have had to wait another eighty years before their merits were praised and recognized if an energetic Jew [Ziv-Av himself] hadn't decided that it was time to honorably remove the yellow stain of Boaz" (Lapid, 1962). The "stain of Boaz" stuck to those farmers involved in early twentieth century labour disputes with Jewish workers who protested their employment of Arab labourers. The term came from a comment by Ahad Ha-ʿAm (Asher Ginzburg), who in 1912 compared private farmers to Boaz in the biblical book of Ruth, who hired and oversaw labourers but did not undertake manual labour. Ahad Ha-ʿAm used the term ambivalently at the time, criticizing the private farmers' approach but praising them as "close to the land" and "very different in [their] inclinations from the urban Jew." Soon, however, it became a wholly derogatory Labor Zionist epithet for the First Aliyah farmers and their communities (Ahad Ha-ʿAm 1912).

In practice, however, the Year of the First Ones was not specifically a celebration of the "First Aliyah" but rather a broad celebration of Zionist settlement that could be claimed by multiple parties. The Israel Coins and Medals Corporation put out a commemorative medal that depicted a Jewish man planting in a swamp, coupled with the text of Leviticus 26:45: "I will remember the covenant of their ancestors [lit: first ones, brit rishonim]." The image evokes the sense of the land's emptiness: aside from the swamp, the pioneer, his planting, and his water tower are the only active forces on an otherwise blank space. The English language version of the pamphlet advertising the medals printed the text "First Settlers Year" in a woodblock-style font that evokes the Old West and strongly alludes to the mystique and heroism of the American frontier, likely in an appeal to American Jewish buyers.[3] A modern rhetoric of settler firstness thus draws from an ancient sense of restarting the temporal clock in law and in space through settlement of the Land of Canaan. In the 1950s, Prime Minister David Ben-Gurion gathered together a study group on the book of Joshua, which describes the ancient Israelites conquest of settlement in a multiethnic Canaan, as his government developed the vision of divinely mandated settlement and conquest that led to national cohesion and strength (Havrelock 2020, 163).

After approving the commemoration, Ben Gurion used the occasion to pen a long introductory essay to that year's Government Yearbook. In it, he undermined First Aliyah claims to primacy both by situating them in a longer history of Jewish Aliyah (literally, ascent) and by reconfiguring the nature of "firstness" itself so as to elevate later arrivals over earlier ones. This was a longstanding Labor Zionist strategy: their ambivalent view of the colony farmers and desire to claim primacy had led Labor Zionists to construct the idea of the "First Aliyah" in the first place. Labor leader Berl Katznelson had said in 1944, "Firstness is not related to chronology, not the merit [zekhut] of the one who had the luck to come first to make Aliyah." Firstness, Katznelson had said, is proven through personal characteristics including "firstness" in "volunteering, exploratory thinking [gishushei mahshavah], drawing from the source [she'ivah min ha-makor], taking down divisions [hapalat mehitzot], digging deep to the essence" (Katznelson 1953). Without the Second Aliyah, Ben Gurion had written in 1955, we would have remained "exilic and atrophied, subjugated to foreigners and dependent on the goodwill of the Arab majority, like the Yishuv that was established in the twenty-five years before the Second Aliyah" (Ben-Gurion 1955, 268–270). In his 1962 essay, Ben-Gurion also admitted that "the turn to settling the land out of independent pioneering initiative" marked a significant break and that "the crown of the first founders of agriculture" indeed goes to the founders of nineteenth century colonies. But he emphasized that the label "First Ones" [rishonim] should belong to those who brought pioneering innovation.

Any number of generations in Jewish history, he felt, could claim innovation. Moving backwards from 1962, he notes that while 1948 was the founding of the state, it was preceded by "decades of action and pioneering creativity." "The terms common among us now for the First, Second, and Third Aliyah, are incorrect and misleading." They obscure the Yemenite, Sephardic, and Ashkenazi communities that built the longstanding traditional Jewish communities of urban Palestine and who, in some cases, got involved in rural settlement come the late nineteenth century. (Ben-Gurion 1962, ii-iv.). Ben Gurion is ostensibly acknowledging the erasure accomplished by the paradigm of numbered aliyot in obscuring Jewish immigrants who arrived in Palestine before 1882. But his comments about "innovation" suggest that Jewish claims to firstness on the basis of historical continuity are provisional. Palestinian Muslim and Christian populations have no claims whatsoever within this Zionist management of firsts.

In practice, the 1882 and "First Aliyah" referent of the commemoration became largely obscured in the country-wide programmes connected to it. In the Summer of 1963, more than 25,000 children of all ages participated in summer camp activities in Tel Aviv linked to the celebrations. A representative of the Agricultural Laborers Union, affiliated with Labor Zionists, commended "the educational aspect of this project for the second generation."[4] Each morning, children would sing the Labor Zionist song "Anu nihyeh ha-rishonim" (We will be the First Ones) despite the fact, newspapers reported, that educators had warned the Culture Department of the Education Ministry that they didn't want to impose Zionism in such heavy-handed way in the summer camps. As it turned out, "The children were actually very interested in this 'antiquated' topic" and found that the popular songs [shlagerim] from early the days of settlement worked well in a "competition" with more contemporary songs. The programming encompassed multiple periods in the history of the Yishuv, with every group taking on different topics.

Hillel Barzel, head of the city's cultural department, reported that children from multiple socioeconomic and ethnic backgrounds, including Palestinian citizens of the state ("Arabs"), had taken on the activities enthusiastically, likely, in the latter case, out of a desire to establish themselves as loyal citizens within a state that still kept them under the restrictions of a military government (Sorek 2015). In a revealing statement, reporter Aryeh Kinarti noted that "the topic of the First Ones excited the kids in the summer camps no less than that of the Indians [Indianim], Blacks [Kushim], Eskimos [Eskimosim], and the heroes of Anderson and Grimm, and other 'traditional' summer camp topics" (Kinarti 1963). Summer camps for American and European children during the interwar period often involved exoticizing and appropriating the identities of non-white others as a means of escape from the present (Van Slyck 2006, 212). In the United States, they would also reenact iconic elements of America's settler colonial narrative, for example Columbus' "discovery" of America (Paris 2010, 216). Zionist camps seemed to have engaged in the exoticization of both iconic foreign "others" and representatives of the Zionist pre-state settler past who themselves are Orientalized.

The year concluded with a nighttime IDF parade in Petah Tikva on September 4, 1963. The parade route was lined with advanced lighting, barricades, and watchtowers. Prime Minister Levi Eshkol (Labor), Army Chief of Staff Zvi Tzur, and Commander of the Central Command, Yaakov Geva, were in attendance. A few minutes before eight pm, a convoy of twenty-eight elders representing the first fourteen settlements in the country took their places alongside the stage. When the Prime minister gave the sign, the elders would be led by escorts to receive a blessing from him. The elders would then be handed the flags of the first settlements, which would be planted in the middle of the road as the IDF band played songs associated with the First Ones. A large model of a tree would be lit up, symbolizing the "bush of pioneering" that burns and is not consumed "from the days of the First Ones until our days." At the end, the elders would return to their seats and the Oldest of the Guards, Avraham Shapira, then ninety-two, would say the Shehecheyanu prayer (Mitz'ad leili, 1963). In this militarized commemorative event, moshavot became army battalions, and First Ones became their (literal) standard bearers, all as the IDF conducted its central mission to defend the frontiers of Israeli settlement against Arabs understood to be, one and all, outsiders and invaders.

But what standard, exactly, were they bearing? What values or ideologies were encoded in those flags? Ziv-Av and members of the Farmers' Federation would have had no doubt: they stood for private farming and individual initiative that dated back to the late nineteenth century. But the framework of "firstness" was malleable enough that representatives of parties could interpret those flags according to their own self-image. As we will presently see in our treatment of the December 1962 Knesset session, the right wing Herut saw them as banners of early militarism and territorial conquest, religious parties (both Zionist and non-Zionist) as ensigns of piety and Jewish tradition, and the Liberal Party, the bastion of the agriculturalist elite, in relation to the moshava past, present, and future.

Postures of firstness

On December 4, 1962, in the special Knesset session, MKs were given the opportunity to praise and offer reflections on the First Ones (Yeshivah hagigit, 1962). Each, as we will see, interpreted the notion of firstness differently and inserted their own political logic into their framing of the past. That the First Aliyah could be so readily and flexibly appropriated speaks to its malleability as a historical cipher for Zionist authenticity, for firstness, for roots in the land.

The Zionist militant right was reflected in the Herut party, which had evolved from the Revisionist Zionist movement and become the chief opposition to Labor. For decades, it had echoed aspects of the private farmers' narratives of pragmatism, pro-capitalism, and devotion to national interests rather than "political" ones: ethnoreligious solidarity rather than class-based politics. Finding certain of their economic values reflected in "founders" who had preceded both them and Labor Zionists they suggested that Israeli society make a turn to the right not only to reject Labor politics and forge a new path, but to return the Zionist settlement project to its true roots.

Abba Ahimeir, a disciple of Revisionist founder Vladimir Jabotinsky, had already taken to defending the moshavot in the 1950s and attacking Labor for denying them their due. In a series of articles in his party's newspaper, *Herut*, Ahimeir criticized early socialist Zionist immigrants, who "preferred to come to Palestine and not to immigrate to America, a place where it would have been necessary to really work and not chatter and write about work." The Zionist left, he claimed, had imported a detrimental "politics" and "hatred" into the internal dynamics of the Yishuv, "something that was almost unknown until then." The workers' "hatred" was directed against "those who gave them a living, the farmers in the moshavot and the businessmen in Jaffa."

Instead, he believed, the private colonies in all of their stages deserved to be lauded. They established trade in wine and citrus, which became the largest branch of the economy. They employed hundreds of Jews (in addition to Arab workers, whom he did not mention). Not only did the Zionist left "not lift a finger to do any of those things, they related to [the colonies] negatively." "That which the Zionist left got involved with remained weak." (Ahimeir 1954). In another article several years later, Ahimeir accused ideological Labor Zionists of directing their hatred at "the [Jewish] son of the First Aliyah who disliked [Friedrich] Engels' Erfurt Program and [wasn't] ready to delve into the theories of [Socialist Zionist thinker Ber] Borochov" instead of decrying "the Arab thief who killed his guard friend in the middle of the night." (Ahimeir 1957). Denigrating Labor, and their class warfare that seemed to displace the more appropriate ethnic struggle, had been the Revisionist modus operandi since the founding of the party in 1925, but this text is notable for its explicit evocation of the First Aliyah past. As Labor Zionists celebrated the fiftieth anniversary of the Second Aliyah in 1954, Ahimeir suggested that the occasion should be cause for reflection: "How and why did Zionist and settlement history get so distorted?" (Ahimeir 1954) The distortion of the early private colonists mattered to Ahimeir not because they became Revisionists—they generally did not—but because in retrospect they seemed to embody an economically Liberal ethos that had become, alongside militarism, the central calling card of the Revisionist movement. National unity, the ultimate desideratum of right-wing nationalism, could be bolstered through alliance with a group that seemed to sit outside— and, crucially, prior to—the left-right divide (Neumann 1964, 3).

At the 1962 special Knesset session. Herut MK Esther Raziel-Naor painted the colonists with a decidedly militaristic brush: "these First Ones were pathbreakers" not in the sense of an abstract "innovation", but because they deliberately acquired land through the "force of the liberator" [koah ha-meshahrer]. "The lands to which the force of the liberator didn't come are not in our control today, fifteen years after the founding of the state." Speaking five years before Israel's conquests of 1967, Raziel-Naor supported the broad Zionist consensus around "Judaizing" [Yihud] the Negev and Galilee. A few settlements were founded in the Galilee during the "days of the First Ones," she noted, using rhetoric that closely mirrors the "firsting" practices identified by O'Brien, but the region as a whole is "still waiting, standing mostly desolate, waiting for the Jewish Man to come to it" (Yeshivah hagigit, 359). Indeed, she implied, military strength, not Labor ideology or symbolic pioneering, would ensure the Zionist future: "Because days came where the wonderful Conquest of Labor was not sufficient, and it wasn't even enough [simply] to conquer land and own it" it was necessary to adopt the "reverse commandment: 'to beat plowshares into swords'" and to adopt a right-wing platform: "political and military pioneering." Raziel-Naor never mentions the "First Aliyah" specifically and indeed suggests a progression from a failed Labor Zionist paradigm to a Revisionist paradigm of outright aspiration for conquest after World War I. The firsts worthy of recognition, she nonetheless implied, were purely committed to settlement and territorial acquisition, without the distraction of leftist labour ideology.

Religious parties, in contrast, emphasized the distinctive religiosity of First Aliyah colonists, who—in contrast to the Labor Zionist activists who denigrated them—retained their traditional observances, established synagogues, and continued to centre prayer and liturgy in local commemorations of settlement. Yitzhak Refael, representing the National Religious Party

(Mafdal), which had joined Mapai in the governing coalition, emphasized the roots of the so-called "New Yishuv" in the religious communities who immigrated to Palestine in the eighteenth and early nineteenth centuries and established new Jewish communities outside the walls of Jerusalem. All of these developments, in urban as well as rural Jewish settlement, were brought about "by the hand of God, an awakening, and directing hand." Neither Israeli citizens nor observers from abroad should assume that the transformative effect of Zionism came through a secularization process. Quite the contrary: "The First Ones were full and complete Jews, full in their aspirations, and complete in their faith. Everywhere they came, wherever they put down stakes, they also established a tent for the Torah of God, which always accompanied them on their obstacle-ridden journey, and strengthened them on their dangerous mission." Citing the Talmud in connection with the recent foundation of a religious kibbutz in the Beit She'an (Beisan) valley, Mitzpe Gilboa (now Ma'ale Gilboa), he said, "What is the difference between the earlier generation, for whom miracles occurred and us, for whom miracles do not occur? ... The previous generations were wholly dedicated to the sanctification of God's name [while we are not as dedicated to the sanctification of God's name]." (Yeshivah hagigit, 361). Any settlement activity not undertaken by God-fearing Jews would be compromised. A decade later, a similar set of sentiments would animate Gush Emunim, the religious movement that undertook rural settlement in the West Bank and beyond with a similar combination of pioneering sentiment and religious imperative (Feige 2009).

Non-Zionist religious parties, too, could find affinities with the religious settlers of the First Aliyah who, after all, had been motivated in part by piety. Menachem Parush, from the non-Zionist party Agudat Yisrael, initially appeared to disparage the very framework of the event, asserting (like Ben-Gurion) that "Aliyah to the Land of Israel never stopped." Nonetheless, he, too, could find special meaning in the anniversary date being celebrated— 1882—and in the First Aliyah specifically. The Rosh Pinna colony's initial regulations that year, he said, obligated all residents to observe land-based Jewish law related to planting and harvesting and, he added, "the vast majority of the first colonies had regulations like this," built synagogues and ritual baths, and opened houses of Jewish learning. To him the first moshavot were signs not of a radically new political movement, the first step of a transformation, but the inheritors of a spiritual Zionism, a longing for Zion that had nothing to do with statehood or sovereignty. This apparent tension between denial of the First Aliyah colonies' "firstness" claims but emphasis nonetheless on their religiosity had characterized the engagement of the so-called "Old Yishuv" with the colonies from their beginnings, as Yehoshua Kaniel has shown (Kaniel 1981). Similarly, Yaakov Katz from Po'alei Agudat Yisra'el, a splinter group of Agudat Yisrael that represented the interests of ultra-

orthodox workers, stated that the project of Jewish life in Israel could continue effectively only if the next generation based their efforts on a "pure
and refined nationalism [le'umiyut], unmixed and not taken from a non-
Jewish way of life." (Yeshivah hagigit, 365–66). Nationalism is defined here
in a religious sense, "apolitical" in its own way in ostensibly preceding and
transcending modern politics.

While Herut saw militarism and land conquest as the legacy of the first
rural settlers and the religious parties emphasized those Jews' piety and traditionalism, the Liberal Party saw this celebration as uniquely their own. The
Liberal Party had been founded in 1961 through a merger between the urban
professionals of the Progressive Party and the General Zionists, which had
attracted owners of capital and private farmers since the times of the
British Mandate. (Karlinsky 2005; Shamir 2000).

In his comments, Liberal Party MK Joseph Sapir, the prominent citrus
owner and former mayor of Petah Tikva, praised First Aliyah First Ones
explicitly for their "noble modesty which is hard to find these days," a
reference to the "non-ideological" self-image that farmers had been promoting, and which had been pejoratively attributed to them, since the
early part of the century. Alluding to Ben Gurion's effort to sideline
those who "simply" arrived "first," Sapir also insisted that the firstness
of the First Aliyah was not simply chronological; rather, its associated
founders and communities embodied three sets of essential national
characteristics. (Yeshivah hagigit, 359).

First, he said, the First Aliyah had laid the foundations for self-rule and
"independent statist institutions." He clarified what he meant by independent: "not in a communal framework, but through nuclei for building an independent, sovereign, and democratic state." (360). These terms—independent,
democratic—evoked the rhetoric of the General Zionist party in the 1950s,
which held that support of the [Jewish] individual was the true meaning of
democracy (Rozin 2011, 75; Rozin 2016). Moreover, he stressed, the importance of land settlement was not, as Labor ideologues would have suggested,
primarily a method for Jewish cultural revitalization but rather "the foundation of a national economy." (Yeshivah hagigit, 360). Second, the moshavot
set the borders of the country—indeed, the pattern of Jewish land settlement
had shaped the United Nations partition plan. Echoing the comments of the
Herut MK, he lamented, "if only there were more First Ones and if only the
Hebrew plow had been extended out over the remaining parts of the land"
then the shock of Hebrew weaponry, when the time came, could have
burst through new areas and walls [lifrotz tehumim ve-homot]." (ibid) When,
five years later, Israel captured the West Bank, Gaza, East Jerusalem, the
Sinai, and the Golan Heights in the Six Day War, this counterfactual wish
would become a reality. Third, the moshavot seemed to embody an ethos
of security. Their "deep political-security sense," he said, allowed them to

realize the necessity of having "Hebrew weaponry to defend their territorial conquests." Through a selective reading of the moshavot, Sapir created an image of a society defined by its individual initiative, territorial conquest through land purchase, and ethos of security, one that reflected some of the perspectives of Herut, but within a claim to moderation and capitalist pragmatism.

In 1965, the Liberal Party joined with Herut to form Gahal and in 1973 the Likud Party was founded, now an amalgam of traditional capitalist interests and right-wing ethnonationalism. Indeed, the former group's legacy as a moderate, centrist party went far in giving legitimacy to Herut, known for its *lack* of moderation and its non-centrism. The General Zionists, wrote Itzhak Carmin in a 1951 survey, "took pride in standing above the Zionist party battles, in working for the general interests of the Jewish national home" and offering "a balancing factor" that could wield a "wholesome influence" amidst the "extremes of partisanship" (Carmin 1951, 83–84). "There could be no question," writes political scientist Jonathan Mendilow, "of its efficacy in conferring legitimacy on Herut, seeing that it was a long-established, moderate, centrist party" (Mendilow 2003, 40). The First Aliyah, the settlement "first" outside the politics of the present, was thus symbolically integrated into the party that would oversee Israel's ongoing settlement efforts.

The 1982 100th anniversary

The Zionist project of land settlement and development never ceased. Before the conquests of the Six Day War in 1967, the Israeli government began to peg the Negev in the South and Galilee in the North as sites of Jewish population dispersion and funded development towns and other Jewish settlements (Ben-Porat 1989, 28). After Israel's land conquests during the 1967 Six Day War, development and displacement continued in the Galilee and Negev, though a programme Israel called "Judaization" (Ghanem and Ghanem 2001, 88–89) and began in the newly occupied territories. The drive for settlement both before and after 1967 came in part from immigrant demand for housing but its particular urgency and geographic distribution in peripheral and border areas—where most Jewish immigrants did not want to live (Kemp 2002)—reflected ongoing regional threats, militant groups made up of Palestinian refugees who now resided in Jordan, Lebanon, or Gaza, and, within the Israeli political process, Palestinian Citizens of Israel who began to unite across political divides around the threat and practice of ongoing land confiscations (Sorek 2015, 49–59). Many Israeli Jews perceived attacks, anti-Zionist rhetoric, and civil rights organizing, to different extents, as extensions of the anti-Zionist rhetoric and violent resistance that they had faced from within Palestine before 1948. Such incidents continually reminded the state and its Jewish citizens of the precarity of Zionist political control over space despite Israeli military strength. "Settlement is on-going," Kevin Bruyneel writes of American settler colonialism, "because politically the matter of claims to space are not settled. They are contested. Settlement is thus a practice, a status, and a site of conflict" (Bruyneel 2016, 353).

Labor-led governments between 1967 and 1977, though they spoke of captured lands as bargaining chips for eventual peace treaties, saw strategic and security rationales for settlement and initiated construction and infrastructure planning in East Jerusalem, the Golan Heights, the Jordan Valley, and Northern Sinai (Lesch 1979, 35). Settlement throughout the Occupied Territories accelerated through both state investment and retroactively recognized settler initiative after the Likud Party took power in 1977. Settlement after 1977 thus occurred within a broader context of renewed political support for private enterprise and religious Zionism, skepticism about Labor Zionist history and claims, and support for a new movement that saw itself as continuing the story of settler bravery on the new frontier. As the international community called upon Israel to return conquered lands in the context of peace negotiations and reiterated its position that civilian settlements in Occupied Territories constituted a violation of international law, the principle that had animated Ottoman-era settlement now pertained again. In the absence of international approval—in the case of unauthorized settlement, even Israeli state approval—Israel and its settlers established communities on the premise that facts on the ground would ensure Jewish security and primacy, with or without a formal extension of borders, and would shape any borders to be drawn in the future.

By the 1970s, "the dormant codes of the immigrant-settler political culture, "had been reawakened" (Kimmerling 2003, 38). As the settler movement grew, its supporters connected themselves to the historical legacy of Zionist settlement and appealed to a broader, ongoing belief across the Zionist spectrum that settlers and settlement were the uncontroversial bedrock of the Zionist project. On February 8, 1982, the Knesset convened a special session to mark one hundred years of settlement in the Land of Israel. Knesset chairman Menahem Savidor (Likud) praised Yitzhak Ziv-Av, the head of the Farmers' Federation who had promoted the Year of the First Ones in 1962–3 and who also chaired the public committee for this celebration: he had "not allowed history to pass over the mute heroes of the revival. He extracted them from the abyss of forgetting" (Yeshivah meyuhedet, 1982, 7).

Now, too, Knesset members had contemporary settlers on their minds: those in the Occupied Territories. Israel was on the verge of withdrawing around 2,500 settlers from the Yamit corridor in the Northern Sinai in the context of the Israel-Egypt Peace Treaty of 1979 as it continued to expand settlements in the West Bank and Gaza Strip (Anziska 2018). Geula Cohen, a fighter in the mandate-era Revisionist Etzel and Lehi militias, Likud Knesset member, and founder of the pro-settlement Tehiya Party, used the opportunity to make a statement. She suggested that the gathering instead take place "in the only place where the principal fight for preserving Jewish settlement in the Land of Israel is happening: the Yamit corridor." Cohen knew the suggestion would be rejected, but she was using it to grandstand: "If the Knesset doesn't accept this proposal we will be witnesses here to a cynical display by the Knesset, which is using its voice to elevate settlement while taking up an axe in its hand to uproot it" The commemoration of the hundredth anniversary of the First Aliyah was not going to pass in isolation from a debate about settlement. Yet that ensuing session did not feature disagreement about settlement writ large. It confirmed not only that right-wing supporters of settlement in the Occupied Territories saw the settlers of eras past as models, but that all Zionist Knesset members who spoke wished to elevate Zionism's settler origins and settler ideology despite their different strategies regarding contemporary settlement and regional foreign policy (Yeshivah meyuhedet, 2–3).

Likud MKs, in particular, connected nineteenth century settlement to twentieth century settlement in the Occupied Territories. Savidor noted wistfully that, "If the founder of Rishon LeZion, [Zalman David] Levontin had indeed realized his plans near Gaza, or if Yoel [Moshe] Solomon had realized his intentions to strike root near Jericho, as he intended, and not in Umlebes [Petah Tikva], how much blood, how many casualties, and how many debates about the borders of Israel could have been spared from the following generations?" But celebration of "First Aliyah" founders was also a celebration of all Jewish settlers, "all workers and builders of the land in all settlement streams" who "turned a wasteland into a flowering Garden of Eden."(Ibid., 6)

Minister of Agriculture Simha Erlich (General Zionists, and then Likud) echoed Savidor: "Settlement hasn't ceased over 33 years of statehood." On the contrary, the establishment of settlements [yishuvim], which had previously been done, in the British and Ottoman periods, "under the watchful eye of a foreign occupier" now occurs "publicly and without shame" [be-resh galei]. Settlements established hastily in Judea and Samaria [the West Bank], the Golan, and Gaza, he noted with approval, "are now getting more established through increased budgets and a widening of their human population base." Overall, the agricultural sector is producing one billion dollars of export goods through the use of advanced technology including electronic irrigation computers that crunch numbers. "This is the agriculture of today" (Ibid., 16–17). He did not mention that Palestinians had flooded into unskilled agricultural labour. They, too, were responsible for this economic growth, which they benefitted less from (Farsakh 2005; Portugali 2013).

The Labor Zionist Alignment (Maarakh) Party, in the opposition at the time, supported evacuating Yamit but also favoured ongoing settlement in other areas of the Occupied Palestinian Territories. MK Shimon Peres shared in the full-throated praise of the Zionist settlement project and did not explicitly distinguish in his rhetoric between settlement then unfolding within the Green Line and that taking place in the Occupied Territories. He boasted of "861 new settlements, [including] 300 kibbutzim and 400 cooperative settlements and 4.5 million dunams cultivated, considered the best agriculture in the world, with the ability to produce an output of 20 billion shekels a year, [in commodities ranging] from oranges to flowers." (Ibid., 21). In invoking oranges, Peres was celebrating the sector that had been most closely associated with private colonies before 1948. The citrus sector that still existed continued to rely on Palestinian labour. But here, too, he did not mention it. Rather, his rhetoric expressed an ongoing process of Jewish cultivation, improvised settler habitations, and shifting and faceless foes, a narrative in which neither 1948 nor 1967 was a decisive turning point:

> The land that waited for them was arid and exposed. They lived in caves, thickets, tents, cabins, metal and fabric shacks, in camps and transit camps [ma'abarot] and abandoned houses and temporary apartments, small apartments. They worked in swamps, sands, rocks, feverish valleys and unknown hills. They fought against murderers, gangs, foreign powers and the Arab armies. Always few in number, without strategic reserves, lacking manpower, weapons, and resources, and they paid a heavy and cruel price. Until the day that they could turn back and see behind them a flowering and verdant land, whose reputation travelled as far as that of the best agricultural producers, the strongest armies, the most advanced societies (Ibid., 18).

The story Peres, Savidor, and Erlich were celebrating that day did not begin with statehood, with political organizing, or with ideas. It began with acts of settlement and continued with acts of settlement under Ottoman, British, and Israeli rule. Amidst the blistering and ongoing partisan fights over the specific contours of settlement, rival Zionist parties expressed an agreement about its centrality to Zionist memory and ongoing practice.

Just as in the 1962 summer camps, educators used anniversaries to blur the boundaries between Zionist parties as they attempted to initiate youth, many of them new immigrants, into the Zionist settler narrative through "firsting" practices. In the early twentieth century United States, Matthew Frye Jacobson has shown, immigrant children read schoolbooks that emphasized the European conquest of "an otherwise 'savage' continent" and communicated that to be American was "to have arrived on American shores on some kind of journey from Europe" on the basis of a "natural, God-given claim to North America." Pride in the "legacy of conquest" Jacobson writes, is "integral to American nationalism and national belonging" (Jacobson 1998, 214). Newcomer white ethnics in the United States (including Eastern European and some Ottoman Jews) had real, if tenuous, claims to membership in the (white) national collective, unlike Chinese arrivals, formerly enslaved African-Americans, and Native Americans. White ethnics were often especially enthusiastic about the nationalist narrative and resisted having it questioned (Zimmerman 2002, 14–15). Jewish immigrants to Israel may have arrived indifferent to late nineteenth century (or, for that matter, earlier twentieth century) histories, but found them particularly enchanting because they offered a path toward membership in the emerging collective, both against the Arabs of Palestine who had no such path, and diaspora Jews, whose families had (foolishly in the dominant view) not yet chosen it.

In 1985, Ziv-Av authored an educational curriculum for the Israeli Department of Education and the Jewish National Fund. He thought it correct to jointly celebrate three instances of firsting: the plowing of the "First Furrow" in Petah Tikva (1878), the establishment of Rosh Pinna (1882), and the founding of the Jewish National Fund (1901), all of which occurred around Hanukkah time and which Ziv-Av suggested should be marked together on a new holiday called "The celebration of the First Furrow." His pamphlet consisted of a script to be read aloud by teachers and students. "Let us elevate the memory of the first of the First Ones [rishonim], they who established a long chain of colonies within the desolation of the land," it began. The process of settlement to be celebrated was ongoing: "we will elevate the memory of First Ones in every generation … Standing erect, we unite as ones continuing on the path of the First Ones by remembering them." (Ziv-Av 1985, 2–15).

*   *   *

"Recognition of the past is influenced by the present," wrote *Davar* writer (and future Sociology professor) Dan Horowitz in his coverage of the special Knesset session to mark The Year of the First Ones in 1962–3. "The residue of eighty years-worth of arguments and disagreements, ideological disputes and differences in values showed themselves in the Knesset yesterday." This eighty-year history, not only its vaunted origins, "was reflected in the mirror of the Knesset via its many faces." As such, he noted, the proceedings could offer great material for a historian: "Not a historian of the 'First Ones,' the people of the First Aliyah per se, but maybe first and foremost a historian of the history of Yishuv that also continues today" (Horowitz 1998). Horowitz had articulated our core insight: those gathered in the Knesset on the eightieth anniversary of the "First Aliyah" in 1962, like those who gathered in 1982, and those in and beyond the "First Aliyah" colonies who had been commemorating the "First Aliyah" for decades, were not telling the story of the First Aliyah. Rather, they were telling the evolving story of their own political evolution, contemporary anxieties, and future hopes through the malleable substance of the Zionist settler past. But the internal contention that reveals texture and multiplicity within the history of Zionism, which shows us how not all Zionists built the image of the past in the same way or towards the same ends, also confines all claims to firstness to within the national conversation. Zionist firsting, the insistent and ongoing attention to First Ones and First Things, mutes and overwrites competing claims to space and place. The event of "first" settlement becomes a frame through which ongoing settlement is celebrated, negotiated, and justified, and its erasures obscured, within the political dynamics of the present.

Notes

1. Letters from David Ben Gurion to Yitzhak Ziv-Av, July 22 and July 26 1962, CZA A483/74.
2. Letter from David Ben Gurion to Ziv-Av, August 1, 1962. CZA A483/74
3. Israel Coins and Medals Corporation, "Medaliot shenat ha-rishonim 5723" [Year of the First Ones Medallions, 1962-3], No Date. CZA A483/74.
4. Letter from A. Herzfeld, on letter head of Histadrut ha-po'alim ha-hakla'iyim [Union of Agricultural Laborers] to Y. Ziv-Av, Farmers Federation, Tel Aviv, September 13, 1963, CZA A483/74.

Disclosure statement

No potential conflict of interest was reported by the author(s).

ORCID

Liora R. Halperin ⓘ http://orcid.org/0000-0001-6205-0853

References

Ahad Ha-'Am. 1912. "Sakh ha-kol" [All in all], ha-Shiloah 26:3 (Nisan 1912), Dated London 17 Adar 1912, http://benyehuda.org/ginzberg/Gnz_127.html#_ftn1.
Ahimeir, Aba. 1954. [Aba Sirka], "Hiyuv u-shelilah ba-'Aliyah ha-Sheniyah" [Positives and Negatives in the Second Aliyah], Herut, 24 December 1954, 3.
Ahimeir, Aba. 1957. [Aba Sirka], "ha-Shomer," Herut, 31 May 1957, 3.
Anziska, Seth. 2018. Preventing Palestine: A Political History from Camp David to Oslo. Princeton: University Press.
Bartal, Israel. 2010. "'Al ha-rishoniyut: zeman u-makom ba-'Aliyah ha-Rishonah." [On Firstness: Time and Place in the First Aliyah]." In Lesoheah tarbut 'im ha-'Aliyah ha-Rishonah, [Talking Culture with the First Aliyah], edited by Yaffa Berlovitz, and Yosef Lang, 15–24. Tel Aviv: ha-Kibbutz ha-Me'uhad.
Ben-Artzi, Yossi. 1997. Early Jewish Settlement Patterns in Palestine, 1882–1914. Israel Studies in Historical Geography. Jerusalem: Magnes Press, Hebrew University.
Ben-Bassat, Yuval. 2009. "Proto-Zionist–Arab Encounters in Late Nineteenth-Century Palestine: Socioregional Dimensions." Journal of Palestine Studies 38 (2): 42–63.
Ben-Bassat, Yuval. 2013. Petitioning the Sultan: Protests and Justice in Late Ottoman Palestine, 1865–1908. Library of Ottoman Studies 42. London; New York: I.B. Tauris.

Ben-Gurion, David. 1955. "Al he-ʿavar ve-ʿal he-ʿatid" [On the past and the future], in *Hazon va-derekh* [Vision and path]. Vol. 5. Tel Aviv: ʿAm ʿoved, 267–296.

Ben-Gurion, David. 1962. ""Rishonim" [First Ones]." In *Shenaton ha-memshalah* [Government Yearbook], 1962–3, edited by Reuven Alkalai, i–li. Jerusalem: Government Printer.

Ben-Porat, Amir. 1989. *Divided We Stand: Class Structure in Israel from 1948 to the 1980s*. New York: Greenwood Press.

Ben-Porat, Amir. 1999. *Hekhan hem ha-burganim ha-hem?: toldot ha-burganut ha-Yisreʾelit* [Where are Those Bourgeois People?: The History of the Israeli Bourgeoisie]. Jerusalem: Magnes Press.

Bitan, Dan. 1997. "'On sagi poreah': mitosim shel gevurah lohemet be-reshit ha-Tziyonut" ['Exalted Strength is Blooming': Myths of Fighting Heroism at the Beginnings of Zionism]." In *Mitos ve-zikaron: gilgulehah shel ha-todaʿah ha-Yisreʾelit* [Myth and Memory: the Metamorphosis of Israeli Consciousness], edited by David Ohana, and Robert S. Wistrich, 167–188. Jerusalem; Tel Aviv: Van Leer Institute; ha-Kibbutz ha-meʾuhad.

Brog, Mooli. 2010. ""ha-Gimnasya 'Herzliya' megaleh et kivrot ha-makabim 1907–1911: le-heker ʿitzuv shel zikaron kibutzi u-zehut leʾumit" [the Herzliya Gymnasium Discovers the Graves of the Maccabees, 1907–1922: Researching the Making of Collective Memory and National Identity]." *ʿIyunim bi-Tekumat Yisraʾel*, [Studies in the Rebirth of Israel] 20: 169–192.

Bruyneel, Kevin. 2016. "Codename Geronimo: Settler Memory and the Production of American Statism." *Settler Colonial Studies* 6 (4): 349–364.

Carmin, Itzhak. 1951. *The General Zionist World: A Four-Year Report on the World Confederation of General Zionists*. New York: World Confederation of General Zionists, American Office.

Degani, Arnon Yehuda. 2015. "The Decline and Fall of the Israeli Military Government, 1948–1966: A Case of Settler-Colonial Consolidation?" *Settler Colonial Studies* 5 (1): 84–99.

Dowty, Alan. 2012. *Israel/Palestine. 3rd ed., Fully rev. and Updated*. Cambridge, UK. Malden, Mass.: Polity.

Eliav, Mordechai, ed. 1981. *Sefer ha-ʿAliyah ha-Rishonah* [The First Aliyah]. Jerusalem: Yad Yitzhak Ben-Zvi, Israel Ministry of Defense.

Farsakh, Leila. 2005. *Palestinian Labour Migration to Israel: Labour, Land and Occupation*. Vol. 3. The Routledge Political Economy of the Middle East and North Africa Series Series. Abingdon, Oxon: Routledge, Taylor & Francis Group.

Feige, Michael. 2009. *Settling in the Hearts: Jewish Fundamentalism in the Occupied Territories. Raphael Patai Series in Jewish Folklore and Anthropology*. Detroit: Wayne State University Press.

Gertz, Nurith. 2000. *Myths in Israeli Culture: Captives of a Dream. Parkes-Wiener Series on Jewish Studies*. London; Portland, OR: Vallentine Mitchell.

Ghanem, Asʿad. 2001. *The Palestinian-Arab Minority in Israel, 1948–2000: A Political Study*. Albany, NY: SUNY Press.

Guesnet, François. 2004. "Chanukah and Its Function in the Invention of a Jewish-Heroic Tradition in Early Zionism, 1880–1900." In *Nationalism, Zionism and Ethnic Mobilization of the Jews in 1900 and Beyond*, edited by Michael Berkowitz, 227–245. Leiden: Brill.

Halperin, Liora R. 2021. *The Oldest Guard: Forging the Zionist Settler Past*. Stanford, Calif.: Stanford University Press.

Havrelock, Rachel. 2020. *The Joshua Generation: Israeli Occupation and the Bible*. Princeton: University Press.

Helman, Anat. 2006. "Place-Image and Memorial Day in 1920s an 1930s Petach Tivkah." *Journal of Modern Jewish Studies* 5 (1): 73–94.

Horowitz, Dan. 1998. "Petihat 'Shenat Rishonim' ba-Knesset" [Opening of the 'Year of the First Ones' in the Knesset] *Davar*, 5 December 1962, 2.

Jacobson, Matthew Frye. 1998. *Whiteness of a Different Color: European Immigrants and the Alchemy of Race*. Cambridge, Mass.: Harvard University Press. 214.

Kaniel, Yehoshua. 1981. *Hemshekh u-temurah: ha-Yishuv ha-Yashan veha-Yishuv he-Hadash bi-tekufat ha-ʿAliyah ha-Rishonah veha-Sheniyah* [Continuity and Change: The Old Yishuv and the New Yishuv During the Periods of the First and Second Aliyah]. Jerusalem: Yad Yitzhak Ben-Zvi.

Karlinsky, Nahum. 2005. *California Dreaming: Ideology, Society, and Technology in the Citrus Industry of Palestine, 1890–1939*. Albany: State University of New York Press.

Katznelson, Berl. 1953. "Shlomo Lavi ben 70" [Shlomo Lavi turns 70], *Davar*, 21 December 1953, 2.

Kemp, Adriana. 2002. ""'Nedidat ʿamim' o 'ha-beʿerah ha-gedolah': shelitah medinatit ve-hitnagdut ba-sefar ha-Yisreʾeli" ['Human Migration' or 'The Great Conflagration': State Control and Resistance in the Israeli Periphery]." In *Mizrahim be-Yisraʾel: ʿiyun bikorti mehudash* [Mizrahim in Israel: A Critical Observation Into Israel's Ethnicity], edited by Hannan Hever, Yehouda Shenhav, and Pnina Motzafi-Haller, 36–67. Tel Aviv: ha-Kibbutz ha-meʾuhad; Van Leer Institute.

Kimmerling, Baruch. 2003. *Politicide: Ariel Sharon's War Against the Palestinians*. London: Verso.

Kinarti, Aryeh. 1963. "Shenat rishonim be-kaitanot" [Year of the First Ones in the summer camps], *La-merhav*, 16 August 1963, 4;8.

Lapid, Yosef. 1962. "Matanah la-nasi" [A gift for the president]. *Maariv*, December 7.

Lepore, Jill. 2010. *The Whites of Their Eyes: The Tea Party's Revolution and the Battle over American History*. Public Square (Princeton, N.J.). Princeton: University Press.

Lesch, Ann Mosely. 1979. *Arab Politics in Palestine, 1917–1939: The Frustration of a Nationalist Movement*. Ithaca, N.Y.: Cornell University Press.

Lissak, Moshe. 1981. *ha-Elitot shel ha-yishuv ha-Yehudi be-Eretz-Yisraʾel bi-tekufat ha-Mandat: rekaʿ hevrati u-defuse karyerah* [Jewish Elites in the Land of Israel during the mandate period: Social background and career patterns]. Tel-Aviv: ʿAm ʿoved.

Matsuda, Matt K. 1996. *The Memory of the Modern. New York* . Oxford: Oxford University Press.

Mendilow, Jonathan. 2003. *Ideology, Party Change, and Electoral Campaigns in Israel, 1965–2001*. SUNY Series in Israeli Studies. Albany, NY: State University of New York Press.

"Mitzʿad leili shel Tzahal be-Petah Tikva yesayem ha-yom 'Shenat Rishonim'" [A night-ime IDF parade in Petah Tikva today will conclude the 'Year of the First Ones']. *La-merhav*, 4 September 1963, 6.

Neumann, Emmanuel. 1964. *"General Zionism as the Major Unifying Force in the Zionist Movement," Excerpts from the Keynote Addressed Delivered at the Opening Session of the World Conference of General Zionists, Tel Aviv, 26 December 1964*. New York: World Union of General Zionists.

O'Brien, Jean M. 2010. *Firsting and Lasting: Writing Indians out of Existence in New England. Indigenous Americas*. Minneapolis: University of Minnesota Press.

Paris, Leslie. 2010. *Children's Nature: The Rise of the American Summer Camp*. New York: New York University Press.

Penslar, Derek Jonathan. 1991. *Zionism and Technocracy: The Engineering of Jewish Settlement in Palestine, 1870–1918*. Bloomington: Indiana University Press.

Piterberg, Gabriel. 2008. *The Returns of Zionism: Myths, Politics and Scholarship in Israel*. London: Verso.

Portugali, Juval. 2013. *Implicate Relations: Society and Space in the Israeli-Palestinian Conflict*. Dordrecht: Kluwer Academic Publishers.

Robinson, Shira. 2013. *Citizen Strangers: Palestinians and the Birth of Israel's Liberal Settler State*. Stanford Studies in Middle Eastern and Islamic Societies and Cultures. Stanford, CA: Stanford University Press.

Ross, Kristin. 2002. *May '68 and Its Afterlives. May 1968 and Its Afterlives*. Chicago: University of Chicago Press.

Rozin, Orit. 2011. *The Rise of the Individual in 1950s Israel: A Challenge to Collectivism*. Waltham, Mass.: Brandeis University Press.

Rozin, Orit. 2016. *A Home for All Jews: Citizenship, Rights, and National Identity in the New Israeli State*. Waltham, Mass.: Brandeis University Press.

Shafir, Gershon. 1996. *Land, Labor and the Origins of the Israeli-Palestinian Conflict 1882–1914*. Berkeley: University of California Press.

Shafir, Gershon. 2007. "Zionism and Colonialism: A Comparative Approach." In *The Israel/Palestine Question: A Reader*, edited by Ilan Pappé, 2nd ed., 78–93. London; New York: Routledge.

Shamir, Ronen. 2000. "Burganut yehudit be-Palastinah ha-koloniyalit: kavei meta'er le-seder yom mehkari [The Jewish Bourgeoisie in Colonial Palestine: Outline for a Research Agenda]." *Israeli Sociology* 3 (1): 133–48.

Shapira, Anita. 2012. *Israel: A History*. Waltham, Mass.: Brandeis University Press.

Sorek, Tamir. 2015. *Palestinian Commemoration in Israel: Calendars, Monuments, and Martyrs*. Palo Alto: Stanford University Press.

Trofe, Eliezer. 1948. *Reshit: li-melot 70 shanah le-Fetah Tikva* [Beginning: on Petah Tikva's 70th anniversary] *(638–708)*. Petah Tikva: sn.

Trouillot, Michel-Rolph. 1995. *Silencing the Past: Power and the Production of History*. Boston: Beacon Press.

Van Slyck, Abigail Ayres. 2006. *A Manufactured Wilderness: Summer Camps and the Shaping of American Youth, 1890–1960*. Minneapolis: University of Minnesota Press.

Wolfe, Patrick. 1999. *Settler Colonialism and the Transformation of Anthropology: The Politics and Poetics of an Ethnographic Event*. London: Cassell.

Wolfe, Patrick. 2006. "Settler Colonialism and the Elimination of the Native." *Journal of Genocide Research* 8 (4): 387–409.

"Yeshivah hagigit shel ha-knesset le-tziyun Shenat Rishonim" [Festive session of the Knesset in order to mark the year of the First Ones]. *Divre ha-Knesset* 35 (7 December 1962): 353–66.

"Yeshivah meyuhedet be-yom kinun ha-Knesset le-tziyun me'ah shenot hityashvut ba-aretz," [Special Knesset session to mark 100 years of settlement in the Land], the 55th session of the Tenth Knesset—Second Sitting, Monday 15 Shevat/ 8 February 1982, Jerusalem, 16:02. CZA A483/74, 7.

Zerubavel, Yael. 1995. *Recovered Roots: Collective Memory and the Making of Israeli National Tradition*. Chicago: University of Chicago Press.

Zimmerman, Jonathan. 2002. *Whose America?: Culture Wars in the Public Schools*. Cambridge, Mass.: Harvard University Press.

Ziv-Av, Yitzhak. 1985. "Bnei banim be-'ikvot rishonim" [Sons in the footsteps of the Fathers]. Israel Department of Education; Jewish National Fund Teachers Movements. In CZA A483/74, 2–15.

Index

Note: Figures are indicated by *italics*. Endnotes are indicated by the page number followed by 'n' and the endnote number e.g., 20n1 refers to endnote 1 on page 20.